REFORM, REVOLUTION AND FRENCH GLOBAL POLICY,
1787–1791

Reform, Revolution and French Global Policy, 1787–1791

JEREMY J. WHITEMAN
University of Tasmania, Australia

ASHGATE

© Jeremy J. Whiteman 2003

All rights reserved. No part of this publication may be reproduced, stored in a retrieval system or transmitted in any form or by any means, electronic, mechanical, photocopying, recording or otherwise without the prior permission of the publisher.

The author has asserted his moral right under the Copyright, Designs and Patents Act, 1988, to be identified as the author of this work.

Published by
Ashgate Publishing Limited
Gower House
Croft Road
Aldershot
Hampshire GU11 3HR
England

Ashgate Publishing Company
101 Cherry Street
Burlington, VT 05401-4405 USA

Ashgate website: http://www.ashgate.com

British Library Cataloguing in Publication Data
Whiteman, Jeremy J.
  Reform, revolution and French global policy, 1787-1791
  1. France - History - 1789-1793 2. France - Foreign relations
  - 1789-1815 3. France - Politics and government - 1789-1799
  I. Title
  944'.04

Library of Congress Cataloging-in-Publication Data
Whiteman, Jeremy J., 1967-
  Reform, revolution and French global policy, 1787-1791 / Jeremy J. Whiteman.
    p.cm.
  Includes bibliographical references and index.
  ISBN 0-7546-0672-4 (alk. paper)
   1.France–History–Revolution, 1789-1799. 2. France–Foreign relations–1789-1815.
  I. Title.

DC148 . W48 2002
944.04–dc21

2002074732

ISBN 0 7546 0672 4

Printed and bound in Great Britain by MPG Books Ltd, Bodmin, Cornwall

Contents

Acknowledgements   *vi*
List of Abbreviations   *vii*

Introduction: Historiography and the Definition of the Problem   1

PART ONE: THE OLD REGIME

1. France Resurgent: from the Peace of 1783 to the Assembly of Notables   15

2. The Dutch Crisis and the 'Implosion' of Vergennes' Diplomatic System   43

3. The Contraction of French Global Power, 1788—1789   71

PART TWO: THE NATIONAL CONSTITUENT ASSEMBLY

Preface   98

4. The 'Revolutionising' of French Foreign Policy   101

5. Trade and the Regeneration of the French Economy   139

6. The Question of the Colonies   169

7. Defending a 'Regenerated' France   215

8. Conclusion: Continuities and Discontinuities in French Global Policy, 1787—1791   245

Appendix   *257*
Bibliography   *259*
Index   *267*

Acknowledgements

There are a number of people and institutions I must thank for their help in guiding this project through to completion, first as a doctoral thesis, and finally as a monograph. I must first of all express my gratitude for the generous financial assistance I received from the Commonwealth Government of Australia, the Arts Faculty and the School of Graduate Studies at the University of Melbourne. The History Department at the University of Melbourne and the School of History and Classics at the University of Tasmania also provided some assistance in defraying a number of my research expenses.

Secondly, I would like to thank all those who have provided me with personal assistance. My doctoral supervisors, Professor Peter McPhee, Associate Professor Charles Sowerwine and Dr. Alison Patrick were all generous with their advice, knowledge and criticism. I was also fortunate to receive advice from a number of other scholars whom I met in the course of my European travels or in conferences in Australia, including Dr. Munro Price, Dr. John Hardman, and Professors Alan Forrest, Peter Jones and Norman Hampson. Aside from this scholarly advice, I would like also to thank those who were helpful to me in other ways, such as the office staff in the History Department at Melbourne, Caroline Veenendaal at the School of History and Classics at the University of Tasmania, and the staffs at the various libraries and archives I visited over the course of my research.

There are, finally, a number of people whom I would like to thank for their moral support, encouragement and friendship over the past few years, and to whom this work is collectively dedicated: my father Michael Whiteman, my friends and colleagues Simon Cooke, Rachel Jenzen, Anna Johnston, Kate Holden, Katrina Woodland, Bruce Hawkins, Elizabeth Freeman, Kate Kennedy, Joanne Townsend, Anne Diamond, Frank Zelko and all the friends I made during my happy sejour in Paris, most especially Ane Kristin Rogstad, Rebecca Griffiths and Mark Bryant.

List of Abbreviations

AAE	Archives du Ministère des Affaires Etrangères, Quai d'Orsay, Paris
AN	Archives Nationales, Paris
AP	Archives Parlementaires
APs	Archives Privées
BN	Bibliothèque Nationale, Paris
CP	Correspondance Politique
FC	Fonds Colonies
Marine	Archives de la Marine, Vincennes
MD	Mémoires et Documents
NAF	Nouvelles Acquisitions Françaises

Author's Note

In transcribing from French manuscript sources, I have preserved original eighteenth-century spellings, such as the use of 'Anglois' for 'Anglais'. I will hence refrain from using [sic] in reference to quotations throughout the thesis.

Please note also that Chapter Five has previously appeared in modified form as a journal article and is reprinted here by kind permission of Sage Publications Ltd., from Jeremy J. Whiteman, 'Trade and the Regeneration of France, 1789-91: Liberalism, Protectionism and the Commercial Policy of the National Constituent Assembly', in *European History Quarterly*, 31:2 (2001), pp. 171-204 (© Sage Publications Ltd., 2001).

Introduction: Historiography and the Definition of the Problem

It is something of a truism to say that the historiography of the French Revolution has undergone its own revolution in recent times. By the time of the Bicentenary of 1789, the essentials of classic or 'orthodox' Marxist interpretation had been fundamentally challenged by a wave of historiographical revisionism. Regarding the former interpretation as empirically unsustainable, this revisionism was part of a wider review of historical method and understandings of causality. Whereas historiographical analyses and interpretation had predominantly been focused around issues of class, that is, where social and political change was viewed as deriving 'from below' (as Marxists and other materialists believed), revisionist historians called for a return to interpretative approaches to the Revolution which ascribed a far greater autonomy to politics. The subsequent reorientation of French Revolutionary historiography from the social to the political can thus be seen in part as a return to what one might call an empirical and inductive historiographical tradition, represented most eminently by the work of such historians as William Doyle, Timothy Tackett and Alan Forrest. With the work of François Furet, Robert Darnton, Lynn Hunt, Keith Baker and others, this refocusing has also involved a marked revival in intellectual history, and the spawning of a powerfully renewed and more theoretical interest in ideology and its causal potency.[1]

For some historians, such as Lynn Hunt and François Furet, the dynamics inherent in ideology have been seen as the single most important factor in accounting for the ongoing outcomes of the

---

[1] It should be noted that number of 'neo-marxists', such as Colin Jones, Gwynne Lewis and George Comninel have also endeavoured to take account of recent developments in French revolutionary historiography. See Colin Jones, 'Bourgeois revolution revivified: 1789 and social change', in Peter Jones (Ed), *The French Revolution in Social and Political Perspective* (London, 1996); Gwynne Lewis, *The French Revolution: Rethinking the Debate* (London, 1993); George Comninel, *Rethinking the French Revolution: Marxism and the Revisionist Challenge* (London, 1987).

2 Reform, Revolution and French Global Policy 1787—1791

Revolution, at least up until Thermidor. Indeed, Furet and his disciples have seemed to look no further for more significant causal derivations of the Terror than purely ideological conceptions present at the outset of the Revolution, insisting that the increasing violence of the Revolution over the period 1789—94 can be attributed almost entirely to the inherently violent potential of the prevailing revolutionary discourse, rather than to otherwise external or 'circumstantial' factors. In this schema, Revolution itself is seen as tantamount to violence, and ideology therefore its vehicle.[2]

Other historians, such as Darnton, Baker and Roger Chartier have concentrated more closely on the intellectual and ideological origins of the Revolution.[3] While Darnton has taken what might be considered a 'social history of ideas' or 'cultural anthropology' approach to an examination of old regime society, looking at the social and cultural contexts in which ideas were received, transmitted and understood at street-level, other historians like Baker, following the 'linguistic turn', have come to focus more abstractly on textual and discourse analysis, and on the motive force of meaning and signification, irreducible, so it would seem, to social or economic relations and contexts. Baker, working from the premise that all social action is symbolically and discursively constituted, has argued for the central importance of ideology, or discourse, in understanding the origins of the Revolution. Defining Revolution then as a "transformation of the discursive practice of the community, a moment in which social relations are reconstituted and the discourse defining the political relations between individuals and groups is radically recast", the aim for Baker was to examine how a supposed synthesis and transformation of various old regime discourses resulted in and allowed for the creation of a new kind of political language in 1789, one that framed and gave impetus to an insurrectionary mindset and a popular revolutionary will.[4]

In short, with the history of political culture seemingly the dominant current trend in French Revolutionary historiography, recent work on revolutionary origins has tended to focus mostly on an understanding of

---

[2] See François Furet, *Interpreting the French Revolution* (Cambridge, 1981); Mona Ozouf, 'War and Terror in French Revolutionary Discourse (1792—94)', *Journal of Modern History*, 56 (December, 1984).

[3] Robert Darnton, *The Literary Underground of the Old Regime* (Cambridge, Mass., 1982); K. M. Baker, *Inventing the French Revolution* (Cambridge, 1990); Roger Chartier, *The Cultural Origins of the French Revolution* (Durham, N.C., 1986).

[4] Baker, *Inventing*, p. 18.

this 'insurrection of the public mind', in other words, on the cultural creation of a revolutionary constituency. As Michael Kwass has observed in a recent article, the questions currently at the forefront of this historical enquiry would appear to be the following: "Why did royal subjects, especially those in positions of power, re-conceive their political existence? Why did new political mentalities and discourse develop within the confines of absolutism, and how did they become revolutionary?"[5]

If lately there has been a reawakened interest in intellectual and cultural history, one other aspect of this return to the 'political' can be seen in a growing interest over recent years in the geopolitical dimensions of the Revolution and its origins. This has seen the emergence of two interpretative models, one by the historical sociologist Theda Skocpol in her 1979 work *States and Social Revolutions*, and another by Bailey Stone in his 1994 work *The Genesis of the French Revolution: A Global-Historical Interpretation*. Both of these models present radically different interpretations to those above, describing the final crisis of the old regime state as stemming from in its inherent material and structural problems, and precipitated in large part by the pressures of international competition.

In Skocpol's interpretation, the advent of Revolution in 1789 is seen as the natural result of complex geopolitical failure, that is, of the inability of the absolutist state to successfully pursue a policy of military aggrandizement against both land-based and maritime powers. This was largely owing to the allegedly 'backward' nature of its agrarian and pre-capitalist economy—relative to its most powerful rival, Britain—which ultimately allowed France insufficient fiscal resources to maintain its strategic position. This was to lead not only to the virtual paralysis of an already dysfunctional state machinery, and to the disaffection of Old Regime élites, but also to the unleashing of the furious discontent of the overburdened peasantry and the urban poor.[6]

For Skocpol, these structural and external factors were, moreover, not merely central to an understanding of the Revolution's origins, but also to its outcome. According to Skocpol, both the war of 1792, and the massive augmentation of state power and administrative centralisation that subsequently occured under the Jacobin Republic and later under Napoleon, could only be properly understood in the wider

---

[5] Michael Kwass, 'The Kingdom of Taxpayers: State Formation, Privilege, and Political Culture in Eighteenth-Century France', *Journal of Modern History*, 70 (June 1998), p. 296.
[6] Theda Skocpol, *States and Social Revolutions* (Cambridge, 1979), *passim*.

and longer-term context of the European balance of power system.[7] In this way the consequences of the Revolution could thus be connected to its origins, by virtue of a central problematic: the logic of international competition.

Stone's interpretation is similar to that of Skocpol, insofar as he depicts the revolutionary outbreak of 1789 as resulting from the interplay and convergence of external and internal crises. For Stone, the Revolution arose out of "a gradually developing crisis of governmental legitimacy in the domestic sphere paralleling and eventually interacting with the gradually developing crisis of French credibility in the international strategic sphere".[8] This convergence in itself allegedly arose from a failure of the absolute monarchy to adequately mesh its external ambitions with elite concerns, leading to a climate of acute discontent with the royal government in the late 1780s. This crisis manifested itself finally in a challenge to the constitutional authority of the absolute monarchy. As Stone concludes,

> the French Revolution began in 1789 as the result of a convergence in the Gallic kingdom of statist geopolitical and sociopolitical needs rooted deeply in the past. On the one hand, Bourbon statesmen were long mesmerized by the vision of a France not only perdurably secure in the endless competition of the European states but also uniquely positioned to achieve greatness on both the high seas and the continent. On the other hand, the policy makers who sought to realize this vision found, as time went on, that pursuing it forced them to sponsor a kind of domestic change that was ever more difficult to square with the social and political tenets undergirding the ancien régime. By 1789, the French crown was irretrievably undone by its coalescing failures in the foreign and domestic realms: that is to say, its failure to achieve anything remotely approaching its historic goals abroad and its failure to maintain control over rising sociopolitical expectations at home that, paradoxically, owed much in the first place to the crown's very pursuit of international greatness.[9]

These 'geopolitical' approaches of Skocpol and Stone may be said to have their roots in a rich historiography relating to early modern and eighteenth-century state-building and international relations. These are dimensions that would appear to have been strangely neglected by French Revolutionary historiography. For example, in Peter Jones' otherwise fine 1995 study *Reform and Revolution in France*

---

[7] *Ibid.*, p. 186.
[8] Bailey Stone, 'Geopolitical Origins of the French Revolution Reconsidered', *Consortium on Revolutionary Europe, Proceedings* (1988), p. 256.
[9] Bailey Stone, *The Genesis of the French Revolution* (Cambridge, 1994), p. 236.

1774—1791, he takes almost no account of the role of external pressures on the French state, and neglects even to mention the Dutch Crisis of 1787, surely an important event in the Pre-Revolution.[10] One might even say that the history of the French Revolution, and the history of international relations in which this Revolution forms part of a continuum, have seemed almost to occupy different spheres of scholarship, at least until recently.[11]

The keynote of this latter historiography is the importance it attributes to exogenous factors in the early and ongoing formation of European states. Indeed, those who have made studies of general European history across the eighteenth century have rarely failed to emphasise the crucial importance of external pressures and the role of an inherently competitive international system, particularly in the internal development of 'absolutist', dynastic states. For example, earlier in the century Otto Hintze declared that "it is often held that the growth and change of a political constitution dependent on the social developments within society; ... there is of course a germ of truth in this; but one point is overlooked—namely, the development of the state in relation to its neighbours".[12] For Leo Gershoy, many aspects of domestic reform and development could not be extracted from this context, since, as he stated,

> Security and power were [during the eighteenth century] fast becoming the co-ordinates of natural survival in the new technological order where administrative inefficiency as never before threatened the weaker state with disaster. The passage of sound laws and uniform legal procedures, the careful training of civil servants, establishment of orderly financial systems, and the enactment of countless regulations were all necessary security measures against potential aggression on the part of stronger neighbours.[13]

---

[10] Peter Jones, *Reform and Revolution in France: the politics of Transition, 1779—1791* (Cambridge, 1995).

[11] Not all historians of the French Revolution have been so neglectful of the impact of international relations. The impact upon the Revolution of traditional balance of power logics was asserted by Albert Sorel in his landmark late nineteenth century work *Europe and the French Revolution*, a point forcefully reiterated by Tim Blanning in his 1986 work *The Origins of the French Revolutionary Wars* (London, 1986).

[12] Otto Hintz, *The Historical Essays of Otto Hintz*, Felix Gilbert (Ed.) (New York, 1975), p. 158.

[13] Leo Gershoy, *From Despotism to Revolution* (New York, 1944), p. 162.

A succession of other historians, including E.N. Williams, M.S. Anderson, and more recently, Paul Kennedy and Paul Schroeder, have similarly noted that the rise of the central state and gradual centralization of public power that was to occur throughout the seventeenth and eighteenth centuries was closely related to an endemic pressure upon states to compete on a strategic and economic level.[14] Reformist efforts such as those pursued by the 'enlightened despots' of states such as Prussia, Russia, and Austria, in the mid-to-late eighteenth century, though often promoted as demonstrative of a liberal or paternalistic concern for the general welfare, have thus nonetheless been seen as having as their ultimate purpose the augmenting of absolutist military power and the furthering of autocratic government. In most of the countries of Europe, including France, it was thus the central state that has been identified as the instigator of reform and the principal agent of 'modernization', in opposition to the entrenched structures and interests of corporate society.

In spite of this resonance within general eighteenth-century historiography, there still persists among French Revolutionary historians some resistance to the type of 'statist' models or interpretations presented by Skocpol and Stone. Skocpol's "structuralist, nonvoluntarist" model has, in particular, met with criticism from several directions. Some historians simply dismiss the view that France's economy was actually 'backward' in relation to Britain throughout the greater part of the eighteenth century.[15] Others, such as William H. Sewell, highlighted what they saw as Skocpol's unsatisfactory treatment of ideology. This was insofar as ideology seemed to be regarded by Skocpol as a kind of causal epiphenomenon, as a mere indicator of structural change, rather than as an autonomous factor in itself. Sewell also asserted that a depiction of ideology as an autonomous factor was by no means incompatible with Skocpol's structural approach, in that the internal evolution of ideological

---

[14] E. N. Williams, *The Ancien Régime in Europe* (Harmondsworth 1970); M. S. Anderson, *Europe in the Eighteenth Century* (London, 1961); Paul Kennedy, *The Rise and Fall of the Great Powers: Economic Change and Military Conflict from 1500 to 2000* (London, 1988); Paul W. Schroeder, *The Transformation of European Politics 1763-1848* (Oxford, 1996).

[15] Jack Goldstone, *Revolution and Rebellion in the Early Modern World* (Berkeley, 1991), p. 208.

'systems' could be understood as constituting yet another kind of structural phenomenon.[16]

Lynn Hunt, on the other hand (in what Skocpol has dubbed an 'internalist' approach),[17] has seemed to discount material-structural analyses altogether. In her 1984 work, *Politics, Culture and Class in the French Revolution*, she insisted that an understanding of the origins, nature and outcomes of the Revolution could only be divined through a reading of the prevailing ideology and its powerful symbolism, that is, in recognising the causal potentiality of this ideology as almost entirely an autonomous and historically specific phenomenon. She therefore argued the French Revolution's inaccessibility to 'transnational' structuralist analyses.[18]

Stone's attempt ten years later at a 'grand synthesis' of geopolitical and sociopolitical causes in his *Genesis of the French Revolution* has also drawn criticism. Though he has generally been praised for his attempt at such a synthesis, particularly for his review of recent (and mainly revisionist) historiography, some reviewers found themselves unconvinced that his interpretation amounted to a genuine synthesis at all. Rather, they saw it as one still dominated by the functionalist logics of international relations, and hence in their view insufficiently attentive to recent developments in the study of political culture. David Bell, a prominent practitioner of politico-cultural history, has even described the interpretation as "reductionist" and as still only offering a "narrow, determinist model" of revolutionary etiology.[19] Colin Lucas has commented, similarly, that despite Stone's consideration of sociopolitical causes, he remained nonetheless "most ill at ease with social and intellectual issues". Lamenting that there was in Stone's work only the "briefest allusion to the possible autonomy of social change", Lucas concluded that Stone's work provided "no explanation of where

---

[16] William H. Sewell, 'Ideologies and Social Revolutions: Reflections on the French Case', *Journal of Modern History*, 57 (March 1985), pp. 57-96.

[17] Theda Skocpol and Meyer Kestnbaum, 'Mars Unshackled: The French Revolution in World-Historical Perspective', in Ferenc Fehér (Ed.), *The French Revolution and the Birth of Modernity* (Berkeley, 1990), pp. 15-16.

[18] *Ibid.*; Lynn Hunt, *Politics, Culture, and Class in the French Revolution* (California, 1984).

[19] David A. Bell, *Journal of Interdisciplinary History*, 27, (Summer, 1996), pp. 131-132.

the great insurrection of the public mind comes from, other than the geopolitical failure of the state".[20]

Bell and Lucas seem here to be implicitly acknowledging that an attempt at such a synthesis is warranted, although, having criticised Stone's efforts to provide a framework for this, they provide no alternative suggestion about where such a synthesis might be found, or fruitfully pursued. Clearly neither politico-cultural or geopolitical-statist causes can alone account satisfactorily for the complex phenomenon of the Revolution. It is clear then that a fully satisfying account of the Revolution and its origins can only begin with an understanding of the Revolution as essentially multi-faceted, with the integration of both external and internal pressures on the French state.[21]

The source of much of the criticism attached to Skocpol and Stone's interpretations is that they have reduced the state itself to some kind of impersonal, non-voluntarist entity, that simply responded 'automatically' and predictably to certain external stimuli, and where the response could be gauged according to physical rather than cultural or other 'cognitive' outcomes.[22] My own view is that this criticism is somewhat misplaced, at least in regard to Stone, for throughout most of his 1994 work he clearly assumes foreign policy-making to be a subjective and culturally-informed process.

However, if Stone at least appears to argue that the Revolution was not simply the outcome of long-term structural pressures, but also emerged out of a *conscious* and spontaneous response in France to accumulated French humiliations on the international scene, then it is reasonable to expect this to be empirically substantiated. Unfortunately, although Stone in particular has provided a powerfully suggestive and insightful synthesis of secondary literature, neither he nor Skocpol have engaged in any appreciable direct archival or primary source research in

---

[20] Colin Lucas, *American Historical Review* (December, 1995), pp. 1585-1586.

[21] This was the basic theoretical point put forward in my 1993 Masters Thesis, which argued for a more 'co-axial' approach to the Revolutionary causality, one that integrated geostrategic exigencies with the issues or logics internal to ideology and political culture, and in which their differences, connections and interactions could be acknowledged. See Jeremy Whiteman, 'Tocqueville and the Two Faces of Modernity: Current Liberal Historiography and the French Revolution', Unpublished M.A. thesis, University of Melbourne, 1993.

[22] See, for example, Bell's comment that in the concluding chapter of Stone's 1994 work "the state seems to take on a life of its own, with every historical development apparently determined by the hidden logic of its restructuring in the face of international challenge". Bell, *Journal of Interdisciplinary History* (Summer, 1996), p. 132.

order to substantiate and give particular weight to their specific conclusions, in other words, to conclusively support an argument that the Revolution was at least partly inspired and shaped by a desire to restore France's status as a leading international power.

There has been until recently very little consideration of this proposition by historians of the French Revolution, and certainly no in-depth empirical analysis. Taken together, the few and often oblique references made by historians to the connection between French international humiliation and the origins of the Revolution had painted a picture that was only sketchy and inconclusive. The most authoritative and systematic general analysis of the pre-revolutionary *cahiers*, by Beatrice Hyslop, had even seemed to suggest that as 'martial' patriotism appeared in fact to have been only a minor element in the expressions of French patriotism found in the *cahiers*, it did not play a pronounced role in public opinion.[23]

This situation has changed with the recent publication of Orville Murphy's work *The Diplomatic Retreat of France and Public Opinion on the Eve of the French Revolution*, and the work of Gary Savage.[24] Both Murphy and Savage have examined the impact of the crown's foreign policy failures on French public opinion in the period of the Pre-Revolution. Murphy has noted how in the last two decades of Louis XVI's reign a growing public climate of frustration and discontent, focused chiefly around France's Austrian alliance, was encouraged by the appearance of various (sometimes illicit) publications. This was part of a 'public opinion' which was increasingly beyond the crown's ability to control and manipulate, and which was highly critical of its foreign policy. The period following the Dutch crisis of 1787 is considered the point at which this discontent became most acute, and which, as Murphy describes, Louis XVI was seen in this public opinion to have suddenly become a shameful "nullity" in European affairs.[25] For his part, Savage has mounted a comprehensive examination of this increasingly discontented public opinion, focusing similarly around the

---

[23] Beatrice Hyslop, *French Nationalism in 1789 according to the Cahiers* (New York, 1968), pp. 160-163.

[24] Gary Savage, 'Favier's Heirs: The French Revolution and the Sécret du Roi', *Historical Journal*, 41:1 (1998), pp. 225-258. See also, Savage's unpublished PhD thesis, 'Political Culture, Revolution and Foreign Policy in France, 1787-92', Cambridge, 1996.

[25] Orville Murphy, *The Diplomatic Retreat of France and Public Opinion on the Eve of the French Revolution, 1783-1789* (Washington D.C.), 1998.

issue of the Franco-Austrian alliance, and taken in the context of the evolving political culture of the time.[26]

This present study differs from the recent works of Murphy and Savage in three ways. Firstly, it seeks to make a distinction between foreign policy, as applied principally to the European and continental sphere, and what I shall define as 'global policy', including not only foreign policy, but also the 'Atlantic' sphere of maritime, commercial and colonial policy. Secondly, it confines itself mostly to an examination of the work and understandings of the policy-makers themselves, rather than of broader public opinion. Thirdly, the study will focus on the relationship between the Revolution and French international aspirations more from the perspective of political economy than of political culture. The basic questions to be pursued are as follows: if one may regard the Old Regime state as having patently failed in its attempt to sustain its ability to compete strategically and economically with other powers, what then was the attitude and response of the revolutionaries to the question of France's place in the world? To what extent did the idea of French national 'regeneration' after 1789 include not just cultural and civic dimensions, but involve also the question of French national power, and the role of France in a competitive world system? What, furthermore, were their underlying understandings of the nature of the international system, and of its political economy? Finally, what continuities and discontinuities can one perceive between the work of the revolutionary global policy-makers and their old regime predecessors?

One can assume that from the outbreak of war in 1792 the impact of external exigencies on the fledgling revolutionary state was profound, direct, and immediate. For this reason this study will also extend no further chronologically than the period of the National Constituent Assembly, before the work of 'national regeneration' became subordinate to the needs of war, and before it was eclipsed by the struggle between revolution and counter-revolution. Looking specifically at policy-outcomes, the basic hypotheses will be, firstly, that the discourse of 'national regeneration' among the deputies of the Constituent Assembly did place strong emphasis on the *material* regeneration of France. Secondly, it will be proposed that the Constituents did anticipate a revival in French international influence, and pre-eminence in Europe, that was as much material as moral and which they believed would flow from the reorganisation of French society and government. In this way it will be argued that French

---

[26] Savage, 'Favier's Heirs', *passim*.

responses to the demands of international competition played an important role in both fostering and shaping the Revolution of 1789.

The book will be divided into two parts, the first part examining the nature and exigencies of French foreign and global policy-making in the last years of the Old Regime, particularly the period 1787—89. The first chapter will consider the background of French global policy-making from the end of the American War of Independence up until the Assembly of Notables in early 1787. The second chapter will consider the crisis in French foreign policy following the Assembly of Notables, and its impact on the French position in Europe, in particular reference to Stone and Murphy's recent analyses. The third chapter will consider the nature and impact of this crisis for French power in the wider global arena, mostly during the period 1788—89. The second part of the book will examine the combined work of the royal government and the Constituent Assembly following the outbreak of Revolution in May 1789, with separate chapters focusing on the various elements of their global policy: foreign affairs, trade and colonial administration.

In regard, finally, to the primary sources, the study will concentrate primarily on official documentation. For the period of the Old Regime, these sources—including ministerial *mémoires*, minutes and correspondance of the royal government—derive principally from the archives of the French Foreign Ministry at the Quai d'Orsay, the archives of the Naval and Colonial Ministry presently on microfilm at the Archives Nationales in Paris, and the manuscript collections at the Bibliothèque Nationale. For the period of the National Constituent Assembly, I have been particularly fortunate to have available to me at the Baillieu Library at the University of Melbourne a wide range of primary source material, including the Maclure Collection of French Revolutionary Materials and the enormous French Revolutionary Research Collection. For the purposes of the study, this latter collection contained—among a vast range of printed and published material—such important sources as the proceedings both of the pre-revolutionary Assembly of Notables and of the National Assembly, most specifically the *Archives Parlementaires*. The collections also contained voluminous pamphlet material, newspapers, and records of the National Assembly's various legislative committees. I have also been fortunate to have available to me hardbound at the Baillieu Library the *Réimpression de l'ancien moniteur*, a reproduction of the original *Le Moniteur* which contained record of parliamentary debates and legislation, and effectively served the function of government gazette throughout the Revolution.

PART ONE
THE OLD REGIME

1 France Resurgent: from the Peace of 1783 to the Assembly of Notables

The period following the American War of Independence was, for the France of Louis XVI, the high water mark of its diplomatic prestige.[1] Benefitting from the support of the other major maritime powers of Europe, Spain and Holland, and bolstered by Catherine II's 'League of Armed Neutrality', France had managed to isolate and subsequently humble the same power that had humiliated France during the Seven Years' War twenty years before. Britain, having lost its American colonies, and deprived of the European alliances that it had always depended on in order to divert French attention and resources away from the oceanic and colonial sphere, now looked in a somewhat more vulnerable position as a maritime and imperial power. By contrast, France's victory in the war of 1778—82 seemed to offer it the promise of commercial expansion and the strengthening of its own position as a global power.

There were three principal French ministers during this period who can be said to have had a major bearing on the issue of France as a global power: Firstly, the comte de Vergennes, Foreign Minister since 1774, and as such responsible for the direction of foreign affairs and negotiations, including those concerning trade with other powers; secondly, the maréchal de Castries, Minister for the Navy and Colonies since 1780, responsible, as his title suggests, for the direction and administration of all maritime and colonial affairs, including issues pertaining to colonial trade; thirdly, Charles-Alexandre de Calonne, whose duties as Contrôleur-Général since 1783 broadly encompassed the administration of all matters pertaining to the French economy and its finances. These three ministers naturally had differences with regard to policy born of the distinct demands of their separate ministries, as is common to any government. Such, however, was the effective degree of

---

[1] As John Hardman argues in *Louis XVI* (New Haven, 1993), p. 99.

overlap in these ministers' responsibilities, and the lack of policy co-ordination endemic to the government of Louis XVI during this period, that these differences may be said to have had in the end profound consequences for the overall coherence and success of French global policy.

The Policy Outlooks of Vergennes and Castries in the Wake of the American War

Among the more bitter of the rivalries which were exacerbated under the French ministerial system in this period was that between Vergennes and Castries, representatives of differing power factions at the court of Versailles who also had strongly opposing views on the issue of France's general foreign policy. It was the conclusion of the American War that set the stage for the struggle between these two ministers over the future direction of this foreign policy.

Great as the diplomatic gains resulting from France's victory in 1783 seemed, the actual material gains deriving from the Peace Treaty with Britain were relatively modest. A French naval defeat in the 'Battle of the Saints' in the West Indies, though it had failed to change the overall result of the war, nonetheless had considerably lessened French bargaining power at the peace negotiations. Shelburne, the British Prime Minister, had also been able to play successfully on the mistrust existing between the various allied powers, concluding a separate peace with the Americans which only put pressure on the French and Spanish to come quickly to the table to press their own claims. The subsequent peace settlement was the result of hard bargaining and, beyond the loss of its American colonies, saw no other major losses for Britain. In the end, while Britain and the Bourbon powers agreed to the mutual return of territories captured by the other during the war, France had managed to negotiate the return of its trading posts in Sénégal and its scattered establishments in India (which, excepting those in Bengal, it was now permitted to fortify). In addition, the French were accorded the former British possession of the island of Tobago at the base of the Windward Isles in the Antilles, as well as some fishing concessions off Newfoundland. As consolation for not taking Gibraltar, France's ally Spain had to be content with the acquisition of Florida and Minorca, an outcome with which they were hardly satisfied.[2]

---

[2] For a detailed account of the diplomacy surrounding the peace negotiations, see Jonathon Dull, 'Vergennes, Rayneval and the Diplomacy of Trust', in R.

From the French perspective, the greatest impetus to enter into peace negotiations in 1782 came from a realisation of its own financial plight. Despite the optimistic situation presented in Necker's famous 'Compte Rendu' of 1781, it had during the war become obvious to Vergennes that it was simply beyond France's capacity to fund another campaign.[3] Yet, as Vergennes would argue in a *mémoire* to the king in 1784, the conclusion of a 'reasonable' or 'magnanimous' peace with Britain the previous year was in fact completely consonant with the principles and long-term aspirations of French foreign policy, the central plank of which was the maintenance of European stability.[4] That is, for Vergennes, who had come to preside over a French diplomatic 'system' of enormous complexity, peace and possible reconciliation with Britain was both a imperative necessity and a desired object, for upon it depended the strength of France's position in Europe.

Vergennes was a veteran diplomat steeped in the traditions of the balance of power. The keynote of his overall policy, in accord with the views of his master Louis XVI, was that of 'moderation'. Coming to office at the start of the King's reign, the minister had offered Louis XVI a foreign policy that both appealed to the king's personal sense of moderation and yet seemed also to promise a return to France of a role in Europe in accordance with her most cherished traditions. In essence, Vergennes asserted that France's recovery and future destiny as a front-rank power lay in her renouncing territorial aggrandisements in favour of becoming the 'peaceful' and 'moral' arbiter, and preserver of the status quo in Europe as laid down long before by the Treaty of Westphalia. Outlined in a *mémoire* to the king at the start of his term of office in 1774,[5] the essentials of this policy were reaffirmed in another *mémoire* written in the wake of the American War, ten years later. In it Vergennes argued that the protection of smaller states against the predatory ambitions of larger powers was as just and honourable as it was in France's interest. "La France", he declared,

---

[3] Hoffman and R. Albert (Eds), *Peace and the Peacemakers* (Charlottesville, 1986), pp. 101-131; see also Vincent Harlow, *The Founding of the Second British Empire* (London, 1952), Vol. 1, Ch. 7.

[4] Ibid., p. 324; see also Orville T. Murphy, *Charles Gravier, Comte de Vergennes: French Diplomacy in the Age of Revolution: 1719-1787* (Albany, 1982), p. 324.

Vergennes, 'Mémoire présenté au Roi', 29 March 1784, AAE-MD-France-587, f. 207.

[5] Hardman, *Louis XVI*, p. 93; Murphy, *Comte de Vergennes*, pp. 213-218.

placée en quelque sorte au centre de l'Europe, forte par la contiguïté de ses provinces et leur ensemble par la richesse et la population de son sol, environnée de forteresses qui couvrent ses frontières, et de voisins qui pris isolement sont hors d'état de les attaquer, la France dis-je, n'a besoin ni d'agrandissements ni de conquêtes; toutes ses vues et toute son influence doivent donc être dirigées au maintien de l'ordre public, et à prévenir que les différens pouvoirs qui forment l'équilibre de l'Europe ne soyent point détruits.[6]

The recent war with Britain was consistent with this policy in that it formed the first part of a two-stage strategy, in which the maintenance in Europe of a balance of power favourable to France had first necessitated the reduction or removal of British influence on the continent, and the checking of its rapidly expanding maritime and colonial power elsewhere. For this reason Vergennes and Sartines, Castries' predecessor as Naval minister, had continued Choiseul's earlier policy of rebuilding a French navy shattered by the Seven Years' War, and had subsequently intervened in the late 1770s in the worsening dispute between Britain and its American colonies. Although the ostensible objective was to help procure independence for what was later to become the United States of America, the ultimate aim of such a substantial armed intervention was to reverse the trend toward increasing British naval superiority, by bringing about a genuine parity of maritime strength between the British and their Bourbon rivals.[7] Thereafter, in the second and most ambitious part of Vergennes' plan, it was hoped that the chastened British would realise that it was in their interest to co-operate with France in the maintenance of European stability. This would mean the containing of ambitious powers such as Prussia and Austria, and of the alarming growth of newer powers such as

---

[6] Vergennes, 'Mémoire', AAE-MD-France-587, f. no. 210. As most contemporary writers on Vergennes attest, it was perhaps a combination of the Foreign Minister's innate conservatism and his rather 'legalistic' frame of mind that caused him to put enormous store into this objective, for it became the cornerstone of French foreign policy, and the objective which all other elements of French foreign policy were meant finally to serve. See Orville Murphy, 'Charles Gravier de Vergennes: Profile of an Old Regime Diplomat', Political Science Quarterly, 83:3, 1968, pp. 400-417; 'The Conservatism of Charles Gravier, Comte de Vergennes', *Consortium on Revolutionary Europe 1750—1850*, 1981; Munro Price, *Preserving the Monarchy: the comte de Vergennes, 1774—1787* (Cambridge, 1995), Ch. 1; Jean-François Labourdette, *Vergennes: Ministre principal de Louis XVI* (Paris, 1990), Ch. 1.

[7] See Orville Murphy, 'The View from Versailles: Charles Gravier Comte de Vergennes's Perceptions of the American Revolution', in R. Hoffman and R. Albert (Eds), *Diplomacy and Revolution: The Franco-American Alliance of 1778* (Charlottesville, 1981), p. 115.

Russia, which had begun to exercise an influence in Eastern Europe that threatened to supplant that of France.[8] In short, by counter-balancing British seapower in the 'oceanic' sphere, it was hoped that France could then begin to regain its ascendancy in Europe, through the subsequent containment of continental powers.[9]

This policy revealed Vergennes' understanding of the connections between strategic and economic power, and of the particular role of commerce in the pursuit of strategic goals. Although the 'modest' peace settlement with Britain in 1783 was one that, according to Vergennes in his 1784 *mémoire*, accorded with the general principles and aspirations of France's foreign policy, it was clear that the French desire for a peace in 1782 was dictated above all else by France's manifest financial weakness. Such was Vergennes' innate conservatism, however, that he was disinclined to endanger the traditional structures of French society through any major overhaul of its fiscal institutions and practices.[10] Rather, as Orville Murphy has pointed out, Vergennes preferred that it be through a general expansion of trade that France should find the funds sufficient to achieve and maintain a favourable position in the European and global balance of power.[11] This, as Murphy notes, was not to be achieved through further French colonial expansion, an enterprise that Vergennes considered largely unnecessary, perilous and of dubious economic value, but rather through a combination of diplomatic means and an expansion of French shipping.[12]

In fulfillment of this policy, Vergennes sought throughout his stewardship of foreign affairs to foster a web of bilateral trade agreements with other states, with the aim of extending French trade and markets, often at the expense of the British. Such agreements had a

---

[8] Dull, 'France and the American Revolution seen as Tragedy', in R. Hoffman and R. Albert (Eds), *Ibid.*, p. 81.

[9] See Stone, The Genesis of the French Revolution, pp. 111-13. See also Dull, 'France and the American Revolution', pp. 80-84.

[10] Munro Price has recounted the considerable difficulties faced by old regime reformers in their efforts to improve the Royal Government's financial administration, largely because of the internal politics of the court at Versailles, see Price, *Preserving the Monarchy*, Ch. 2, *passim*.

[11] Murphy, *Comte de Vergennes*, p. 432.

[12] *Ibid.*, pp. 456-457. In this conviction, Vergennes echoed a growing sentiment among some elements of French public, and particularly 'enlightened', opinion, ill disposed toward colonialism or colonial expansion for either economic or humanitarian reasons. See Vincent Confer, 'French colonial ideas before 1789', *French Historical Studies*, 7:4 (1972), p. 354; Carl Lokke, *France and the Colonial Question: A Study of Contemporary French Opinion 1763—1801* (New York, 1932), p. 78.

number of perceived benefits. Not only would increased levels of trade stimulate the French economy and provide valuable customs revenue to the French treasury, but the increased level of economic interdependence would hopefully preserve peace and give France greater influence in the deliberations of these other powers. Thus, while commerce could be used to draw various countries away from British influence and more into the orbit of France, commerce with Britain itself could be seen as a means to restrain or otherwise influence the latter's policy.[13] It was this reason as much as any other that prompted Vergennes to include in the peace settlement of 1783 a mutual undertaking between Britain and France to work toward a liberalisation of their trade relationship that would finally take shape in the form of the Eden Treaty of 1786.

Thus, while with Vergennes France had forsaken the idea of any further territorial aggrandisements, and hence confined itself to the preservation of a delicately poised postwar balance of power, it was both to pay for and profit from its policy of the strategic containment of Britain and the continental powers through an *economic* expansion of France engineered in large part through skilful diplomacy.[14] Through the maintenance of this peace and the stability of Europe France would progressively achieve the degree of economic and strategic preponderance necessary to make it in turn the impregnable arbiter of this balance of power. Vergennes' overall foreign policy thus consisted not merely of two basic stages but of two dimensions, on one hand the strategic containment of Britain and the continental powers Prussia, Austria and especially Russia, and on the other hand the economic expansion of France through the promotion of trade with these very countries.[15]

---

[13] Murphy, *Comte de Vergennes*, p. 456.

[14] As Vergennes' chief advisor on economic affairs, Dupont de Nemours, wrote in a 1783 mémoire, "Les marchandises dans lesquelles les Anglois nous surpassent, si l'on en exception leur laines brutes qu'ils ne laissent pas sortir librement, sont des marchandises de main d'oeuvre. Nous pouvons un jour, et avec quelques encouragements, perfectionner notre industrie, égaler par elle, ou même surpasser les Anglois", Dupont de Nemours, 'Mémoire abrégé sur la position actuelle de l'Europe, le changement que la paix y peut apporter et les combinaisons de commerce auxquelles elle peut donner lieu', 1783, AAE-MD-France-587, ff. 76-77.

[15] For more on Vergennes' diplomacy and policy-outlook see Robert Crout, 'In Search of a Just and Lasting Peace: The Treaty of 1783, Louis XVI, Vergennes and the Regeneration of the Realm'. *International Review*, 5 (August 1983), pp. 363-98.

France Resurgent 21

Those in France who had for a generation hoped for a simple war of revenge that would strike a mortal blow to the global power of Britain were to be sorely disappointed. Britain, it was true, had suffered humiliation in being forced to recognise the independence of her former American colonies, but as Franklin Ford has noted, despite some concessions made in the Treaty of Paris, Britain still retained more or less the web of strategic bases that were vital in supporting its naval power around the world.[16] Thus, despite the French and allied victory, the outcome of the Seven Years' War was not in any substantial way reversed, a fact that excited considerable criticism during the period of Vergennes' Ministry. At the forefront of this criticism was Vergennes' colleague the Minister for the Navy and Colonies, the maréchal de Castries. This minister was a classic 'Choiseulist' in that he believed that France's deadliest enemy was Britain rather than any continental power, and that the true test for France as a great power lay in its competition with Britain on the high seas and in the struggle for the acquisition of colonial and maritime trade.[17]

French intervention in the American War has been condemned by historians such as Marcel Marion as having fatally overburdened the fragile financial structures of the royal government, and thus having played a significant role in the subsequent demise of the Old Regime.[18] The Contrôleur-Général, Turgot, had argued against participation in this war, warning that an involvement on such a scale was beyond France's financial capacity. With his removal in 1776, these warnings had gone unheeded.[19] Castries' view was the opposite, in that he argued after the war that France's efforts in the American War had not gone nearly far enough. In a *mémoire* apparently read to the King and the Conseil d'Etat by Castries in 1786, Vergennes' conclusion of the peace in 1783 was criticised as unnecessary and premature, in that France had supposedly been only one campaign away from scoring a decisive and comprehensive victory over Britain in both the West and East Indies.[20]

---

[16] Franklin Ford, *Europe 1780-1830* (London, 1970), p. 68.
[17] See Duc de Castries, *Le Maréchal de Castries* (Paris, 1956), Ch. 4-5, passim.
[18] Marcel Marion, *Histoire financière de la France depuis 1715* (Paris, 1914), Vol. 1, pp. 289-90.
[19] Jonathon Dull, *The French Navy and American Independence: A study of Arms and Diplomacy 1774-1787* (Princeton, 1975), pp. 44-49; Stone, *Genesis of the French Revolution*, p. 116.
[20] Cited in J-L Soulavie, *Mémoires historiques et politiques du règne de Louis XVI*, 6 vols. (Paris, 1801), Vol. 5, p. 20. There is some doubt as to the authenticity of this document, the original having been lost. Soulavie and Labordette accept it as authentic, and as having been read to the Conseil d'état by Castries in both the king's and Vergennes' presence, a situation which John

It concluded by declaring that recent history had witnessed the rapid degradation of French credit and influence, and, "par conséquent son rang à la tête des puissances du premier ordre", a situation which the meagre gains of the peace treaty of 1783 had done nothing to redress.[21]

Such criticism of Vergennes' foreign policy demonstrated a crucial difference in Castries' and Vergennes' respective conceptions of the then present and future needs of French national power. On the question of the need for at least a continuing parity of naval strength with Britain, they were more or less agreed. Both anticipated that the strength of British finances would allow the British to rearm vigorously, and that France and its allies ought to maintain sufficiently powerful naval forces to prevent any British attempt to wage a return war of revenge for the loss of their American colonies. Beyond this their views sharply diverged. While Vergennes had wished for Britain's waxing power to be checked, he had strategic and economic reasons for not wishing it to be collapsed entirely. In contrast, Castries, in a *mémoire* of 1784 to the King, stated his belief that the American War ought to be merely the first of a two-stage campaign that effectively aimed at the destruction of Britain as a front-rank colonial and maritime power. Declaring that "c'est toujours avec une sorte de honte qu'on entend parler de la rivalité de l'Angleterre et la France", given that France's population was three times that of Britain's, Castries believed, as did many Frenchmen, that Britain was an 'inflated' power that deserved to be reduced to its 'real' proportions:

> Plus de deux siècles d'expérience ont fait connaître que la puissance qui dominait sur la mer pervenait à maîtriser le continent; c'est par l'emploi de ce moien puissant que l'Angleterre est sortie de la ligne que ses forces naturelles lui assignait et qu'elle a détruite l'équilibre maritime qu'il importe si fort de rétablir.[22]

Hardman, a recent biographer of Louis XVI, has asserted (in discussion with me) as highly unlikely, given the king's great dislike of confrontation, and the lack of supportive evidence. On balance, I am inclined to accept Munro Price's view that if it was not actually presented to the Conseil d'état, it may nonetheless have been sent to the king privately. In any case, for our purposes it is sufficient to establish that although the mémoire may have been written by Grimoard, it was not only endorsed by but actually conveyed the views of Castries, a point which is not in dispute. See Munro Price, *Preserving the Monarchy*, p. 209-212.

[21] Soulavie, *Mémoires historiques et politiques*, p. 89.
[22] AN 306 APs-21-16, pp. 2-4.

Much as Choiseul had done two decades previously, Castries argued that it was essential for the future power and prosperity of France that she shift the focus of her endeavours from the continent to the struggle for naval and colonial ascendancy. Not only had France's long and regrettable neglect of her navy ultimately compromised its continental security, but from the perspective of political economy, such a concentration on Europe had proven extremely unremunerative:

> Je doute qu'aucun des chapîtres de dépenses de Votre Monarchie, Sire, présente à Votre Majesté, d'aussi grands dédommagements, jamais une guerre sur terre n'a donné de résultats aussi utiles qu'une guerre de mers peut en produire. Ainsi, à gloire égale, il reste dans la balance à l'avantage des succès maritimes, un accroisement de prospérité qu'une guerre dans la continent ne donnaît jamais. On peut donc articuler, sans crainte, que c'est une dépense bien entendu que celle d'une marine puissante, et qu'elle seule peut assurer la gloire et la prosperité d'une nation.[23]

Thus any resources devoted to the development of French maritime and colonial power were investments that would eventually reap substantial dividends, effectively paying for themselves, whereas continental conflicts could only ever be a heavy and relatively unproductive drain on the country's finances. Already, he pointed out, it was only colonial trade that France had to thank for it sustaining a favourable balance of commerce. Naval wars, moreover, were not only far more profitable than land wars, but, he argued, would also ultimately give France greater political influence in Europe.[24] Hence, in contrast to Vergennes' cautious and moderate approach, Castries was convinced that France could only succeed as a great power if the power of its primary maritime rival Britain could effectively be broken, an objective that only war could procure.[25]

Calonne, Vergennes and the Question of Trade Liberalisation

If Vergennes and Castries were both concerned to constrain the strategic growth of Britain and other rival powers, it should be noted that Calonne, as Contrôleur-Général, was concerned more narrowly with improving the economic and financial health of the French state,

---

[23] *Ibid.*, p. 15.
[24] *Ibid.*, p. 16.
[25] On the views of Castries, see also Price, *Preserving the Monarchy*, p. 68.

regardless of wider political considerations.[26] In this respect, however, his policy goals seemed to dovetail to a large extent with those of Vergennes, in so far as they together co-operated in the task of promoting the expansion of French foreign trade, primarily through the provision of trade treaties of a more liberal nature with two of France's more serious strategic rivals, Britain and Russia. This move from a regime of high protectionism toward more liberal economic relationships with other powers undoubtably constituted a major shift in the traditional pattern of international competition. French policy during most of the eighteenth century had continued to follow traditional mercantilist precepts, wherein military force was considered a primary weapon in the race for economic advantage, and governments had been concerned to deny, where possible, all economic or commercial advantages to their strategic rivals.[27]

It is difficult to determine what role economic theorists may have played in the reformulation of French commercial policy during this period. Certainly, with the increasing level of international trade during the latter part of the eighteenth century, mercantilist conceptions had progressively lost much of their cogency, challenged first by the physiocratic faith in 'free trade', and the writings of such influential authors as Montesquieu and Adam Smith. These thinkers contributed to a growing conviction among intellectual elites that it was only through heightened reciprocal and interdependent commercial activity that states could fulfil their potential for internal economic development.[28] A natural concomitant to this view among such theorists was the belief that aggressive war, rather than being a prime instrument of economic gain, was in fact gravely injurious to the wealth, power and future prosperity of states. The eminent Physiocrat Dupont de Nemours, economic advisor to both Vergennes and Calonne, typified this view when he stated, in a *mémoire* to the former, that

---

[26] Wilma J. Pugh, 'Calonne's "New Deal"', *Journal of Modern History*, 11:3 (September 1939), p. 294.

[27] On Anglo-French commercial rivalry during the eighteenth century, see Jeremy Black, *Natural and Necessary Enemies: Anglo-French Relations in the Eighteenth Century* (London, 1986), Ch. 5. See also M.S. Anderson, 'Eighteenth-Century Theories of the Balance of Power', in R. Hatton and M. Anderson (Eds), *Studies in Diplomatic History* (London, 1970), p. 194.

[28] For the views of Montesquieu on international relations and commercial competition, see Merle L. Perkins, 'Montesquieu on National Power and International Rivalry', *Studies on Voltaire*, 238 (1985), especially pp. 52-55; Stephen Rosow, 'Commerce, Power and Justice: Montesquieu on International Politics', *Review of Politics*, 46:3 (1984), pp. 346-366.

toutes les Puissances ont également intérêt à maintenir la Paix, parceque la Guerre, même la plus heureuse, épuise les Capitaux, rallentir les travaux de l'agriculture et du commerce, nécessite des emprunts qui absorbent les revenus publics et qui obligent de multiplier les impôts: de sorte que les Conquêtes même ne valent jamais ce qu'elles ont coûté, et laissent les Nations qui les ont faites, moins puissantes et par conséquent moins imposantes qu'elles ne l'étaient auparavant.[29]

Despite the cogency given to this view by the state of mutual debt that Britain and France had found themselves in after the American War, it may nonetheless be argued that government policy during this period, as at most other times, was ultimately determined less by the convictions of economic theorists than by the demands of immediate reality. The conclusion in 1786 of a more liberal trade treaty between Britain and France, as proposed in the peace negotiations of 1782—83, had, from the French perspective, a number of different motives. Firstly, it may be seen as a simple recognition of the growth in both legitimate and illicit Anglo-French trade over previous decades. Both governments adopted the view that it was better to have a far smaller customs duty that one could actually collect, than a prohibitively high tariff that had only encouraged large scale evasion and smuggling, and which, in failing to staunch the flow of illicit trade either way, had proven counter-productive. Secondly, as already indicated, Vergennes' desire for economic rapprochement with Britain, and for closer trade links with other powers, was motivated in large part by specific political considerations, in particular, the desire to extract maximum political and diplomatic gains from greater levels of economic interdependence. This policy of rapprochement was demonstrative both of his short term and longer term objectives. Peace and stability between the European powers, particularly Britain and France, was considered both necessary on account of the state of French domestic finances and integral to the vision of the future of French strategic power as outlined by Vergennes in his *mémoires* to the king.

In the case of Britain, the proposed trade treaty was to be the anchor for that peace. As Vergennes' senior economic adviser Dupont argued in another *mémoire*, such was the degree of comparative economic advantage existing between Britain and France that they could not only benefit from peace with one another and closer economic ties, but would also be in a position, as the two wealthiest and foremost trading nations, to help maintain the peace and stability of all Europe by ceasing to

---

[29] Dupont de Nemours, 'Réflexions sur le bien que peuvent se faire réciproquement la France et l'Angleterre', n.d., AAE-MD-Angleterre-65/3.

subsidise the war-making capabilities of the other continental states. France and Britain were thought to be the only two European countries able to subsidise other countries in this way. As Dupont affirmed in another *mémoire*, written in 1783, the economic interests of Britain and France were not only more or less compatible, but the threat of potential shifts in the balance of power in Europe—in the guise of a possible Austrian, Prussian and Russian powerbloc—meant also that they now had common strategic interests to defend.[30]

In the case of Russia, the commercial treaty that Vergennes was negotiating in 1786 was similarly complex in its motives. On the one hand, it was hoped that lower trade barriers between Russia and France would allow French trade to expand into both the Baltic and the burgeoning Black Sea trade, helping to displace Britain in its dominance of the northern trade and strengthening French commerce in the Mediterranean and Levant. This, it was hoped, would in turn give France a commensurate diplomatic weight in the Russian imperial court, enabling her to act as a restraining influence on the ambitious Catherine II, drawing her away from the influence of the British, who depended on the Baltic trade for some of their more vital strategic resources, such as naval stores. Above all, the curbing of Russian expansionism would perhaps allow France to fulfil its ambition to act as the 'arbiter' of Europe, by returning to France much of the influence in Eastern Europe of which the rise of Prussia, and more latterly of Russia, had progressively deprived it.

The third factor was more specifically economic, in that Calonne and Vergennes assumed that a move toward a closer and freer trading relationship with Britain would ultimately be of greater economic benefit to France. Assuming that the treaty would be truly reciprocal, it was argued by Dupont in particular that any rise in French consumption of British manufactured goods would in the first place be offset by the

---

[30] "L'Angleterre et la France elles-mêmes," wrote Dupont, "si elles jugent bien leur position et leurs intérêts futurs, peuvent trouver des avantages immenses à se faire des faveurs réciproques, qui de part et d'autre accroitraient leur population et leur richesse, qui tariraient entre elles la source et l'occasion des guerres, qui établiraient un lien dont elles peuvent avoir le plus grand besoin." Referring to the "projets ambitieux" of the House of Austria and the prospect of a growth in the power of her Empire, and also to Prussian opportunism, he went on to declare thus that "dans le cas d'une confédération de ces deux puissances avec la Russie, il arriverait que la Suède, le Dannemarc, la Pologne, la Turquie, les Princes d'Allemagne seraient en danger. La nécéssité d'une alliance entre la France, l'Espagne, l'Angleterre, la Hollande, les petites puissances du Nord, et la Turquie serait alors indispensable". See Dupont de Nemours, 'Mémoire abrégé', ff. 72-74.

advantages gained through expanded markets in Britain for French agricultural exports, which would thus in turn stimulate increased agricultural productivity.[31] In the second place, the heightened competition of British imports in French home markets would soon act as an effective spur to greater efficiencies in the French manufacturing and industrial sectors, hence improving their general export competitiveness. Ultimately, as the potential for rapid economic growth and development was thought to be far greater in France than in Britain, it was believed that increased interdependence would eventually see the French economy outstrip that of its neighbour and long-term rival.

Such a policy of closer trade relations with Britain may thus be seen as demonstrative of a changing understanding of the nature and dynamics of international competition. It could also perhaps be seen as something of a victory for Physiocratic and more 'liberal' principles: firstly, in its emphasis on the benefits to economic development of more liberal and competitive trade arrangements, and secondly, in the conviction that French economic power could only ultimately be sustained and augmented through the development of the France's own domestic resources, rather than relying on the exploitation of cheap colonial produce as the mainstay of France's exports.

Calonne's approach in encouraging French economic development was, however, marked more by pragmatism than by any strict adherence to theoretical principles. That is, Calonne was by no means a devotee of complete free trade, but rather was concerned at all times to protect fledgling elements of French manufacturing and industry from the immediate rigours of competition with British and other imports, at least until such time as they could develop sufficiently so as to be able themselves to compete effectively and unassisted.[32] Whether he was actually successful in this endeavour would become a matter of debate and controversy within France. Furthermore, although Calonne was convinced of the need for France to expand its own internal productive and industrial potential, he also recognised the continued importance to France of a strong and mostly monopolised colonial trade, thereby rejecting the exhortations of those such as Dupont who had called also

---

[31] *Ibid.*, f. 77. See also Dupont de Nemours, 'Observations sur les motifs particuliers qui peuvent déterminer le traité de commerce', n.d., AAE-MD-Angleterre-65, ff. 3-24; see also Orville Murphy, 'Dupont de Nemours and the Anglo-French Commercial Treaty of 1786', *Economic History Review*, 19:2 (1966), pp. 569-580.

[32] Pugh, 'Calonne's "New Deal"', *Journal of Modern History*, 11 (September 1939), No. 3, *passim*.

for the French colonies in the West Indies and Indian ocean to be opened to foreign trade.[33]

French Policy and the Question of India

One major locus of tension between these three ministers, and an issue of great import for Anglo-French global rivalry, lay in their respective views with regard to French policy in India. Prominent among Castries' criticisms of Vergennes was that he had failed to take advantage of the successes gained by the French naval squadron sent to India under Suffren in 1781, in order to work toward a re-establishment of French power in India such as it had previously enjoyed under the Governorship of Dupleix.[34] Merely to settle for a re-establishment of the French position as it had been before 1763, when the great territorial gains made by Dupleix had mostly disappeared, and France had returned to having simple trading posts in various points around the country, took no account in Castries' view of the rapid territorial expansion that Britain had since made in the rich and fertile region of Bengal, and the degree of dominance over Indian trade that that had allowed it.[35] As the

---

[33] Dupont, AAE-MD-France-587, ff. 76-78. See Pugh, 'Calonne's "New Deal"', regarding the 1784 arrêt partially opening Saint-Domingue to US trade; see also, Frederick Nussbaum, 'The French Colonial Arrêt of 1784', *South Atlantic Quarterly*, 27 (January 1928), pp. 62-78.

[34] See Stone, *Genesis of the French Revolution*, pp. 125-126; Murphy, *Comte de Vergennes*, p. 325; Labourdette, *Vergennes*, pp. 120-121. Dupleix, Governor-General of Pondichéry during the War of Austrian Succession (1744-48), had tried to take advantage of the outbreak of hostilities between the English and French Compagnies in India, attacking in 1746 British bases on the Carnatic. With the help of Indian allies, he captured Madras, but eventually had to yield before the greater resources and more skillful diplomacy of the British. He was recalled to France in 1754. D.K. Fieldhouse, *The Colonial Empires*, p. 165.

[35] While the relative balance of power between Britain and France in the West Indies had remained more or less stable for many decades, the situation with regard to India continued to be different in several respects. Firstly, while the European powers had been able to dominate outright the various small and moderately sized islands of the Antilles, establishing any kind of foothold in India had always been far more difficult. The sheer distance of India from Europe and the existance there of local rulers of considerable power had prohibited any comparable monopoly of force on the Indian subcontinent. However, as Dupleix had initially suggested, and the English had subsequently demonstrated, the attainment of any degree of substantial military and territorial power in India in areas that could yield considerable revenue, gave one a level of strength and bargaining power in matters of trade far greater than that possible through commercial agents alone.

colonial minister pointed out, the peace of 1782 only seemed to confirm the vastly subordinate position that France had been confined to in India.

For Castries this disparity in the relative position of France and Britain in India had enormous implications. As various *mémoires* addressed to the French Foreign Ministry as early as the 1770s had attested, it was, above all, the gaining of lucrative territorial revenues in Bengal that was increasingly providing Britain with the means to assert its will not merely within the Indian subcontinent, but also on the oceans and in Europe itself. On this point French Ambassadors and diplomats to Britain concurred.[36] At the end of the American War Castries himself was clearly of the belief that it was India that had become the bulwark of British global power, and that it was the relative position of British and French power in India that would now be crucial in determining the general balance of power between them.

Castries proposed in his 1784 *mémoire* to the king that it would be India that would be the focal point for any new contest between France and Great Britain, and one that ought thus to prove decisive in re-establishing French global ascendancy. As an obvious swipe at the economy-minded Vergennes and his post-war policy of restraint, Castries warned direly against what he called "dangerous economies". As the balance of land forces was currently in favour of France in the West Indies, he proposed that France should now similarly build itself a strong *offensive* capability in the East Indies. Although the British had greater ground forces in India, he argued that with the effective acquisition of Holland as an ally (a formal alliance would be signed in 1785), the balance of power in the Indian Ocean had now swung toward France. "Si on veut considérer la position menaçante de Ceylan", Castries declared, "les ressources qu'on peut tirer de la position intermédiaire entre l'asie et l'Europe, du Cap et de l'isle de france, et selon leurs circonstances politiques, des Philippines, on jugera, sans doute, que la destruction de l'empire des anglais en asie, n'est pas une chimère".[37]

However, in a backhanded acknowledgement of the superior ability of the British to sustain a longer-term war effort, Castries asserted that the key for France would lie in an overwhelming French assault on British possessions, both in the West and East Indies, from which Britain, possibly attacked also on its own shores and in its possessions in

---

[36] See, for example, Barthélemy to Montmorin, 30 October 1787, AAE-CP-Angleterre-562, ff. 50-54.
[37] AN-306-APs-21, f. 30.

Europe, would find it impossible to recover.[38] As he wrote in a letter to the Marquis de Bussy,

> Ainsi nous ne pouvons espérer de plus grands avantages dans le commerce tant que les Anglois y auront l'excessive prépondérance qu'ils y ont acquise: il faut donc préparer sourdement une meilleure situation pour la développer à la premiere guerre; tirer de celle actuelle, le meilleur parti que nous pouvons, et faire nos dispositions de manière à pouvoir frapper vigoreusement les Anglois dès la première campagne.[39]

In its most basic terms, what Castries was proposing in his mémoire was a high-risk, high-gain strategy wherein it would be either Britain or France that would emerge as the complete victor, holding a dominant and virtually unassailable position in trade and the global balance of power.

In making this plea in his 1784 *mémoire* for considerable increases in troop and naval forces in the East Indies, Castries was following in the footsteps of those such as Duprat and Saint-Lubin who had for many years petitioned the government for a renewed and more concerted effort to combat the British in India.[40] However, since the recall of Dupleix and the subsequent disastrous expedition of de Lally in 1760, there had also grown among some elements of the French court a strong prejudice against any substantial military commitments in India, or any pretentions to major territorial power there, there being the conviction that such ambitions were doomed to failure. As Roger Glachant has remarked,

> En somme la France tenait à croire qu'aucun empire européen ne pouvait exister en Inde et que toute prévision contraire était illusoire. L'Inde anglaise, qui s'échafaudait grâce à la méthode même de Dupleix, l'exaspérait plus qu'elle ne l'inquiétait. Les Anglais d'ailleurs n'avaient pas mieux compris leur propre succès, dont le seul Clive avait été responsable, mais ils s'enrichissait avec appétit. Versailles essaya d'imaginer qu'ils allaient à la catastrophe, puisque nous y étions allés. Qu'une domination européenne sur l'Inde fût inéluctable,

---

[38] *Ibid.*, ff. 27-30.
[39] AN-FC-C2-165, f. 215.
[40] Le Chevalier de Saint-Lubin, 'Mémoires sur l'état de l'Hindoustan et un projet de conquête de l'Inde anglaise', April 1775, AAE-MD-Angleterre-18, f. 132; Le comte Duprat, 'L'expulsion des anglais de l'inde', 1782, *Ibid.*, f. 248. Duprat notes here that "parmi tous les moyens qui se présentent d'affaiblir la puissance anglaise; le plus sûr, celui qui va la plus directement au but est sans contredit de l'attaquer dans les Indes Orientales. L'Angleterre descendroit promptement au rang des puissances de second ordre", *Ibid.*, f. 249.

on ne s'habituait à cette evidence que lentement, avec stupeur et mauvaise grâce.[41]

Whether or not Vergennes conformed to this view, it was nonetheless clear that for him a policy of outright aggression and confrontation in the East Indies was out of the question. It not only contravened the 'moderate', gradualist approach of French foreign policy he had laid down, but it represented simply too much of a gamble, given its wider implications for French power elsewhere, and especially given the meagreness of France's financial resources when compared to the robust credit system open to the British.[42] Although it might be hoped that local Indian princes such as those of Hydrabad or Mysore could work to curb and possibly diminish British landed power, all that could reasonably be expected from Vergennes' point of view, taking into account the support they hoped to find in the Dutch possessions in the region, was a containment there of British expansion.

In the meantime this containment could be furthered by the restoration and expansion of French trade opportunities in India. For this reason Vergennes had sought from the British in 1782, and had been granted, a free hand for French trade in India, within certain restrictions.[43] As for Calonne, the return to France of its various factories and trading posts in India, such as Chandernagor in Bengal, offered the opportunity for an exploitation of Indian trade simply in terms of commercial profit, a project which he felt was best served by the re-establishment of a French East India Company, to be granted by necessity a privileged monopoly of Indo-French trade.[44]

Vergennes initially supported this project, encouraged by a mémoire written in 1782 by Moracin (later an agent of Vergennes', resident at Pondichéry, on the board of the India Company) on the possibilities for

---

[41] Roger Glachant, *Suffren et le temps de Vergennes*, Paris 1976, pp. 149-150.
[42] In response to comments, firstly, that depriving England of India would relegate it to the ranks of secondary powers while raising up forever the power of France, and, secondly, that allowing England to keep India gave it the means constantly to threaten France in Europe, Vergennes replied on 13 March 1785 that "le Conseil du Roi, Monsieur, est certainement aussi pénétré que vous pouvez l'être d'avoir un oeil attentif sur ce qui se passe dans l'Inde, et il sent de même que l'Inde peut devenir, pour l'Angleterre, la source d'une grande prospérité. Mais ces vérités, quelques importantes qu'elles soient, ne le sont pas assez pour que nous nous livrions aux risques et aux hasards d'une nouvelle guerre", in F. Pluchon, *Histoire de la Colonisation Française*, Vol. 1 (Paris, 1991), p. 752.
[43] Harlow, *The Second British Empire*, pp. 325, 330-42, 361-84.
[44] Frederick Nussbaum, 'The Formation of the New East India Company of Calonne', *American Historical Review*, 38:3 (1933), *passim*.

a re-establishment of French commercial activity in India.[45] However, the structure of the new company as proposed by Calonne soon brought out the tensions between the Contrôleur-Général's aim for straight profit and the political or strategic aims that Vergennes hoped this renewed trade would serve. Seemingly guided by pure commercial considerations, Calonne had proposed a company organised along the lines of what Frederick Nussbaum has described as a "modern international cartel", which would agree to buy many of its goods from the increasingly preponderant English East India Company.[46] Although, in order to avoid the possibility of military conflict, Vergennes had insisted that the French company be restricted to purely a commercial function, he demurred at an arrangement that left it subordinate to and dependent on the English Company, and which would only contribute to the profitability and success of the latter, when his political aims demanded precisely the contrary.

Louis XVI and the Expansion of French Navigation

Ever since his childhood, Louis XVI had showed an avid interest in geography and maritime affairs. This strong and abiding personal interest was later to prove significant in the shaping of French global policy. An admirer of the British explorer Cook, the king oversaw an expanding program of naval exploration and cartography in the wake of the American War, particularly in the north and south Pacific. He even took care to draft the instructions for what became the most famous of these expeditions, that of La Pérouse from 1785 to 1788. The purpose of these expeditions was predominantly scientific. The La Pérouse expedition, for instance, included among its principal members a number of scientific experts, such as naturalists, botanists, astronomers, engineers and a mineralogist and meteorologist.[47]

Many of these exploratory voyages, while ostensibly scientific, also contained an economic and strategic dimension, the desire to explore the possibilities for trade in the Asia-Pacific region, and to monitor the naval and colonial activity of other European powers, most of all, Britain. One may look, for example, at the instructions written by Louis

---

[45] Moracin, 'Mémoire sur l'établissement de la puissance française dans l'Inde', 26 Octobre 1782, AAE-MD-Asie-17, ff. 52-86.

[46] Wilma J. Pugh, 'Calonne's "New Deal"', p. 295. See also Nussbaum, 'French Colonial arrêt of 1784', pp. 482-490.

[47] Catherine Gaziello, L'Expédition de Lapérouse 1785—1788 (Paris, 1984), p. 281.

for an early voyage of D'Entrecasteaux.[48] The primary purpose of this particular mission appears in fact to have been explicitly strategic and commercial. D'Entrecasteaux's task was, firstly, to investigate whether the British were adhering to the Anglo-French agreement restricting the number of their respective warships operating in the Indian Ocean, secondly, to reconnoitre Trincomalee and the Indian coast as far north as Bengal, and above all, to ascertain the needs and strategic possibilities for French defence and navigation (including combined operations with Dutch and Spanish forces) should war once again break out with Britain.[49] Thereafter D'Entrecasteaux was directed to make his way to Canton in China, in order to examine the respective positions there of French and British trade and to reinforce that of the former where possible.[50]

Aside from the commissioning of exploratory and reconnaissance expeditions, the king also oversaw during the 1780s a program of intense naval construction, and a series of reforms of the French navy. This was largely the brainchild of Castries, who urged Louis in 1784 to continue the program of naval expansion begun by his predecessor Sartine prior to the American War. The goal, as defined by Castries, was to achieve, with France's Bourbon allies, a rough parity of naval strength with that of Britain. This meant expanding the French fleet from sixty-odd to around eighty capital ships.[51] Castries' subsequent success in securing royal funding for this intensive program brought him into collision, however, with Vergennes, and eventually Calonne.[52] Each of these ministers had in truth desired an expansion in the scope and

---

[48] See the 'Mémoire du Roy, pour servir d'instruction particulière au Chevalier D'Entrecasteaux, capitaine du vaisseaux, commandant les forces navales en station aux Indes Orientales', AAE-MD-Asie-18, undated, f. 200. See also, Frank Horner, *Looking for La Pérouse: D'Entrecasteaux in Australia and the South Pacific 1792-1793* (Melbourne, 1995), p. 20.

[49] 'Mémoire du Roy', AAE-MD-Asie-18, ff. 200-206.

[50] 'Mémoire sur le commerce de Chine', n.a., 3 May 1786, AAE-MD-Asie-18, 237-238. It was stated in this mémoire, in essence an instruction to D'Entrecasteaux, that "indépendamment de recouvrement des dettes considérables que reclament les Négociants françois, l'apparition de Pavillon du Roi dans les mers ne pourra qu'augmenter la considération dont la Nation françois ne jouit peut être pas à Canton au degré qui lui est dû", *Ibid.*, p.238. D'Entrecasteaux eventually arrived in Canton in February 1787, before proceeding back to the Indian Ocean.

[51] Castries, 'Mémoire pour le roi sur la marine', AN-306-APs-21 ff. 53-55. See also Dull, *The French Navy*, pp. 336-338; William Cormack, *Revolution and Political Conflict in the French Navy 1789-1794* (Cambridge, 1995), p. 22.

[52] Vergennes made concerted efforts to block Castries' funding for naval expansion through the creation of a Comité des finances in 1783. See Hardman, *Louis XVI*, pp. 73-74.

size of French navigation and maritime power. The difference between Vergennes and Castries was that the former believed that this should occur as a natural complement to a gradual expansion in French overseas trade, while the latter had instead insisted on an aggressive policy of naval armament. Vergennes considered such a policy to be manifoldly dangerous: firstly, it was far beyond the capacity of French finances, already burdened by the accumulated debts of the last war; secondly, it would compete in terms of precious manpower with the merchant marine; and thirdly, it would severely compromise his efforts to build confidence in a peaceable Anglo-French relationship by threatening to bring about a sizable inbalance in naval strength in favour of France and her allies.[53]

The Signing of the Anglo-French Trade Treaty and the Construction of Cherbourg Harbour

Central to Vergennes' grand plan for the consolidation of France as the arbiter of Europe was hence the maintenance, at least for the forseeable future, of peace with Britain. Vergennes, and his first assistant Rayneval, even continued to hope that a degree of harmony between Britain and France might possibly give way to actual co-operation in maintaining the status quo in the general European balance of power, increasingly menaced by Russian territorial ambitions. The signing of the new Anglo-French commercial treaty on 26 September 1786 was viewed by Vergennes as a major step in achieving such a degree of rapprochement with Britain, its role being to increase the level of mutual confidence and interdependence between the two countries.

Despite the regular diplomatic expressions of good faith and desire for peace between Versailles and the Court of St. James throughout this period, there remained an undercurrent of hostility and suspicion between the two powers. The persistence of such feelings at a high level was unsurprising, given the long history of rivalry and enmity between the two countries, and the experience of the recent conflict. These suspicions, however, were not simply the product of traditional prejudice. Though the British shared the French desire for peace, from their perspective the diplomatic aftermath of the American War—centred specifically on the growing Franco-Dutch accord—presented enormous potential dangers. It gave rise to understandable suspicions that French overtures for closer and more

---

[53] AAE-MD-France-587, f. 224; Dull, *The French Navy*, pp. 337-338.

amicable relations were merely a ruse, and that the French were in fact endeavouring both to challenge and even supercede Britain as a maritime power and to galvanise themselves for a further assault on British colonial possessions, this time in India.[54]

In this regard, the factional infighting and lack of basic policy coherence within the French cabinet was not helpful. While, on the one hand, Vergennes' hopes for the 'peaceful' containment of British seapower was effectively undermined by Castries' aggressive approach to French naval expansion, on the other hand, his control of French foreign policy was also increasingly compromised when it came to the question of Holland. Vergennes had in fact been reluctant even to formalise the Franco-Dutch relationship by a military treaty, but the pressure brought to bear by the more bellicose elements in the French court, chief among them Castries, and insecurity about his own personal position, had forced him to concede on this point.[55] The difficulty was that the strength of this alliance was entirely dependent on the continued ascendancy of one particular faction in the ongoing civil strife in Holland, the 'Patriots', who for some years had been endeavouring to deprive the Stadtholder of his erstwhile dominance over the government of the Dutch Republic, but whose future was, however, clouded by the increasing prospect there of full-scale civil war.[56] Much to Vergennes' consternation, his own agents sent secretly to liaise with the Patriots had encouraged that party—at the behest, partially, of

---

[54] In respect of British suspicions, the tone was set as early as July 1784, when in writing to the Duke of Dorset, the Ambassador to the French court, the British Foreign Secretary Carmarthen stated that "The present situation of France in regard to its finances as well as commerce might furnish a reasonable ground of hope for the continuance of the public tranquility so far at least as may depend upon the will of France, were it not for that restless and ever enterprizing spirit of ambition, which in spite of every idea of their own real interests is perpetually at work in forming new plans of intrigue if not of conquest, and which, as Your Grace well observes, seems now to direct its course towards the East Indies. As far as any progress has been made in the projected alliance between France and Holland, the most serious consequences to this country (in regard to our oriental possessions) are to be guarded against, the mutual guarantee of foreign possessions being plainly concerted with a view to future hostilitys with us in that quarter of the world; at least such is indisputably the fairest construction we can put upon the measure, and I flatter myself that no assurances, however friendly or pacific, may ever deceive us into a false security on this most important subject." In L. Wickham Legg (Ed.), *British Diplomatic Instructions 1689-1789*, Volume VII. France, Part IV, 1745—1789 (London, 1934), p. 251.

[55] Murphy, *Comte de Vergennes*, pp. 464-465.

[56] Simon Schama, *Patriots and Liberators* (New York, 1977), pp. 120-128.

Castries—to adopt an increasingly intransigent and radical demeanor with regard to the Stadholder, on the promise of French support.[57]

Even more alarming to Vergennes, were the efforts in late 1785 of French agents such as the comte de Grimoard, to convince the Patriots to support a prospective Franco-Dutch offensive aimed at ousting the British from India. Grimoard had earlier submitted a bold plan to this effect to Vergennes in September 1785, a plan that soon became the subject of a bitter controversy between Vergennes and Castries. In response to Castries' adoption and promotion of this project for a Franco-Dutch expedition, Vergennes warned his ministerial colleague of the dangers of arousing British suspicions to the point where it might provoke war, stating that "since our alliance [with Holland] is purely defensive, we must carefully avoid anything which could alter its nature and give it a more alarming appearance". He insisted that it was the king's desire to maintain the peace.[58]

This tension within French global policy and appearance of contradiction cannot, nonetheless, be reduced just to inter-ministerial rivalry or policy conflict. Rather, it should also be seen as reflective of the difficulties and contradictions inherent in Vergennes' own policy, toward Britain, of simultaneous rapprochement and strategic containment. Jonathon Dull and Bailey Stone have stressed the basic contradiction represented by Vergennes' attempt to secure British co-operation in Europe by means of an initial attack on their Empire (during the American War). "Had Britain been an absolutist state", notes Dull, "such a contradiction would not have been fatal, but British diplomacy was ultimately dependent on Parliament and Parliament dependent on public opinion—a ground on which the American War sowed seeds of further hatred and suspricion which future diplomacy could not uproot".[59] Vergennes' 'British Policy' was also based, as Dull and Stone further point out, on the assumption that in the wake of the American War Britain's Atlantic trade, and hence its seapower, would be substantially reduced. This hope was soon dashed, for it became

---

[57] Murphy, *Comte de Vergennes*, p. 470.

[58] Price, *Preserving the Monarchy*, p. 201. Grimoard had, in negotiation with the Patriots, reportedly declared that the aim of the project was to "chase the English out of India, reduce Great Britain to the same condition of weakness as Denmark or Sweden, and make the United Provinces the dominant power in India, which will enable them to become a first-rank European power". "One can imagine", says Price, "Vergennes' horror at reading this", p. 208. For a fuller discussion of the wrangle between Vergennes and Castries over their respective views of the Dutch-Indian axis, see Price, pp. 200-211.

[59] Dull, *The French Navy*, pp. 342-343.

apparent by the late 1780s that Anglo-American trade had not only recovered after the war, but in fact flourished as never before.[60] As Stone concludes, "depriving the proud insular adversary of its American colonies did not restore the overall strategic balance between London and Versailles".[61]

In identifying the flaws and misconceptions inherent in Vergennes' long-term strategy, one should also make reference to the British perception of their own strategic and economic exigencies. It was, in the first place, axiomatic to the British that they had owed their growing success over the century to the preponderance of their own maritime power, a fact that was always vulnerable to change. From the British point of view, the question of apparent French intentions might be seen as immaterial; it was threatening enough that their rivals should have simply the *capability* to mount a serious challenge to British naval ascendancy. Thus, while the French saw the forming of a French-Spanish-Dutch coalition as a salutary correction to a perceived imbalance in the maritime balance of power, the British were never likely to regard such a coalition as anything other than a direct threat to their own prosperity and survival as a front-rank and imperial power. For the British, even peaceable 'containment' held the seeds for them of ultimate catastrophe.

Vergennes was sufficiently aware of British sensitivities on this front that from 1783 he endeavoured to maintain a fine balance between working toward the continued isolation and containment of British power, and avoiding any direct military confrontation that might lead again to all out war. Having secured in the negotiations of 1782—83 a reduction and future limit in the number of French and British warships permitted to operate in the Indian Ocean, he thenceforth strove to assuage any further anxieties of the British in this region, studiously avoiding posing any direct threat there to British trade, and emphasising the strictly defensive nature of the Franco-Dutch relationship.[62]

Nonetheless, in the case of India, the line between containment and outright provocation would prove increasingly difficult to sustain. Given their own lack of substantial military power there, the French had long relied as much or more on diplomatic means to stem the growth of British landed power on the Indian sub-continent, by encouraging the foremost independent Indian powers—the Marathas, Mysore and Hyderabad—to put aside their own mutual rivalries in order to form a

---

[60] *Ibid.*, p. 341; Stone, *Genesis of the French Revolution*, pp. 119-123.
[61] *Ibid.*, p. 129.
[62] Alan Frost, *Convicts and Empire* (Melbourne, 1980), p. 90.

united front against the British.[63] In British strategic calculations, however, particularly with regard to India, there was little to distinguish between a French policy of 'peaceful' strategic containment and the potential threat of outright aggression against British colonial interests, for although their position in India was gradually strengthening, it was still very much vulnerable to any concerted offensive against them on behalf of the major local Indian powers. The British were, moreover, keenly aware of the vital importance of their eastern possessions to their overall strategic and economic interests, and the fact that the advantages derived there hinged on their predominance over the other European powers present in India.[64]

As a result, France was in India as in Holland, always to be walking a difficult tightrope between provoking the British, on the one hand, and, on the other hand, alienating current and prospective allies, who had their own agendas and exigencies. The French relationship with Tippoo Sultan of Mysore was a case in point. Tippoo, an able and ambitious ruler with considerable military resources, had been encouraged by France in the war of 1778—82 to enter into an alliance with them against the British, but had then felt deserted and compromised when the French withdrew from hostilities at the news of peace from Europe. It had taken all the statesmanship of the legendary French agent Bussy then to encourage Tippoo himself to come to terms with the British, with as little damage as possible incurred to France's reputation as a reliable ally among the Indian powers.[65] By 1786, and the resumption of the Mysore war, Tippoo was once again pressing the French for an alliance, only to be told by Souillac, the Governor of Pondichéry, that it would be best for him that he make an 'accommodation' with his enemies, lest the British enter the fray also, and to wait until "circumstances would permit the French to assist him".[66]

Castries' own handling of this issue was testament to the difficulties faced by the French in India. While he hoped and anticipated that France, with its new Dutch allies, might one day be in a position to "chase the English out of India", he was determined in the interim to preserve, on the one hand, the potential for an anti-British coalition,

---

[63] S. Sen, *The French in India* (New Delhi, 1971), p. 323.
[64] Frost, *Convicts and Empire*, Ch. 4-5, *passim*. See also, B. Kennedy, 'Anglo-French Rivalry in India and the Eastern Seas, 1763-93: A study of Anglo-French Tensions and of their impact on the consolidation of British power in the region', Unpublished Ph.D, Australian National University, 1969, *passim*.
[65] Sen, *The French in India*, pp. 381-384.
[66] 'Copie de la lettre de M. le Vicomte de Souillac, à l'Isle de France le 11 Novembre 1786', AAE-MD-Asie-18, f. 409.

while preventing, on the other hand, war with the British from breaking out prematurely (before the French could properly assist them). In a dispatch of April 1786 to Souillac, Castries, as the responsible minister, commented that

> Il parait, quant à la politique des princes de l'Inde, qu'il n'y a rien à faire en attendant que des dispositions nouvelles nous donnent de la consistance en Asie, et qu'il faut se borner à entretenir leur haine contre les Anglais sans prendre d'engagements avec eux. Il ne seroit ni juste ni politique de les commettre par des espérances prochaines à s'engager dans une guerre dont l'illusion de dissiperoit peu après et dont le discrédit le plus entier serait la suite indispensable.[67]

The sense of frustration and unease in the correspondence among local French agents on this matter is palpable; agents such as Souillac, Monneron, Cossigny and Chauvigny knew that it was only for so long that they could attempt to restrain Tippoo, before such Indian rulers finally lost faith in the French altogether. At that point the preponderance of British power in India, and on the oceans, and hence in Europe, would be assured.

If the respective situations in Holland and India demonstrated brewing tensions within French global policy, then the contradictions apparent in this policy were exemplified still further by another event of 1786, the visit of Louis XVI to view work on the construction of Cherbourg Harbour.[68] Few projects could have been better designed to damage the cause of genuine Anglo-French reconciliation, at the same time as the French were hoping, with the conclusion of the Eden treaty, to inaugurate a new era of peaceful co-existence with that country. Already wary about French ambitions in the East Indies, the British were then positively alarmed by the intensification of French efforts to construct a naval harbour in the channel, for this presented by far the most immediate threat not merely to their wider strategic interests, but to the very security of their homeland. The experience of the last war had already shown to what degree British control of the seas had been

---

[67] Castries to Souillac, 14 April 1786, AN-FC-C4-94, f. 279.

[68] Although one might argue that the building of Cherbourg harbour may been seen as part of Castries' campaign to augment French maritime power, this was a project that had also long been patronised by Vergennes, before Castries had even come to office. Labourdette, *Vergennes*, pp. 265-267. The king's visit to Cherbourg shows the degree of interest of Louis XVI had in this project, and the importance he placed in it, for aside from the later episode of the Flight to Varennes, this was the only time in his reign that Louis travelled to the French provinces.

threatened by the combined seapower of France and Spain, made more dangerous at the time by Britain's diplomatic isolation from Europe.

The placement of a major French port in the channel seemed now to alter the strategic equation that had once brought Britain a naval superiority over the Bourbon powers; with even a moderately sized French fleet stationed at Cherbourg, the possibility of an attack on the principal English ports in the channel, or of an invasion crossing, were ever greater. Faced with this threat, the British would not only be severely constrained in their ability to disperse and deploy their fleets, something which their imperial system had always relied upon, but they would now have to divert substantial resources to the establishment of sufficient land forces to fend off potential invasion by the far larger land forces of France.[69]

This again demonstrates the fundamental contradiction inherent in Vergennes' conception of French global policy, and the great flaws in the assumption that Anglo-French reconciliation and the strategic containment of British maritime power could be pursued simultaneously. The result of this policy was that, instead of diminishing, Anglo-French tensions would actually increase throughout the 1780s, endangering the peace made in 1783. The role in this of the Franco-Dutch Alliance—the very pivot upon which Vergennes' policy of containment rested—was central. Aside from the mistaken assumptions about the post-war British naval strength, the basic problem with this containment policy was that the balance between supposedly peaceful containment and outright provocation would prove extremely difficult to sustain at *both ends* of what might be described as a 'Dutch-Indian axis'. On the one hand, the political situation of the Dutch Republic was both volatile and inherently unstable: as the brewing tensions within the Republic threatened to boil over into civil war, it would become increasingly obvious by 1786—87 that France would have to intervene there militarily if it wished to maintain the Dutch alliance, most likely provoking Britain into a declaration of war. From the British perspective, France could have the Dutch alliance or peace with Britain, but it could not have both. On the other hand, the theatre of domestic Indian politics—being multipolar—was also inherently unstable, making it increasingly difficult to prevent the sparking of open war there between British and French forces, and their respective allies among the local Indian powers.

---

[69] The prospect for a 'descent' by combined Franco-Spanish forces was only foiled in 1779 by the allies' own mismanagment and the devastating effects of scurvy on their respective fleets. See Murphy, *Comte de Vergennes*, pp. 277-279.

In conclusion, one must again note that global policy, insofar as it may be deemed to encompass not merely foreign affairs but also naval and colonial matters, was a shared responsibility within the French Ministry. Though it would be Vergennes' overall conception of French global policy that would largely prevail in the 1780s, there were, in practice, significant tensions within the Ministry over global policy issues, especially between Vergennes and Castries. Added to these tensions was the fact that Vergennes' own global strategy was in itself beset with significant internal contradictions, particularly in regard to Anglo-French relations. By 1786, these interministerial tensions and internal contradictions would together only exacerbate the dangerous lack of cohesion within French global policy, and threaten, moreover, the sustainability of Vergenne' overall strategy.

Finally, it is important to note that aside from threatening another Anglo-French war, the development of the 'Dutch-Indian axis' into two separate and dangerous 'faultlines' would also put pressure on France to maintain its capability even to project military power. Vergennes himself recognised, in his *mémoire* of 1784, that his whole diplomatic 'system' hinged on one crucial factor: the continuation of the French government's financial solvency, and hence the sustaining of France's reputation as a great power.[70] That is, provided that France could continue to appear internally strong and play the role of an imposing power, Vergennes' system could take on a self-reinforcing character: if peace in Europe would allow France to concentrate its resources on containing Britain at sea, this could, in turn, reinforce French dominance in Europe by keeping Britain isolated and quiescent. Yet, as shall be shown in the following chapter, it was precisely this most crucial pivot of Vergennes' diplomatic system that would be the first to give way and collapse. Following the convocation of the Assembly of Notables in February 1787, it was the inherent fragility of French financial and fiscal structures, and the expanding debt of the French government, that would propel the French state into domestic crisis, a crisis that would have immediate and profound international repercussions.

---

[70] Vergennes, 'Mémoire', 1784, AAE-MD-France-587, f. 223. See also Donaghay's comment that "Vergennes' success as arbiter of a European status quo favorable to France rested not only on clever diplomacy but also a reputation built up over the years and French ability, more apparent than real, to pay for whatever it took to maintain his 'pacific system'". Marie Donaghay, 'The Vicious Circle: The Anglo-French Commercial Treaty of 1786 and the Dutch Crisis of 1787', *Consortium on Revolutionary Europe 1750—1850* (1989), p. 450.

2 The Dutch Crisis and the 'Implosion' of Vergennes' Diplomatic System

On 13 February 1787 the sixty-eight year old Vergennes died after a short illness and apparently weakened by overwork. Louis XVI, who appears to have been acutely aware of how important the support of Vergennes was to his hopes for the success of the Assembly of Notables, would subsequently have reason to rue the loss of his long-serving foreign minister.[1] Aside from Vergennes' achievement in restoring to France much of its former international prestige—through the instrument, firstly, of arms, and then through peaceful diplomacy—the foreign minister was no less important for his role as a pillar of the regime. Not only had Vergennes been a 'strong hand' within the ministry, but he had also been a faithful supporter of monarchical authority, and indeed the last minister, according to Calonne, to have shared Louis' own conception of the absolute monarchy.[2]

Not long after his death, however, as Bailey Stone and Orville Murphy have recently argued, Vergennes' elaborate 'system' quickly began to unravel. Firstly, the public exposure, during the Assembly of Notables, of France's deep financial problems and the royal government's failure to resolve them, would produce an impression of profound internal weakness that would seriously compromise France's reputation and capability as a great power. Secondly, as this chapter will argue, following Stone and Murphy, the subsequent collapse of France as an imposing financial and military power would, in turn, rapidly expose the latent contradictions within French continental diplomacy. This

---

[1] In January 1787, Louis wrote to the bedridden Vergennes, expressing his "peine" that the foreign minister had been taken ill, and exhorting him to take better care of himself, if only because Louis was so dependent on him, especially in view of their "grande affaire du dedans". See P. and P. Girault de Coursac (Eds), *Louis XVI à la parole* (Paris, 1989), p. 131; Hardman, *Louis XVI*, p. 111.

[2] Hardman, *Louis XVI*, p. 112.

would result in the crippling paralysis of French foreign policy within the European theatre, a paralysis that would be as much diplomatic as it was financial in origin.

Calonne and the Notables

"War", M.S. Anderson declared in 1961, "was the greatest single factor in the history of eighteenth-century Europe".[3] For Anderson and many other historians of the period, the process of European state-building—the internal expansion and centralisation of state functions—was a direct response to the demands of international rivalry, and the single most important conditioning factor on the development of state power and political regimes. The costs of fighting wars and maintaining large armies and navies were very great, and had been increasing over the course of the early modern era, regularly consuming by far the greater part of these states' yearly expenditures.[4] The strain of these costs had become particularly burdensome by the end of the Seven Years' War in 1763. As Paul Kennedy has commented, this particular war "had so overstrained the taxable capacity and social fabric of the Great Powers that [henceforth] most leaders frowned upon a bold foreign policy; introspection and reform tended to be the order of the day".[5] Paul Beik has shown that if in France the Seven Years' War led to a more aggressive policy toward Britain, and the building up of France's naval establishment, it also brought forth a heightened interest in issues of political economy and fiscal policy.[6]

In such a context, access to credit was becoming increasingly important to the governments of states such as Britain and France, especially in their attempts to fund wars, when expenses always tended to far outweigh existing—and often chronically inadequate—fiscal resources. Aside from the practical necessity of maintaining confidence in national creditworthiness, this need for credit was accompanied by the growing public conviction that states ought to honour even the

---

[3] M. S. Anderson, *Europe in the Eighteenth Century*, p. 151.
[4] Geoffrey Best, *War and Society in Revolutionary Europe* (London, 1982), p. 29.
[5] Paul Kennedy, *The Rise and Fall of the Great Powers*, p. 149. See also, William Doyle, *The Old European Order 1660-1800* (Oxford, 1978), p. 295.
[6] Paul Beik, *A Judgment of the Old Régime: Being a survey by the Parlement of Provence of French Economic and Fiscal Policies at the Close of the Seven Years War* (New York, 1944), pp. 15-36.

most burdensome of their debts, and not effectively repudiate them through partial bankruptcies, as had previously been the practice. As John Hardman comments, Louis XVI himself seemed to share this conviction, renouncing the recourse to such measures at the beginning of his reign.[7] Yet by 1786, only three years after the French victory in the American War, Calonne informed the king in a secret *mémoire* that the French state was threatened with an impending bankruptcy of a more complete and catastrophic kind. Credit was rapidly drying up, and further taxation within the existing system was virtually impossible.

The origins of the final crisis that was to overwhelm first the financial then the political structures of the absolute monarchy has been the subject of a long and complex debate among historians.[8] Different historians have pointed to various contributing factors, some with conflicting interpretations. The long-held conventional view is one that is generally supportive of Calonne's own diagnosis, in that it was chiefly Necker's reliance on massive borrowing rather than on increased taxation during the American War that precipitated the financial crisis. The recourse particularly to expensive, short-term credit by Necker produced before too long what might be called a spiralling debt crisis, wherein debt-service was threatening to consume ever greater proportions of revenue, and where the existing tax base was too small, and too exhausted, to make up the increasing shortfall. This view has, however, been challenged by Robert Harris, who, concerned to rehabilitate Necker, singled out as the chief catalyst of France's financial crisis of 1787 the allegedly 'extravagant' expenditure on public works initiated by Calonne between 1784 and 1786 (as a means partly of restoring public confidence in the Crown's creditworthiness).[9] From another perspective, Jack Goldstone has asserted that the real root cause of this financial crisis was not the accumulated war-debts of the royal government, but rather the longer-term strain placed on traditional fiscal structures by the demographic and inflationary pressures of the eighteenth century.[10]

Although there may be some dispute as to the specific catalysts of the financial crisis, very few historians would disagree that the problem was at its core an institutional one, that the traditional fiscal

---

[7] Hardman, *Louis XVI*, p. 36.
[8] For an overview and analysis of this debate, see Doyle, *Origins of the French Revolution* (Oxford 1980), part one.
[9] See Robert Harris, *Necker, Reform Statesman of the Ancien Regime*, (Berkeley, 1977), p. 154.
[10] Goldstone, *Revolution and Rebellion*, p. 250.

institutions of the French state proved manifestly inadequate to the growing needs of its government. Whereas Britain had over the century been well served by a reasonably sound and efficient system of public finance that had been brought about by the rigours both of imperial competition with France and parliamentary scrutiny, management of the French finances had been, on the contrary, increasingly hamstrung by the rigid, corporative structure of public institutions in France. As John Bosher has argued, even to label the French financial crisis of 1787 as a 'budgetary' one would be something of a misnomer, since, unlike Britain, no such thing as an annual budget had ever even existed in France; nor had a central treasury, a national bank, or anything resembling a system of central financial control. Instead, state finances had traditionally been conducted through a cadre of semi-independent, profit-seeking venal accountants, with little or no co-ordination in financial matters between even the various royal ministries.[11]

Although, as Bosher asserts, Calonne must bear some responsiblity for the persistence of the system of venal accountants, few historians would also dispute Calonne's own diagnosis, exposed to the king in the secret *mémoire* of 20 August 1786, that the problem of French finances stemmed largely from a faulty system of revenue collection.[12] This problem was in itself rooted in the very structures of Old Regime state and society, and the potentially fatal flaws of its political culture and economy. "La disparité, la discordance, l'incohérence des différentes parties du corps de la monarchie", he expounded, "est le principe des vices constitutionnels qui énervent ses forces et gênent toute son organisation". This, he concluded, had resulted in a situation whereby

> l'administration générale est excessivement compliquée, la contribution publique inégalement répartie, le commerce gêné par mille entraves, la circulation obstruée dans toutes ses branches, l'agriculture écrasée par des fardeaux accablans, les finances de l'état appauvries par l'excès des frais de recouvrements, et par l'altération des produits.[13]

Thus, not only had the French system of taxation failed to keep pace with the growing expenditure needs of the royal government, but it had also acted as a severe blight on the development of the French economy.

---

[11] Bosher, *French Finances 1770-1795* (Cambridge, 1970), pp. 23, 41-46.
[12] *Ibid.*, pp. 57-58.
[13] Alan Goodwin, "Calonne, the Assembly of Notables of 1787 and the Origins of the 'Révolte Nobiliaire'", *English Historical Review*, 61, (May-September 1946), pp. 209-210.

Calonne then instructed the king, and later the Assembly of Notables, that the threat of state bankruptcy could no longer be staved off through traditional expedients or half-measures. Only a complete and unprecedented overhaul of the French system of administration and taxation, a revivification of the French state through a root-and-branch rationalisation of its internal structures, could, he believed, provide the financial strength and general stability that France required for its future vigour and prosperity.[14]

These proposals of Calonne constituted the most comprehensive and far-reaching reform program ever attempted under the Old Regime, remarkable alone for their challenge to the concept of fiscal privilege, which had long been regarded as a sacrosanct and inherent feature of French political society.[15] What made this program all the more remarkable, as Hardman has noted, was the "enthusiasm with which the King embraced it and made it his own".[16] The most important feature was the proposed replacement of the only existing direct tax, the *vingtièmes*, with a uniform and universal land-tax, to be paid by all landowners without exemption. A system of local, district and provincial assemblies, elected by these landowners, would be charged with administering this tax, and ensuring an equitable distribution of the tax burden. Secondly, to encourage trade and economic growth, Calonne proposed the abolition of internal customs barriers and other constrictions on internal trade. Thirdly, Calonne proposed, like Turgot, that the grain trade once again be allowed to operate freely and without restriction, for both internal and external trade.[17]

Whatever may be the causes of France's financial crisis in the late 1780s, it was clear to the royal government that the soundness of its finances, and the efficiency of its fiscal structures, would greatly affect France's capacity to be a great power. In his opening address to the Assembly of Notables on 22 February 1787, Calonne made it clear to the assembled high dignitaries of France that their country was at the crossroads of its destiny as a great power, in both strategic and

---

[14] *Ibid.*, pp. 210-215.

[15] For a discussion of reformist efforts during the reign of Louis XVI, see Jones, *Reform and Revolution in France, passim.*

[16] Hardman, *Louis XVI*, p. 103. Louis even took the unusual step of allowing himself to be identified personally with these reforms, with the aim of adding to the pressure on the Assembly to support them. The Notables took umbrage at this tactic, since it went against traditional convention of the 'king's religion' which had previously enabled the crown to distance itself from ministerial initiatives. *Ibid.*, pp. 122-123.

[17] Doyle, *Origins of the French Revolution*, pp. 96-97.

economic dimensions. France, the Contrôleur-Général argued, had been able to capitalise on its victory in the American War to conclude a series of commercial treaties with Holland, Russia and Britain, treaties which, in his view, heralded a new era for France of stability, security and growing prosperity. He thus lauded, as prudent and necessary, the government's efforts since 1783 to encourage and nurture local industry, agriculture and commerce. He also defended expenditure on major public works on roads, canals and ports such as Cherbourg. In an effort to placate the supporters of his rival and predecessor, Necker, he even went so far as to defend the borrowings made during the American War, in spite of the ruinous effects he alleged that they had had subsequently on public finance, stating that:

> Vous savez, Messieurs, combien ces emprunts étoient nécessaires. Ils ont servi à nous créer une Marine formidable; ils ont servi à soutenir glorieusement une guerre qui, d'après son principe & son but, a été appelée avec raison, Guerre nationale; ils ont servi à l'affranchissement des Mers; ils ont servi enfin à procurer une paix solide & durable ...[18]

Yet, on the other hand, as he forcefully argued, all that stood in the way of this glorious future was the current disorder of the government's finances, the continuance of which, he warned, would undoubtably lead to a devastating state bankruptcy with grave consequences for the power, prestige and future prosperity of France in the international arena.[19]

Throughout the life of the Assembly, the Notables were to be reminded of the importance of reform to the future power and prosperity of France in this international arena. For instance, in his own opening speech, Miromesnil, Louis' Keeper of the Seals, had announced that ensuring the good order of the state's finances would allow the king "enfin de se préparer des ressources pour repousser ... les efforts d'ennemis étrangers qui voudroient un jour troubler la paix que la Majesté a donnée à l'Europe".[20] Louis had himself, on 23 April, and following the dismissal of Calonne, made a special appeal to the Notables to approve the proposed reforms, declaring finally that "il s'agit de la gloire de la France dont la mienne est inséparable, & de montrer à l'Univers l'avantage que j'ai de commander à une Nation

---

[18] *Procès-verbal de l'Assemblée des Notables, tenue à Versailles, en l'année 1787*, Paris, 1787, p. 70.
[19] *Ibid.*, pp. 56-57.
[20] *Ibid.*, pp. 54-55.

fidèle & puissante, dont les ressources, comme l'amour pour ses Rois, sont inépuisable".[21]

From the opening of the Notables, however, it became clear that the Assembly would not be quite the compliant instrument that Calonne had anticipated. Although it accepted in principle that fiscal privilege should be abolished, after weeks of deliberation the Assembly hardened in its criticism of the specifics of Calonne's proposed land-tax. Resistance soon turned into deadlock. Faced with mounting opposition to this reform, and by a barrage of court intrigue directed at him personally, Calonne had, finally, no option but to resign on 8 April, in the hope that the reform process could perhaps continue under the direction of a successor. Subsequently, Brienne, Archbishop of Toulouse and one of Calonne's fiercest critics, was appointed to head the revamped Royal Council of Finances, and charged with carrying on the task of addressing France's financial problems.

Much has been written about the Assembly of Notables and their reaction to Calonne's reforms. For their opposition to the basic element of these reforms, they have since been variously depicted as selfish, vindictive reactionaries concerned to safeguard their own privileges, or, alternatively, as mostly conscientious property-owners concerned to curtail what they saw as the growth of royal or ministerial 'despotism', particularly in matters of taxation and financial administration.[22] Whether their motives were indeed selfish or public-spirited, or a mixture of both, it is clear that their opposition was ultimately political. It reflected not only their mistrust of the royal government and its basic financial competency, but also their desire to thwart the goal of generations of reformers under the crown, the development of a centralised, 'administrative' monarchy.

The attitude of the Notables to the government's pleas for co-operation on grounds of national interest was typified by the response of the Bureau of the Prince de Conti.[23] Stating that it was their ardent wish that the king solve the problem of the deficit, upon which they agreed that "la gloire du Roi, & la sûreté de l'Etat" depended, they nonetheless contested the need for the proposed new taxes, attributing

---

[21] *Ibid*, p. 265.

[22] For examples of these contrasting interpretations, see Goodwin, 'Calonne, the Assembly of Notables', and Vivian Gruder, 'A Mutation in Elite Political Culture: The French Notables and the Defense of Property and Participation, 1787', *Journal of Modern History*, 56 (December 1984), pp. 598-634.

[23] For deliberation the Assembly was divided into seven Bureaux, each presided over by a Prince of the Blood.

the state's fiscal problems to the various 'abuses' and excessive expenditures within the royal government itself. Departmental expenditures, particularly those of the War Ministry, had grown, they asserted, to enormous and exorbitant dimensions when compared to expenditures of twenty or thirty years before. The royal government was, to them, basically incompetent and inefficient. Conceding then "la necessité de la conserver sur un pied proportionné aux forces des autres grandes Puissances de l'Europe", they thus argued that strict economies ought and could be applied to the armed forces, as to the other departments, without diminishing their actual strength and capability.[24]

Ultimately, the king would be amply vindicated in his insistence that mere economies, however strict, would not be enough to solve France's financial problems. For the time-being, however, Louis and his government were unprepared to pay the price for élite acceptance of these reforms, namely, an independent scrutiny of government accounts, or the effective sharing of legislative power with aristocratic élites through the instrument of an Estates-General.[25] Consequently, by the time the Government dissolved the Assembly on 25 May 1787, the situation of the monarchy was altogether worse than it had been prior to the Notables. As Doyle notes, the "failure to win the Notables' support showed the world that the French king's government could not command the confidence of its most eminent subjects; while the revelation of the disorder in the finances suggested that this lack of confidence was well merited".[26] This very public failure would not only expose the absolute monarchy to a deepening and paralysing domestic crisis, but it would soon have the most serious external consequences.

The Dutch Debacle and the Humiliation of France

Shortly after the death of the comte de Vergennes in February 1787, his first assistant Gérard de Rayneval prepared a memorandum on the current state of France's foreign relations for the newly appointed Foreign Minister, the comte de Montmorin.[27] In it he gave an account

---

[24] *Arrêtés des Bureaux de l'Assemblée des Notables; présidés par Monsieur et par la Prince de Conty*, s.l., 1787, pp. 10-13.
[25] William Doyle, *Origins of the French Revolution* (Oxford, 1980), p. 103.
[26] *Ibid.*, pp. 104-105.
[27] Armand-Marc, comte de Montmorin de Saint-Herem derived from a family of ancient noble lineage and carried the added distinction of having been chosen as one of Louis' childhood playmates. He subsequently became ambassador to Spain during the critical time of the War of American Independence, returning

of the basic outlines and progress of Vergennes' broad strategy, that is, the increase in French influence and commerce to be won from the diplomatic isolation of Britain from the continent, and the relative weakening there of its commercial ties. Although Vergennes may earlier have been concerned about the provocative nature of the Franco-Dutch alliance, Rayneval here emphasised how much this alliance had become pivotal to the anticipated success of Vergennes' overall strategy:

> Le coup d'oeil le plus léger suffit pour sentir l'importance de cette alliance, et la nécessité de la maintenir. Elle a oté un allié à l'Angleterre; elle nous a prouvé un point d'appui dans la mer-germanique et dans l'Inde, et elle a rendu moins nécessaire pour nous l'alliance avec la Cour de Madrid.[28]

He thus identified and stressed the importance of the continued security of Dutch possessions in and around India, and the effective combination there of French and Dutch power. A commercial treaty with the Republic was, furthermore, recommended as a means of reinforcing Franco-Dutch ties and as a way of furthering the cause of French commerce, particularly in Northern Europe and the Baltic, where British trade had long held a dominant position.

At the same time, however, Rayneval expressed his hopes and expectations for the maintenance of peace with Britain. Though, he believed, Britain still harboured an underlying "hatred and jealousy" toward France, which required the latter to continue to take the utmost precautions with regard to its security, current circumstances seemed to militate against the prospect of aggressive moves from the British Ministry. Not only had Britain recently signed a commercial treaty with France which was entirely in its interest to maintain, but, as Rayneval concluded, the apparent bad state of English finances and its current lack of any continental allies seemed to ensure the continuance of peace.[29] Elsewhere, reports from the French Embassy in London, in February and early March, seemed to confirm the peaceful dispositions of the British Ministry; Landsdowne, the Chancellor of the Exchequer,

---

to France in 1783 as a marshal and governor of Brittany. He became Foreign Minister in 1787 at the age of forty-one. Masson describes him as being a worldly and uxurious man, an "esprit honnête, mais faible; dévoué, mais timoré". Frédéric Masson, *Le département des affaires étrangères* (Paris 1877; Reprint: Geneva, 1977), pp. 55-60.

[28] Gérard de Rayneval, 'Résumé de l'Etat actuel relativement à la France des cours et des Pais qui sont dans mon département', February 1787, AAE-MD-France-587, f. 252.

[29] *Ibid.*, ff. 257-258.

had even publicly rejected the 'system of national animosity' between Britain and France, declaring that it was in their mutual interest to keep the peace in Europe.[30]

Subsequent events would, however, reveal the fundmental miscalculations upon which Rayneval's (and Vergennes') strategic conceptions, and their hopes for peace, had been built. Most of all, they finally revealed the patent failure of the French policy of simultaneous rapprochement and containment; for although the dispositions of the British Government at the time may have been peaceful, they were by no means passive. French efforts under Castries to maintain an enlarged peacetime navy, and the fears of combined Franco-Dutch offensive operations in the East Indies, had driven the British, as Vergennes had foreseen, to intensify the rebuilding of their navy and to strengthen their colonial defences.[31] Barthélemy, the French *chargé d'affaires* at the London Embassy noted in May 1787, that prior to the French intervention in the American War, the English "s'étoit completment négligée dans ses mesures de défense, à une époque où fiere de sa supériorité et méprisant l'univers, elle croyoit impossible que nous puissions secouer le joug de son orgueil". Now, he believed, "les choses sont bien changées. La dernière guerre et ses malheurs, nos travaux de Cherbourg, nos constructions dans nos ports, l'intérêt précieux des Indes Orientales, la tiendront désormais constamment éveillée".[32] Fox's parliamentary denunciation of the Eden Treaty on 23 January 1787 gave voice to English doubts and suspicions about the French desire for peace, and the need for Britain to galvanise itself against any further assault on its maritime and colonial power.[33] Even Landsdowne, in his plea for genuine Anglo-French rapprochement, had not failed to

---

[30] Adhémar to Montmorin, 2 March 1787, AAE-CP-Angleterre-559, ff. 194-196.

[31] Daniel Hailes, chargé d'affaires at the British Embassy, had in October 1786 reminded Carmarthen in a despatch of the recent French efforts to the "increase and improvement of their marine establishment", estimating that there were then "sixty three or sixty four ships of the line which might be put in a condition for sea in a short time", in Oscar Browning (Ed.), *Despatches from Paris 1784-1790*, Vol. 1 (London, 1909), p. 152. The expansion of French navy, and combined with Spanish and Dutch forces, would give them potential preponderance over British maritime power, a threat to which the British government were compelled to respond. See Dull, *The French Navy*, pp. 336-338.

[32] Barthélemy to Montmorin, 22 May 1787, AAE-CP-Angleterre-560, f. 94.

[33] See W. O. Henderson, 'The Anglo-French Commercial Treaty of 1786', *Economic History Review*, 10:1 (August 1957), p. 109.

complain of the French constructions at Cherbourg, which he alleged, gave indication of hostile intent.[34]

In this developing arms-race one of the chief differences between the two countries was in their respective financial situations. It had been the general belief after the American War that the war debts of Britain and France were roughly the same.[35] For their own part, the French had hoped that the British would be deterred from seeking a renewal of the conflict by the scale of the British debt, and by the potential interruption once again to British trade that such a conflict would undoubtably cause. However, French faith that the 'equality' of their respective debts would help sustain an approximate balance of power between the two countries was grossly misplaced, for with the obstruction by the Notables of any serious fiscal reform, the contrast in the health, actual and perceived, of British and French finances could not have been greater. As Adhémar reported to Montmorin in April 1787, while the Notables had revealed the "alarming state of our finances", Pitt had just presented a balanced budget that required no borrowing, a remarkable achievement. In desperate tones the ambassador urged that the King should thus put an end to the resistance of the Notables, and somehow manage to resolve his financial difficulties before the British moved to take advantage of it.[36]

If the French policy of rapprochement through expanded commercial ties had thus failed to stem British fears about the potential and ongoing growth of French diplomatic influence and strategic power, then it was the deterioration in the internal affairs of Holland over the summer of 1787 that would propel both countries into a period of rapidly escalating tension. An alliance with Holland, with its maritime

---

[34] Adhémar to Montmorin, 2 March 1787, AAE-CP-Angleterre-559, f. 196. Suspicions about French intentions were thus by no means confined to the English Opposition, but were prevalent with the Government itself, the Foreign Secretary Carmarthen being notable for his almost paranoid view of France. See Jeremy Black, 'The Marquis of Carmarthen and Relations with France, 1784-1787', *Francia*, 12 (1984), pp. 283-304. In any case, the Government of Pitt could not but respond to concerns of a British public opinion suspicious of French intentions.

[35] Robert Harris, 'French finances and the American War, 1777-1783', *Journal of Modern History*, 48 (1976), pp. 233-58; see also John Bosher, *French Finances 1770-1795: From Business to Bureaucracy* (Cambridge, 1970), p. 23.

[36] "J'espère", wrote the Ambassador, "qu'en dernière analyse le Roi pourra montrer à l'Europe attentive et de bons français et de bonnes finances. C'est après la double conviction de la fermeté du Roi et des ressources de la France que nous obtiendrons une paix durable ... ", Adhémar to Montmorin, 24 April 1787, AAE-CP-Angleterre-559, ff. 342-348.

forces, its strategic position in Europe and its colonial possessions in the East Indies, was regarded by both Britain and France as a critical factor in the attainment of a favourable position in the global balance of power. This the Naval Minister Castries knew only too well:

> Angleterre ni la France ne peuvent se dissimuler que la Hollande ne forme dans la balance maritime de l'Europe un poids qui décidera cette supériorité navale entre les deux puissances; ainsi le plus grand intérêt de la France est de conserver l'alliance de la Hollande, comme celui de l'Angleterre est de parvenir à faire rompre le traité que le Roi a fait avec cette République.[37]

Now that the troubles in Holland seemed ready to descend into civil war between the contending Patriot and Orangist forces (who respectively favoured France and Britain), and that the control and future direction of Dutch foreign policy would thus be at stake, the brewing tensions within the Anglo-French relationship came to a head. For both countries, it was clear that the ultimate issue at stake was the strategic position of each with regard to India, for it was upon this contest that their global rivalry was hinged. This was certainly the belief of the British Ministry. Although Pitt was thought by the French to be an advocate for peace, he well understood the crucial value of India to Britain.[38] Barthélemy, in a despatch to Montmorin, noted, for his part, that the question at the heart of the worsening crisis was the British fear that France might, through their Dutch alliance, acquire Trincomalee or the Cape of Good Hope. This, the British knew, "prépareroient des circonstances essentiellement funestes à la Grande Bretagne".[39]

Caught within a logic of mounting tension, both countries began to mobilise their fleets during June and July, inaugurating a period of 'brinkmanship' between the two powers; while both parties talked, and no doubt desired, peace, they nonetheless continued to prepare for

---

[37] Castries, 'Réflexions sur les dernières nouvelles arrivées d'Angleterre et sur la situation actuelle', 1787, AAE-CP-Hollande-571, f. 45. See also, AN-306-APs-19, f. 5.

[38] Frost, *Convicts and Empire*, Ch. 4, *passim*.

[39] Barthélemy to Montmorin, 7 Aug 1787, AAE-CP-Angleterre-561, f. 24. Britain did not itself possess its own ports between West Africa and Bombay in India. For France then to possess or have easy access to secure port facilities at either the Cape of Good Hope or at Trincomalee would give the French, who already possessed Ile de France and Bourbon in the Indian Ocean, the ability to sever or severely constrict the sea lanes connecting Britain with the riches of India. This was a factor that could prove decisive in any contest in the region, as the earlier activities of Suffren in the last war had given good indication.

war.[40] In this situation, each side was naturally desperate to ascertain the intentions of the other. The difficulty was, however, that in such a climate of uncertainty, where any of the full range of immediate outcomes—war, peace, confrontation, mediation—seemed possible, neither side wished to be at a disadvantage. They thus took action that was only in the end likely to produce the opposite of what either side desired, the compounding of tensions and an increase in the cycle of action and reaction. The French were at a loss to determine whether current British efforts were confined to an attempt to break the Franco-Dutch alliance, or were part of a larger plan designed to exploit France's internal troubles and "pour saisir le moment de reprendre sur la globe la prépondérance qu'elle a perdue". They felt compelled, in anticipation of a possible conflict, to send out warnings to colonial stations in both the western and eastern hemispheres, with orders to forestall any attempted British seizure of Dutch possessions, particularly Trincomalee or the Cape of the Good Hope.[41] Such orders, of course, only made the actual outbreak of war all the more likely.

It was, however, only within Holland that the issue of the Franco-Dutch alliance and the future direction of Dutch foreign policy would be settled. In this respect the looming prospect of civil war between Patriot and Orangist factions produced a sharp dilemma for France: would it intervene militarily to support the Patriots if that became required, or would it otherwise abandon them? That France, in fact, ultimately abstained from any direct involvement in the Dutch affair, leading to the eventual rout of the Patriots, was a matter that would

---

[40] French diplomatic despatches from the London Embassy throughout this period regularly referred to the increasing activity in the English ports, and the sending of more (and sometimes new) vessels to reinforce the naval and land forces in the East and West Indies. From the other side, Dorset had hastened to instruct the British Foreign Secretary Carmarthen that in spite of France's own internal problems and distractions, "the French navy is in good condition; their Ships being in such a prepar'd state that they have it in their power to put to sea a considerable Force in a short time: the greatest attention having been paid to their marine and Dockyards ever since the conclusion of the war". Dorset to Carmarthen, 28 June 1787, *Despatches from Paris*, Vol. 1, p. 209; See also: Dorset to Carmarthen, 19 July 1787, in which he quotes Louis XVI as stating that he had "nothing so at heart as the continuance of the Peace of Europe, but that whenever Great Britain or any other Power shall arm, He will feel Himself under the necessity of doing the same; that it is not his design to take the lead, but to follow the example the other Powers may give ...", in *Despatches from Paris,* Vol. 1, pp. 219-220.

[41] Castries, 'Reflexions sur les dernières nouvelles', AAE-CP-Hollande-571, ff. 45-50.

outrage many in the French court, such as the comte de Saint-Priest, who launched bitter recriminations against the man whom they would hold responsible for that decision, the principal minister, Brienne.[42]

This attribution of responsibility has subsequently been confirmed by historians such as Alfred Cobban and Jean Egret, who pointed to the role of Brienne in 'vetoing' the intervention desired by the ministers Castries and Ségur, basically on financial grounds.[43] That financial reasons were the basic cause of this abstention, Egret points out, was the view held by contemporary observers, one of whom wrote that "it is not credible that the Versailles ministry, in such straits, would risk getting involved in a war that would make bankruptcy inevitable".[44] Such may well have been the case. Quite clearly there *was* division in the French cabinet about French intervention, between the staunch advocates of intervention, Castries and Ségur, and those, such as Brienne and Malesherbes, who were determined to prevent this for financial reasons.

Curiously, much less attention has been paid by historians to the role of Montmorin in the backdown over Holland. As foreign minister, Montmorin would have played a central role in formulating the French response to this affair. However, the scant references that do exist regarding Montmorin's stance on intervention appear to paint a somewhat confused picture. While the historian of the French department of foreign affairs, Frédéric Masson, describes Montmorin as having "désira vivement la guerre", but who was then overruled by Brienne, Murphy, in contrast, describes Montmorin as supporting

---

[42] In Saint-Priest's highly coloured *mémoires*, he denounces Brienne's intervention, declaring that "hélas, la guerre, en ce moment, nous aurait problablement épargné l'horrible révolution qui a suivi, en tournant d'un autre côté l'attention et l'ambition de tous ces jeunes Français revenus d'Amérique et principaux acteurs des troubles qui suivirent", François-Emmanuel Guignard, comte de Saint-Priest, *Mémoires*, 2 Vols (Paris, 1929), vol. 1, p. 204. See also, Murphy, *Diplomatic Retreat*, p. 92.

[43] Cobban, *Ambassadors and Secret Agents*, London, 1954, p. 165.

[44] Egret, *The French Prerevolution 1787-1788* (Chicago, 1977), p. 41. As Egret notes, Brienne received support for this stand in a pamphlet by the future radical revolutionary, Brissot, who wrote: "I like to believe ... that France, wiser than in the past, will slowly withdraw into herself, disengage herself from all those foreign interests, which have cost her so much blood, treasure, and tranquility; that she will concentrate her strength and wealth within herself, in order to repair all the internal ills caused by the erroneous system of past centuries", *Ibid.*, p.42.

Brienne and Malesherbes' opposition to intervention.[45] Which of these seemingly contradictory statements are we to believe? Was Montmorin in fact opposed to, or supportive of intervention? Clarification on this point is important, for a clearer picture of Montmorin's own assessment and recommendations to Louis might more fully explain the dilemmas with which the French were faced during this crisis.

Firstly, it is certainly evident that Montmorin fully appreciated the importance to France of its Dutch alliance. On this issue Montmorin addressed the Conseil d'Etat on 6 September, just as tensions over Holland were beginning to reach a peak. Montmorin instructed the Conseil that the East Indies had become for Britain, since the loss of its American colonies, "la principale source de sa grandeur et de sa prospérité", and that any future war fought between Britain and France would necessarily be focused there. He then asserted, echoing Castries, that it was only the Franco-Dutch alliance that would give France any hope of success in this theatre. "Ce traité", he said, "que nous avions desiré pendant plus d'un siècle, a donc rempli l'objet le plus important de l'intérêt politique de Sa Majesté".[46] In stark terms (and in an assessment that would later prove highly accurate) Montmorin then outlined the devastating consequences for French global power of a failure to act in support of the Patriots and the subsequent loss of the Dutch alliance to Britain: "Cette puissance", he argued,

> aura opéré cette révolution par la seule expression de sa volonté, et, exempte de toute inquiétude dans l'Inde, elle nous bravera tranquillement en Europe; le Roi aura perdu sans retour tout crédit et toute considération; il ne trouvera plus ni alliés ni amis; les autres puissances de l'Europe croiront pouvoir donner sans contrainte et sans réserve l'effort à vües ambitieuses; non-seulement le Roi n'influera point sur leurs déterminations, mais il ne sera pas même consulté ...[47]

---

[45] Masson, *Le département des affaires étrangères*, p. 62; Murphy, *Diplomatic Retreat*, p. 90. It is surprising that Egret in the *French Prerevolution* does not mention Montmorin's role in the decision at all.

[46] Montmorin, 'Mémoire lu au Conseil d'Etat', 6 September 1787, AAE-CP-Hollande-574, ff. 304-305.

[47] *Ibid.*, ff. 306-307. Barthélemy, in a despatch of 17 September, fully concurred that 'Si le Parti Stathoudérien triomphe, nous verrons Trinquemale passer entre les mains des Anglois ... et avec cette possession ils s'assurent à jamais l'empire des Indes Orientales et notre éternelle humiliation dans cette partie du monde'. Barthélemy to Montmorin, 17 September 1787, AAE-CP-Angleterre-563, f. 62.

In other words, so pivotal was the Franco-Dutch alliance, and so important was French support of it, that any submission in this crisis could lead to the effective nullification of French diplomatic influence in the rest of Europe, and to the partial disabling of France as a prime global contender.

What Montmorin then recommended to the Conseil was, however, something less than direct military intervention. The foreign minister stated that:

> dans la supposition que le Roi regardera la guerre, si elle devient nécessaire, comme moins fâcheuse que les conséquences qui résulteroient de la résolution invariable de l'éviter, Sa Majesté pourra articuler d'un ton ferme et décidé quoique conciliant son opinion sur les différends qui divisent les Provinces-Unies; Elle rétablira par là la confiance et le courage parmi les patriotes. Les deux Cours qui protègent M. le Stadholder calculeront probablement avec plus de précaution leurs démarches et leurs exigéances; et il est probable qu'en prévoiant la guerre, elles ne voudront point en courir les hazards pour une cause aussi peu importante que celle de M. le Prince de Nassau.[48]

In other words, Louis and his government should call the British bluff and trumpet their support for the Dutch Patriots. In the meantime they would hope that the British need for peace, and the Prussians' own desire to retain their good relations with France, would sway these powers into accepting a mediation of the Dutch dispute that would leave French interests in Holland more or less intact, and which would hence preserve the broader strategic status quo.[49]

Montmorin was certainly not advocating an action that might likely lead to war. Although Montmorin, in his *mémoire* of 6 September, only referred passingly to the "fâcheuses conséquences" of a war over Holland, both he and Louis could have been in little doubt about how catastrophic such a war would be to France. The twin and chief elements of Vergennes' policy of containment of British power, the diplomatic isolation of Britain from the continent, and the adherence to France of Dutch maritime and strategic resources, had been designed to deny to the British their traditional recourse of distracting France from its maritime endeavours through the instrument of a hostile continental

---

[48] Montmorin, 6 September 1787, AAE-CP-Hollande-574, ff. 307-308.
[49] As Montmorin opined, "L'Angleterre, malgré le bon état apparent de ses finances a comme la france un besoin réel de la paix, et elle n'a point de motif national assez puissant pour la rompre, et pour déranger, pour une succès incertain, l'ordre qu'elle s'efforce de retablir dans ses affaires intérieures", *Ibid.*, f. 308.

alliance. The possibility now that actual intervention by France in Holland might spark a land war with Prussia and a maritime war simultaneously with Britain (and, hence, a probable renewal of the Anglo-Prussian alliance) was precisely the kind of danger that Vergennes' system had been designed to avoid. Such a war would effectively reverse any strategic or diplomatic gains France had made since Vergennes had taken office at the start of Louis XVI's reign, and what is more, as Montmorin had noted on 3 August, would most likely plunge Europe into a general war.[50] This would have meant, finally, a total and ignominious defeat for the shining vision of Vergennes and his master Louis XVI of a peaceful, 'balanced' Europe of which the arbiter was an impregnably strong France. From this defeat, British power both on the continent and on the seas could only profit, maximising its potential economic and strategic power while France, the wealthiest country in Europe, would quite conceivably cease to play a significant role in Europe or elsewhere.

French intervention in Holland would thus not have been a mere "military diversion" as Egret describes,[51] but could well have resulted in a combined European and colonial war, with potentially disastrous consequences for French global power, and for the future strength of the French state. In view of their current relative financial strengths, France would hardly have been capable of embarking even on a limited naval war with Britain, let alone a simultaneous war on the continent. It is in this context that one must place the French government's chronic financial problems, for it was clear to Montmorin, as it had been to Vergennes, that France had not, without fundamental reform of her taxation structures, the financial wherewithal to compete effectively in such a conflict. Furthermore, given the recent Notable and *parlementaire* resistence to reform, there seemed little prospect of an imminent and marked improvement in the French financial situation. Thus, if military intervention in Holland was likely to result in a general war, such an option was for France financially impossible and strategically undesirable.

It is hence unsurprising that in the Conseil d'Etat Castries' persistent advocacy of French military intervention in Holland should have met with such a resounding lack of enthusiasm.[52] At the end of August he resigned, realising that with his failure to succeed Vergennes as the head

---

[50] Montmorin to Vérac, 3 August 1787, AAE-CP-Hollande-574, f. 17.
[51] Egret, *The French Prerevolution*, pp. 40-42.
[52] Jeremy Black, *British Foreign Policy in an Age of Revolutions* (Cambridge, 1994), p. 148.

of the Royal Council of Finances, his position and his plans for the continued expansion of the French navy, had become untenable.[53] Calonne had on his own departure from office in April accused Castries and his naval expenditures of being principally responsible for the current crisis in French finances, while Brienne, Calonne's effective successor, had continued to urge restraint.[54] In this extremely difficult situation, where the likely consequences of both intervention and non-intervention in the Dutch crisis seemed catastrophic, there was thus little more that Montmorin could do but continue to bluff, broadcasting an implacable resolve to defend French interests, while at the same time desperately seeking some kind of diplomatic solution that might somehow preserve the status quo in Holland.[55]

Montmorin's recommendation to the Conseil d'Etat on 6 September that France continue to take a strong stand with regard to Holland, while seeking a mediation of the crisis, was thus based on the hope that the British and the Prussians would wish to avoid the risk of war. In relation at least to Prussia, this, as Orville Murphy has noted, was a grave miscalculation on Louis and Montmorin's part.[56] As Murphy writes,

> Louis XVI's grave diplomatic errors during these years grew from a mistaken confidence that Prussia would remain in the French orbit. France and Prussia had for so long cooperated to keep the ambitions of Joseph II in check, it seemed reasonable to assume the cooperation would continue. But Louis XVI and Montmorin seemed not to have understood how thoroughly Frederick William II was personally committed to the support of his sister and the stadholder in the Dutch Republic. Consequently, at the very moment when Prussia and Britain were concluding a secret accord to guarantee support for the stadholder, Montmorin continued to nourish the hope that France could regain Prussia to her side.[57]

---

[53] Hardman, *Louis XVI*, p. 128-130. The post of the head of the Royal Council of Finances was actually abolished as an 'economy measure'; see Duc de Castries, *Le Maréchal de Castries* (Paris, 1956), p. 146.

[54] *Ibid.*, pp. 147-151.

[55] Montmorin, 'Mémoire lu au Conseil d'Etat', 6 September 1787, AAE-CP-Hollande-574, f. 307. Part of this bluff, and one directed specifically to deter Prussian intervention, was the establishment in June of a French military camp at Givet, positioned as a platform for possible French intervention in Holland. It should be noted that following Castries' resignation, Montmorin also took on the role as caretaker minister for the navy and colonies while they waited for Castries nominated successor to arrive from the West Indies.

[56] Murphy, *Diplomatic Retreat*, p. 172.

[57] *Ibid.*

To this point one may also add that Montmorin's strategy of 'bluff' was based one other serious miscalculation: that there existed a genuine 'balance of terror' between Britain and France. The reality was different; for, while Britain may well have much preferred to avoid war, the British and Prussians were together aware that it was France for whom the prospect of war held the greatest dangers, and who thus had by far the greatest desire to maintain the peace—particularly in view of its domestic problems. This gave Britain and Prussia the crucial moral advantage in this telling game of international brinkmanship. As a result, France was hardly well positioned in this confrontation to force or otherwise engineer any mediation that would produce a favourable result for French interests. In any case, as Montmorin reported to Barthélemy on 13 September, the indignities associated with the temporary detention of the Stadtholder's wife by Patriot forces had destroyed any remaining hope for mediation of the crisis.[58] Whether or not there were any such hopes left to destroy, this incident brought matters to a head. Infuriated by the treatment meted out to his sister, the Princess of Orange, Frederick William had promptly issued an ultimatum to the Patriots. Several days later, on 13 September, the Prussian king ordered his army to invade the Dutch Republic.

The moment of truth had finally arrived for the French government. Though Montmorin had reaffirmed French support for their Dutch allies on the same day that the Prussians invaded, it soon became apparent that no further French involvement in the Dutch crisis was to be forthcoming. On 22 September Louis wrote to the Patriots, advising them that France would not intervene.[59] Left to their fate, Patriot resistance in Holland quickly faded before the might of the advancing Prussian army.

This rapid *dénouement* did nothing to ease the escalating naval tension between Britain and France for, despite this effective 'settlement' of the Dutch crisis, both sides remained no less poised for war.[60] In October the British government ordered the preparation of a further forty ships-of-the-line for active duty.[61] From the Embassy in London, Barthélemy informed Montmorin of the progress of these accelerated British naval preparations, and the high pitch of 'war fever' being stirred up by the English press, warning that, in the apparent state

---

[58] Montmorin to Barthélemy, 13 September 1787, AAE-CP-Angleterre-563, f. 59.
[59] Murphy, *Diplomatic Retreat*, p. 90.
[60] Dorset to Carmarthen, 12 October 1787, *Despatches from Paris 1784-1786*, pp. 251-252.
[61] Jeremy Black, *British Foreign Policy*, p. 154.

of French impotence, "l'arrogance angloise crie dans toutes les parties de cette isle que le ministère doit profiter de l'occasion pour se venger de nous".[62]

Although Montmorin, in a letter to the British Foreign Secretary Carmarthen, continued to justify French naval armaments as a necessary response to those of Britain, he was clearly alarmed and even nonplussed by the scale of these British armaments.[63] On 14 October he wrote to Barthelemy that:

> il serait difficile de deviner pourquoi le Ministère Anglais a été au delà de toute mesure pour ses armements: car les affaires de hollande n'exigeoient pas tant de démonstrations et de dépenses pour prendre la tournure qu'elles ont prise; et nous ne connaissons aucun objet qui ait pu porter la Grande Bretagne à la guerre.[64]

It may have seemed to Montmorin that France might finally be forced into a war she neither wanted nor could afford. The British diplomat Hailes confirmed the apparent bleakness of the situation, reporting that "I have been told, and I fear it is too true, that the [French] Ministers have no longer any confidence in what is said to them on the part of England; - M. de Montmorin is said to have declared in a tone of resignation, that if the English were resolved upon War, they must have it".[65]

The subsequent arrival in France of Grenville, an emissary sent by the British government to help defuse heightening tensions, and the subsequent conclusion on 27 October of an agreement for mutual naval disarmament to the relative levels as of 1 January 1787 was, therefore, a subject of considerable relief at Versailles.[66] In reaching this agreement, France had, at the eleventh hour, managed to avert a

---

[62] Barthélemy to Montmorin, 2 Oct 1787, AAE-CP-Angleterre-561, f. 320. See also Barthélemy to Montmorin, 5 October, ff. 332-333.
[63] Montmorin to Carmarthen, 3 Oct 1787, copy attached to despatch Montmorin to Barthélemy, 7 Oct 1787, AAE-CP-Angleterre-563, f. 77.
[64] Montmorin to Barthélemy, 14 October 1787, AAE-CP-Angleterre-563, f. 79.
[65] Hailes to Carmarthen, 11 October 1787, *Despatches from Paris 1784-1786*, p. 251.
[66] The conclusion of this agreement would have been the cause of especial relief, for on 23 October the French secret agent Morande sent Montmorin a letter which gave further detail of British war preparations, which suggested that Britain was placing itself on a strong war-footing in both the East and West Indies. He quoted the Duke of Richmond, Britain's Master General of the Ordnance, as supporting an attack upon Cherbourg. AAE-CP-Angleterre-562, ff. 26-31.

catastrophic war with Britain. In so doing, however, its humiliation was complete. Not only had Britain managed to assert its will in Holland whilst avoiding war, but France was then compelled in this agreement to declare that it had never even had any intention of intervening in Dutch affairs. For the French, this was all a most bitter pill to swallow; as Castries put it, "We have lost everything".[67]

The Eastern War: The Paralysing of French Diplomacy

Historians of the Pre-Revolution, such as William Doyle and Jean Egret, have tended to view the French 'retreat' across 1787—88 as a direct consequence, or even 'symptom', of France's internal problems, specifically the French government's crippling financial weakness, which, in the eyes of Louis' finance minister Brienne, made any kind of military adventure impossible.[68] More recently, Bailey Stone and Orville Murphy have sought to emphasise that, while the collapse of French power and influence in Europe during this period may indeed have stemmed in large part from a basic incapacity to go to war, where France failed more broadly was in its inability to restrain other powers from going to war. This was most evident in the eruption of the so-called 'Eastern War' in mid-to-late 1787. Although financial—and consequently, military—paralysis may be considered as a crucial catalyst to the collapse of French diplomatic influence in Europe, both Stone and Murphy argue that it is in fact only by reference to the *context*, that is to say, to the specific structure of French diplomacy and foreign policy-making in the 1780s, that one can properly explain why this collapse was so sudden and comprehensive. It is this wider European context of the French foreign policy-making to which we will now turn.

---

[67] Donaghay, 'The Vicious Circle', p. 453; As Hailes later wrote from Paris, "A sentiment of shame at the impotence betrayed by France in the late contest in Holland and the disgraceful political Defeat that followed it, is strongly and generally impressed on men's minds, and is accompanied, no doubt, by the conviction that it is in vain to attempt to struggle with so vicious a government against a power that possesses an innate and constitutional superiority", Hailes to Carmarthen, 17 April 1788, *Despatches from Paris*, Vol. 2, p. 30.

[68] Egret, *The French Prerevolution*, pp. 40-42. Note also Doyle's comment that "totally absorbed in their internal problems, the French abandoned foreign affairs [after the Dutch Crisis]", *The Old European Order 1660-1800* (Oxford, 1978), p. 291.

Montmorin's dark forebodings about the devastating effects of the Dutch crisis on French power, prestige and influence were soon borne out by the views of the other rulers and statesmen of Europe. The Prussian minister Hertzberg wrote that France "has lost the alliance of Holland and the remnants of her prestige in Europe", while Joseph II of Austria concluded that "France has just fallen, and I doubt that she can be raised up". Catherine II of Russia was no less severe in her own assessment: "Who", she asked, "will believe in people who have neither will, vigour nor entreprise?".[69] This perceived 'abasement' of France would soon be borne out in fact. Having already received a severe bodyblow to her global aspirations, France was hence now to be reduced to little more than a passive spectator on immediate developments even in Europe. These developments would see, through the effective dissolution of what remained of Vergennes' system, the utter nadir of French power and influence.

The key to Vergennes' 'system', as it pertained to Europe, had been its attempt, through shrewd diplomacy, to manage and carefully balance a complex network of continental tensions, to maximise French influence and restrain the ambitions of other European powers, notably Austria and Russia. This was a policy that in itself was replete with internal contradictions. Firstly, while on the one hand France persisted with its domestically unpopular alliance (gained during the 'Diplomatic Revolution' of 1756) with its erstwhile rival and enemy, Austria, it also endeavoured to maintain its links with the powers that traditionally had been instrumental in helping it to contain Austro-Hapsburg expansion—Sweden, Poland and Turkey—even keeping an interest in the preservation of Austria's now deadliest enemy, Prussia.[70] Secondly, Vergennes aimed to complete Britain's isolation from the continent by subverting British influence in Russia through a Franco-Russian trade treaty; at the same time, paradoxically, he hoped and anticipated that France could nonetheless engage Britain in a co-operative effort to contain the growth of Russian strategic power.

As Vergennes identified in his 1784 *mémoire* to the king, the growing accord between Austria and a restless and increasingly powerful Russia presented a grave threat to this delicate continental 'balance', primarily through their mutual designs upon the Ottoman Empire (the Czarina Catherine desired to 'liberate' Orthodox Greece from its Ottoman overlords, turning it into a Russian client-state, and to expand

---

[69] Albert Sorel, *Europe and the French Revolution* (Trans. 1969), p. 549; see also *L'Europe et La Révolution Française*, 5th Ed. (Paris, 1902) Vol. 1, pp. 520-521.

[70] Vergennes, 'Mémoire présenté au Roi', 1784, AAE-MD-France-587, ff. 218-219.

Russian power and influence into the Black Sea region).[71] In so doing it also focused the manifold contradictions inherent in Vergennes' diplomatic system, presenting the French with an enormous dilemma.[72] This came in the form of an Austro-Russian offer to France of a 'Quadruple Alliance' between Austria, Russia, France and Spain, with the initial aim of dividing up the spoils of a defeated and dismembered Ottoman Empire; Austria and Russia would gain territorially in the Balkans and the Crimea, while trade in the Levant would also be shared, mostly between Russia and France.[73]

While anxious not to alienate either Austria or Russia, France had had various reasons for rejecting this proposal. Firstly, such a warlike and aggressive position was entirely contrary to the spirit of Louis XVI's foreign policy, to which he held steadfast, and which aimed at a 'peaceful' retention of the status quo in Europe. Furthermore, the great changes in the European balance of power that would result from such a project were deemed also to be contrary to France's strategic and economic interests. Rayneval, in a *mémoire* of June 1783, wrote that although Turkey was a declining and 'apathetic' power, it was best for France that she be preserved in her present state, for although France might profit materially from the division of the Ottoman Empire, this would come at the cost of both Austria and Russia acquiring a dangerously expanded strategic power.[74] Above all, as Rayneval noted, these manouvres would no doubt bring France into collision with Britain.[75] This would be doubly dangerous for France, for it would trigger not only a general war in Europe, but also, unavoidably, a global maritime and colonial war, at a time, soon after the American War, when France had otherwise an imperative need of peace, consolidation and financial recovery.

Vergennes' response to this dilemma had been to promote, with his characteristic ingenuity, closer trade and diplomatic relations with Russia, at the same time as maintaining France's traditional links with the Ottoman Porte. This was a policy, however, that would in effect

---

71 Vergennes, 'Mémoire présenté au Roi', 1784, ff. 209-210.
72 See Orville Murphy, 'Louis XVI and the Pattern and Costs of a Policy Dilemma: Russia and the Eastern Question, 1787-1788', *The Consortium on Revolutionary Europe 1750-1850* (1986).
73 Black, *British Foreign Policy*, pp. 171-172.
74 Gérard de Rayneval, 'Motifs qui doivent déterminer le Roi à s'opposer à la destruction de l'Empire Ottoman, et indication des moiens à emploïer pour rendre l'opposition de Sa Majesté efficace', June, 1783, AAE-MD-Turquie-15, ff. 32-37.
75 *Ibid.*, f. 37.

only deepen the inherent contradictions within France's diplomatic system, placing ever greater importance on the need for France to ensure that neither the Russians nor Austrians went to war with the Ottomans, lest those deepening contradictions be suddenly exposed. France's reputation as a great power had been the key to this maintenance of peace and the management of simmering tensions in Europe. France had, under Vergennes, managed with some adroitness to impose its will by reconciling Austria and Holland in a potentially disastrous conflict in 1784 over access to the Scheldt river.[76] Unfortunately, by 1787, with Vergennes now dead, and France increasingly preoccupied with the Dutch crisis, this was precisely what it was unable to prevent, for in August, after the building of Russo-Turkish tension over the Crimea, the Ottomans issued a pre-emptive declaration of war on Russia. This was soon followed by the entry of the Austrians into the burgeoning conflict, Joseph declaring war on the Porte in February 1788 after ordering, in December 1787, an earlier surprise attack on Turkish held Belgrade.[77]

The sudden and terrible bind in which France was placed by this outbreak of war was well expressed at the time in a *mémoire* by Montmorin to the king. In it he concluded that France now had several different choices, all with far-reaching consequences: firstly, Louis could co-operate with both Austria and Russia in their projected dismemberment of the Ottoman Empire; secondly, he could actively oppose this project; or, thirdly, he could simply do nothing. As Montmorin noted gravely, the first and second options both entailed the likely prospect of a major European war, while the third "porterait une atteinte irréparable à Sa considération, comme à son intérêt politique".[78] In other words, France would—as in Holland—again be faced with a war which it feared and desperately wished to avoid, or, alternatively, if it did not act, with the complete evaporation of its own influence within European affairs.

Faced with such disagreeable and stark choices, what was France to do? This was by no means just a regional conflict, confined to the

---

[76] In 1784 Joseph II defied traditional Dutch restrictions on traffic using the Scheldt river, with the aim of opening up access to the sea for the Habsburg city of Antwerp. This campaign brought a hostile response from the United Provinces, and threatened war. With deft mediation and offers to Joseph II of compensation, Vergennes was, however, able to resolve the dispute. See Murphy, *Comte de Vergennes*, Ch. 33, pp. 405-416.

[77] Albert Sorel, *Europe and the French Revolution*, p. 550.

[78] 'Mémoire sur la Turquie, par le comte de Montmorin, ministre des Affaires Etrangères', 1787, AAE-MD-Turquie-15, ff. 136-139.

Balkans and the Black Sea, but one which was integral to the overall European balance of power, and France's place within that delicate balance. Moreover, the difficulties of this dilemma were compounded by the French government's fear of Britain and its diplomatic machinations in the Eastern courts. Here the innate contradictions and ironies of French foreign policy were perhaps most painfully felt: on the one hand, Vergennes and Rayneval had long promoted the possibility of Anglo-French co-operation in containing Russian expansionism against the Ottoman Empire; yet, on the other hand, it was, as French diplomatic correspondance reveals, the British whom the French suspected of intriguing in the Ottoman court, promoting conflict, with the supposed aim of 'embarrassing' France and checking its influence among the major powers.[79]

Alarmed by the prospect that the British might use the outbreak of war between Russia and the Porte to regain the favour of Catherine II, and thus overturn the good work of the diplomat Ségur in promoting French influence at the Russian court, Montmorin now put out secret feelers to the Russians. If, after all, war between Britain and France could not be avoided in the wake of the Dutch Crisis, then Montmorin was anxious to make sure that Russia became a French rather than British ally, even if this meant, as a last resort, France abandoning its previously staunch support of the Ottoman Empire in its struggle against the territorial ambitions of Austria and Russia.[80] Under instruction by Montmorin, from late 1787 Ségur (now ambassador) secretly endeavoured to interest the Russian court in the possibility of closer Franco-Russian co-operation, more or less intimating that the French government had had a major change of heart in regard to the Ottomans, particularly as they had gone to war contrary to French advice.[81]

Whether this apparent shift to a more pro-Russian and less pro-Ottoman position should constitute a 'revolution' within French foreign policy (suggestive of the later Napoleonic policy) is, however,

---

[79] Montmorin, 'Mémoire pour servir d'instructions au S. Chev. de la Luzerne, Maréchal des camps et armées du Roi, allant à Londres en qualité de son Ambassadeur auprès de S.M. Britannique', 7 January 1788, AAE-CP-Angleterre-563, f. 106; Barthélemy to Montmorin, 15 May 1787, AAE-CP-Angleterre-560, f. 72; Montmorin to Barthélemy, 9 September 1787, AAE-CP-Angleterre-563, f. 58; Barthélemy to Montmorin, 17 Sept 1787, *Ibid.*, f. 62.

[80] Hugh Ragsdale, 'Montmorin and Catherine's Greek Project: Revolution in French foreign policy', *Cahiers du Monde russe et soviétique*, 27:1 (1986), pp. 32-35.

[81] *Ibid.*

debatable. While there were certainly some voices in Louis XVI's court promoting a French acquisition of Ottoman Egypt—for strategic and as well as commercial reasons[82]—Louis and Montmorin were far from enthusiastic about the further decline and possible dismemberment of the Ottoman Empire, even if less than optimistic about its future. Rather, Montmorin's preference was for a French-mediated peace between the Austro-Russian coalition and the Ottomans, whereby France would not be compelled to make a decisive choice between its client, Turkey, and its prospective ally, Russia. In other words, he wished to maintain, where possible, the policy and diplomatic system of his recent predecessor Vergennes. Such a mediation would, however, not be easy, he conceded in his *mémoire* to Louis XVI, for it was hardly likely that the Imperial powers—Austria and Russia—would be bought off cheaply, but would demand major territorial concessions that might prove unacceptable to the Turks.[83]

Montmorin's diplomatic communications with Austria during this period also offer evidence that while the French government was preparing for a Turkish collapse, it nonetheless desired to restrain the Imperial powers in their assault upon the Ottoman Empire in Europe. In early December 1787, the Austrian Ambassador to the French court, Mercy-Argenteau, reported to Vienna what he had been told by Montmorin, that France would discontinue active military support of the Turks and undertake secret negotiations with the Russians. Thereafter, however, Montmorin went on to seek information and reassurances from the Austrians about the extent of the Imperial powers' ambitions regarding Ottoman territory, to urge caution and restraint regarding Catherine's 'Greek project', and, finally, to offer France's good offices as an international mediator.[84]

As the Dutch crisis had similarly revealed, France was here driven to place this faith in the possibilities for a mediated peace by the desperate hope that, in spite of its current powerlessness, the diplomatic status quo so carefully engineered by Vergennes would somehow be preserved. As in Holland, however, this policy was also to be a comprehensive failure. Not only was French pressure for mediation adversely affected by the perception of France's crippling weakness, but this weakness now also exposed the multiple contradictions in France's continental policy.

---

[82] T. C. W. Blanning, *The Origins of the French Revolutionary Wars* (London, 1986), p. 57.

[83] 'Mémoire sur la Turquie, par le comte de Montmorin, ministre des Affaires Etrangères', 1787, AAE-MD-Turquie-15, ff. 136-139.

[84] Ragsdale, 'Montmorin and Catherine's Greek Project', pp. 37-38.

These contradictions carried within them a circular and self-defeating logic. Firstly, the failure of France to declare itself conclusively in support of either side in the Eastern struggle, while being neither entirely neutral (France was still seen to be giving a degree of actual support to both), only compromised its credibility in both Russian and Ottoman courts.[85]

Secondly, French diplomacy was also increasingly constricted by the innate contradictions within its continental policy with regard to Britain. When the British, under the auspices of Pitt, floated the idea of joint Anglo-French mediation of this crisis, the French were only propelled into another agony of indecision: whether this offer was sincere or merely a ploy, would it in any case have the effect of alienating France from both Austria and Russia, who might then be free to fall once again into the diplomatic orbit of Britain, effectively isolating France? With the growing probability of a formal 'Triple alliance' between Britain, Holland and Prussia, France was, on the one hand, increasingly anxious to avoid ruling out, as a necessary counterweight in the European balance of power, the possibility of a Quadruple alliance.[86] Yet, on the other hand, the forming of such an alliance would, as Rayneval had earlier warned, more than likely push France into a potentially catastrophic war with Britain. This was a war she was not only ill-equipped to fight, but in which she had far more to lose than just her interests in the Levant. Her future as a colonial and global power seemed also at stake.

In such a situation, French diplomacy seemed virtually paralysed. Once the capacity of France to project its own power had been disabled by its domestic financial and political crisis, the ability of France to maintain a diplomatic system riven with internal tensions had become severely compromised. In the space of a year France had gone from being the aspiring arbiter of European politics to being a virtual 'nullity'.[87] Where was France to go from here? Should, or could, it gamble on war, or, alternatively, eschew war to retreat into a humiliating isolation?

Ultimately, the Royal Government had little option but to pursue the path of peace, however humiliating this appeared. As Stone and

---

[85] Murphy, 'Louis XVI and the Pattern and Costs of a Policy Dilemma', *passim*.; See also Dorset to Carmarthen, 1 November 1787, *Despatches from Paris*, Vol. 1, p. 262.

[86] Black, *British Foreign Policy*, p. 158. As Black points out, this was, at this stage, actually more of a 'triangular' than a 'Triple' alliance.

[87] Murphy, *The Diplomatic Retreat of France*, Ch. 10, *passim*.

Murphy have similarly argued, the reality of the situation was that France was forced into such a 'diplomatic retreat' not just by its dismal financial situation, but by the combination of financial and diplomatic paralysis.

3 The Contraction of French Global Power, 1788—1789

The ultimate object of Louis XVI and Vergennes' foreign policy had been the creation of a new *Pax Francia* in Europe. As Bailey Stone and Orville Murphy have argued, this vision appeared to fade when in 1787 France's diplomatic system succumbed under the weight of its own massive contradictions. In supporting this argument, one should, however, note that Stone and Murphy have mostly confined their examination of French foreign policy to the European theatre.[1] It is important to expand the geographic scope of this examination for, as the previous chapters have shown, not only did this foreign policy contain an important global dimension, specifically focusing on the Indian Ocean region, but the contradictions within France's strategic and diplomatic framework in the 1780s may also be considered to have been global in scope. The purpose of this chapter is to consider the outcome of the exposure of these global contradictions, principally the response of the French government to the sudden collapse of France's international standing in 1787, and the impact of this 'implosion' of French power beyond Europe, particularly in the context of Anglo-French rivalry.

The Persistence of Anglo-French Tensions

The conclusion of the Dutch Crisis, and the signing of agreement between Britain and France for mutual naval disarmament, did not lead to a significant abating of tensions between the two powers, despite their separate desires for peace. Indeed, the atmosphere of confusion and uncertainty in international affairs that continued into 1788 only contrived to perpetuate a climate of intense suspicion between the two powers. In such a climate, the powers seemed to interpret each other's

---

[1] In *Genesis of the French Revolution*, Bailey Stone makes only one detailed reference to Anglo-French rivalry in India (p. 127); Orville Murphy, in his *Diplomatic Retreat of France*, barely discusses it at all.

understandable caution as evidence of calculating intent. That is, while Carmarthen had voiced his suspicions, in view of Montmorin's apparent 'reserve', that France was "preparing to pursue a line of policy directly contrary to that which she holds to us on this subject", the French were similarly wary of British intentions. Montmorin instructed the marquis de La Luzerne in January 1788 that despite the peaceful resolution of the Dutch crisis, and the French desire for good relations, "le Roi ne sauroit de longtems regarder que comme une trêve la paix qui existe aujourd'hui; et la cour de Londres lui a prouvé qu'il devoit s'attendre à la voir rompue dis qu'elle croiroit y trouver son avantage et pouvoir se le procurer impunément". French diplomats in London were equally, if not more, pessimistic in their assessments.[2]

A major source of continuing French anxiety was the slow and fitfull progress of British naval disarmament in the months following the Dutch crisis. This was exasperating for it obliged the French to maintain their own navy at some level of readiness, the cost of which was even more of a burden than usual given the current state of French financial distress. Moreover, it was clear to the French ministry that the British had emerged from the Dutch crisis stronger, in military terms, than ever before, both at home and in its colonies. The stockpiling alone of supplies and munitions in English ports was cause for concern, for even if the active British fleet was reduced to its former proportions, it gave it the ability to mobilise more rapidly in future. French diplomats in London, however, could only speculate as to actual British intentions. Versailles thus continued its demands on its agents for the close monitoring of both the British fleet and the British cabinet.[3]

---

[2] Carmarthen to Dorset and Eden, 18 December 1787, AAE-CP-Angleterre-562, f. 227; Montmorin, 'Mémoire pour servir d'instructions au S. Chev. de La Luzerne, Maréchal des camps et armées du Roi, allant à Londres en qualité de son Ambassadeur auprès de S.M. Britannique', 7 Jan 1788, AAE-CP-Angleterre-563, f. 106; Barthélemy, in a despatch from London on 4 November 1787, had even stated his belief that it was no longer possible to re-establish harmony between the two powers, or that peace should last long: "La déchirement qu'on veut y effectuer de notre alliance pour y substituer celle de l'Angleterre doivent amener des crises intérieures pour lesquelles la Cour de Londres se fondant sur la suite de nos embarras et sur l'effet de ses démonstrations, sera prête à les renouveller à la premiere occasion ...", Barthélemy to Montmorin, 6 November 1787, AAE-CP-Angleterre-562, f. 95.

[3] Throughout 1787-89 French diplomats sent to Versailles, as requested, detailed and regular reports of the state of the British Navy. See, for example, 'Etat général de la marine anglaise', 4 April 1788, AAE-CP-Angleterre-565, f. 29. See, also, Montmorin's 'Mémoire pour servir d'instructions au S. Chev. de la Luzerne', f. 106.

From the British perspective, there were two items of particular concern, as Dorset and Eden outlined to Montmorin in a meeting in early January 1788. The first concerned the situation in the Balkans and Levant, and the possibility of the French either co-operating or actively joining with the imperial powers in their efforts against the Ottoman Empire.[4] The issue was focused by the Russian intention of sending a naval squadron from the North Sea to the Mediterrenean via the Strait of Gibraltar, a project that the British Ministry seemed determined to frustrate. Would the French and Spanish, the British Ministry enquired, assist the Russians in this endeavour? The second major item concerned the intentions of the French Ministry with regard to the East Indies, and whether it could make reassurances that no hostile projects were being fomented there. With regard to Anglo-French relations, Dorset and Eden had reminded Montmorin of his earlier statement that France had only two options: they could either perpetuate the 'system' of mutual jealousy and misunderstanding with Britain, or enter into good and frank relations. France was thus being pressured to commit itself one way or the other.[5]

On this occasion, and later on, Montmorin could only endeavour to reassure the British Ambassador that France had no desire other than to see the maintenance of peace in Europe, and similarly, that France held no hostile projects whatsoever against British establishments in the East Indies. Montmorin even evinced surprise that Britain should still be so suspicious of France, whose most earnest and expressed desire, he said, was for peace and good relations.[6] However, unfortunately for

---

[4] By early October 1787, British diplomats were seriously speculating that France, unable really to prevent the demise of the Ottoman Empire, was already planning to join the Imperial Powers against the Turks. Hailes presumed, in a despatch to Carmarthen, that a large part of French motivation in this regard was to secure an alternative route to India for the purposes of trade. Hailes to Carmarthen, 4 October 1787, *Despatches from Paris*, Vol. 1, p. 244-245.

[5] Montmorin to Barthélemy, 13 January 1788, AAE-CP-Angleterre-563, ff. 110-111; Dorset and Eden to Carmarthen, 6 January 1788, *Despatches from Paris*, Vol 2, p. 4-8. The French government was under pressure also from Russia in early 1789 to join Russia and Austria in Quadruple alliance against Britain and Prussia, see Sorel, *Europe and the French Revolution*, p. 560-61; Black, *British Foreign Policy*, p. 172.

[6] AAE-CP-Angleterre-563, f. 111; Dorset to Carmarthen, 17 January 1788, *Despatches from Paris*, Vol. 2, p. 10; In February, in response to British accusations that France had harboured hostile projects in India in association with the Dutch, Montmorin told La Luzerne that he had proof that Vergennes had had no such plans, even going so far as to deny that the comte de Grimoard had ever even been a secret agent for France in Holland, Montmorin to the marquis de La Luzerne, 12 February 1788, AAE-CP-Angleterre-564, f. 175.

Montmorin, it was precisely with regard to these two areas of concern—the Eastern War and India—that events across the early months of 1788 would conspire to frustrate any moves toward genuine Anglo-French accord, continually undermining the increasingly desperate French assurances of peaceful intentions and further fuelling the climate of suspicion between the two powers.

Throughout 1788 the British were mindful of the contraints placed on French action by their internal difficulties, but they could not rule out the possibility that some joint French-Spanish-Russian naval effort still remained in the offing. Increased Spanish naval preparations and activity in the early part of the year were of particular concern, for if they and the French were to join up with the sizable Russian fleet heading southward for the Mediterrenean, this would present a formidable threat and potentially fatal blow to the Turkish cause.[7] French claims that they harboured no such designs against the Turks, that they were indeed equally opposed to the passage of the Russian fleet into the Mediterrenean, and even that these Spanish armaments were directed primarily as a *reaction* to the prospective Russian presence there, consistently failed to quell British unease and suspicion about the possibility of a Quadruple alliance.[8]

It was, however, the situation in the East Indies that proved by far the greatest stumbling block in Anglo-French relations.[9] French diplomats had regularly remarked upon the 'excessive jealousy' and 'obsessiveness' with which the British viewed the French presence in the East Indies,[10] and which only seemed to increase with the conclusion of

---

[7] As Hailes commented from Paris, "the naval preparations universally understood to be carrying on in the ports of Spain, cannot fail however to occasion uneasiness; for, exclusive of the apprehensions that must necessarily arise from any powers putting itself in a posture of hostility as this moment, France must be assured of the difficulty she will have to persuade the rest of Europe that, in the present instance, she has no influence in the counsels of His Catholic Majesty, but that Spain is acting an entirely independent part". Hailes to Carmarthen, 3 April 1788, *Despatches from Paris*, Vol. 2, p. 22.

[8] Regarding the suggestion from the French Ministry that the British government be told that Spanish armaments are directed against Russians, see Barthélemy to Montmorin, 1-4 April 1788, AAE-CP-Angleterre-565, ff. 3-20. It should be noted that from July 1788 the Eastern War spread into the Baltic, when hostilities broke out between Sweden and Russia. The ensuing conflict also involved Russia's ally Denmark. See Murphy, *The Diplomatic Retreat of France*, pp. 128-130.

[9] See also Jeremy Black, *British Foreign Policy*, pp. 162-166.

[10] See, for example, Barthélemy to Montmorin, 5 October 1787, AAE-CP-Angleterre-561, f. 332.

the Dutch crisis. Indeed, it was clear to the French that, despite their earnest avowals of peaceful intentions, there was still a real anxiety in Britain that France might seek revenge for the Dutch affair through an attack on British possessions in India. To the French, this was simply preposterous; as Montmorin wrote to the marquis de La Luzerne in London, French forces in India, under the command of the comte de Conway, had neither the instructions nor even the means to carry out such an assault.[11] However, several factors seemed to belie these French assurances and to give apparent credence to British fears: firstly, the sending of the 'Walsh' Regiment to reinforce the French position on the Ile de France, secondly, French objections to the newly proposed Anglo-Dutch defensive pact, and thirdly, the prospective arrival in France of a long awaited ambassadorial delegation from Tippoo Sultan, whose forces were reported to be massing in India against those of Britain's allies. Combined with ongoing anxieties about the possibility of a Quadruple alliance, and the belief in the current state of readiness of the French navy, these fears were aroused to the point where, by June 1788, war fever seemed to be again taking hold in London.[12]

It was in this context that the British and French governments became separately alarmed at the reports filtering in from India during July and August. One of the prime difficulties facing the colonial powers was, of course, the sheer amount of time it took to transmit news and instructions to colonial operatives—a round trip to India and back could take upwards of a year. At the beginning of the year Dorset had stated his belief in the existence of hostile French intentions, and alleged that a French seizure of Trincomalee may already, unbeknownst to them, have been effected.[13] Not only was Tippoo Sultan reported to be, as of March, at the head of a confederation of Indian powers, whose forces could become more formidable than those under the direction of the British, but, just as Dorset had feared, the first reports came that the

---

[11] Montmorin to the marquis de La Luzerne, 20 April 1788, AAE-CP-Angleterre-565, f. 89.

[12] Hailes to Carmarthen, 10 April 1788, *Despatches from Paris*, Vol. 2, p. 27; Montmorin to La Luzerne, 20 April, CP-Ang-565, f. 89; marquis de La Luzerne to Montmorin, 22 April 1788, AAE-CP-Angleterre-565, f. 97; 3 June 1788, *Ibid.*, ff. 222-232; 20 June 1788, *Ibid.*, ff. 299-304. Reporting, in near hysterical tones, on the rumours of impending war in London, La Luzerne commented that little comfort could be taken from the fact that British ports had remained tranquil, for once the British parliament had adjourned, he warned, up to twenty-five warships could be quickly placed in readiness, *Ibid.*, f. 304.

[13] Marquis de La Luzerne to Montmorin, 5 February 1788, AAE-CP-Angleterre-564, f. 170.

French had indeed embarked on an expedition to seize Trincomalee (following instructions sent out the previous year to safeguard it from capture by the British).[14]

The reception of such reports also compounded French anxieties. The French government had indeed continued to hold great concerns that as a result of the Anglo-Dutch pact the port of Trincomalee might pass into British hands, thus making impregnable the British hold over India, and giving them a vital springboard for further incursions into Asia. However, such was the French desperation to avoid providing the British with a pretext for declaring war, that they gave them every assurance that once the outcome of Conway's expedition had become known, they would not hesitate to restore Trincomalee to its Dutch rulers.[15]

It was during this time that the French were also further discomfited by the arrival in France of Tippoo's ambassadors, which they knew would aggravate British anxiety about French activity in India.[16] On the one hand the French were still happy to encourage (at least, secretly) an anti-British stance among the Indian powers, and viewed Tippoo as a valuable ally against the expansion of British interests in India. On the other hand, in view of France's mounting financial difficulties, domestic turmoil, and the situation in the Balkans, the French government had been also increasingly anxious not to be drawn into actual conflict with the British through the actions of such a restless and aggressively warlike ruler. Tippoo's offer to France of trading privileges in return for an offensive alliance against Britain and the help of 3,000 French soldiers could not thus have been more ill-timed. Though the ambassadors were received with some ceremony by Louis XVI at

---

[14] Marquis de La Luzerne to Montmorin, 12 July 1788, AAE-CP-Angleterre-566, ff. 37-40.

[15] Montmorin to Barthélemy, 24 August 1788, AAE-CP-Angleterre-563, f. 159. As Dorset reported from Paris, Montmorin had as early as May 1788 promised "that if it shall be found that any act of hostility was committed in India during the uncertainty of events last year in respect to the Affairs of Holland, His Most Christian Majesty would not hesitate to issue immediate orders for restitution to be made, in cases of capture, and reparation for such injuries as a premature zeal upon the occasion may possibly have produced". Dorset to Carmarthen, 1 May 1788, *Despatches from Paris*, Vol. 2, p. 37.

[16] Tippoo's Ambassadors arrived at Toulon on 9 June 1788. As Montmorin wrote in May to the marquis de La Luzerne in London, the arrival of such a delegation would no doubt cause 'absurd speculations' in England. Montmorin to the marquis de La Luzerne, 14 May 1788, AAE-CP-Angleterre-565, f. 180. However, one might argue, in view of Castries' earlier aspirations with regard to France in India, that such speculations were not, in fact, unreasonable.

Versailles on 10 August, and dined over successive days with the comte de La Luzerne—brother of the Ambassador in London—Brienne, and Montmorin, their offer was politely but firmly declined.[17]

One can imagine the surprise and bafflement of Tippoo's ambassadors at such a rebuff. From the moment of their arrival in France the authorities had seemed to spare no expense in honouring their visit, and impressing upon them the might and grandeur of France.[18] From this, and the messages implicit in Castries' Indian policy, they would thus have had every expectation that their offer would have been seriously considered, if not accepted with alacrity. Now, having been shown the rounds of Versailles, they were being effectively shown the door. The savage irony of this situation would not have been lost on Montmorin, who seemed barely able, according to Hailes, to conceal his contempt for the whole charade.[19]

As a result of these events, the British government continued to respond coldly to French assurances of peaceful intentions. Pitt and his cabinet knew all too well how vulnerable their position still was in India to the vagaries of local politics, and how little it would take to possibly reverse Britain's otherwise growing might on the sub-continent. The British cabinet thus continued throughout the remainder of 1788 to maintain an extreme wariness in regard to French intentions, and to press for further information regarding French dispositions in India. So

---

[17] Hailes to Carmarthen, 11 August 1788, *Despatches from Paris*, Vol. 2, p. 85.

[18] Pierre-Victor Malouet, *Mémoires* (Paris, 1874), Vol. 1., p. 206; Dorset to Carmarthen, 14 August 1788, *Despatches from Paris*, Vol. 2, p. 88. In July Dorset had reported the great effort and expense being made by the French to entertain and fête these Ambassadors, concluding that "great care will... be taken to prevent any impressions being given to these People that can in any shape diminish their ideas of the Power and authority of the Sovereign of this Country, as the confidence of Tippoo Sultan might be lessened was He to be made acquainted with the real State of the Affairs in France". Dorset to Carmarthen, 2 July 1788, *Ibid.*, p. 74. Later on, Daniel Hailes wrote similarly that the "honors and attentions that have been shewn to these people during their residence in this capital have been very remarkable and it is hoped no doubt that by conveying an idea of riches and splendour of this country to the Power by whom this mission is deputed, he may be inclined still more to strengthen his alliance with it...". Hailes to Carmarthen, 25 September 1788, *Ibid.*, p. 106.

[19] Hailes to Carmarthen, 21 August 1788, *Ibid.*, p. 93. On the 14 August Dorset wrote to Carmarthen that Montmorin had, in assuring him of France's pacific intentions with regard to India, denied that these Ambassadors had in fact made any offer at all, insisting that their visit was indeed merely 'complimentary'. Dorset to Carmarthen, 14 August 1788, *Ibid.*, p. 88.

intense were these British suspicions that Barthélemy finally wrote in exasperation to Montmorin that:

> Quoi que nous fassions, nous ne calmerons jamais les inquiétudes du Ministère Anglais sur les vues qu'il sera toujours porté à nous suposer sur l'Inde. Sa disposition à cet égard est si injuste, que je ne pense pas l'être envers lui en les croyant tourmenté de la jalousie qui veut ne voir que piège et dissimulation dans les bons procédés.[20]

The Implementation of the Anglo-French Commercial Treaty

Another significant source of friction between France and Britain in this period concerned the terms and implementation of the recently concluded Anglo-French commercial treaty which, paradoxically, had been initially intended as the motor for future amicable relations. It had been the understanding of Vergennes and Rayneval that the negotiations for such a treaty would procede on the basis of full reciprocity, but as the treaty came into force during 1787 it became apparent to French merchants and their government that this was not the interpretation being followed in Britain.[21] Furthermore, in both Britain and France the treaty soon became the subject of intense debate over whether it was beneficial to either country, a debate which took greater force in France, then experiencing, in contrast to Britain, worsening economic conditions.[22]

The provisions of the treaty which accorded the British manufacturing and industrial sector much greater access to French markets than ever before attracted the most criticism. Vergennes, Rayneval and Dupont's rationale for allowing such an increased access for British industrial goods had been that this measure would be offset by

---

[20] "Mais", as Barthélemy went on, "ce ne sera pas une raison pour nous cesser de les continuer; et il suffira pour le bien de nos affaires que, si de puissantes considérations ne nous ont pas permis d'entamer des négotiations avec les Ambassadeurs de Tippoo, S.M. ait au moins la certitude de pouvoir contracter des liens avec ce redoutable ennemi des Anglais, lorsque leur conduite à notre égard pourra rendre cette ressource nécessaire". Barthélemy to Montmorin, 11 November 1788, AAE-CP-Angleterre-563, ff. 190-192.

[21] Issues of reciprocity had indeed nearly stalled the negotiations altogether, with Castries particularly aggravated about the lack of reciprocity apparently evinced by the British with regard to the issue of trade consuls; see Marie Donaghay, 'The Maréchal de Castries and the Anglo-French Commercial Negotiations of 1786-87', *Historical Journal*, 22:2 (1979), pp. 295-312.

[22] Doyle, *Origins of the French Revolution*, pp. 58-68.

several factors, namely, a greater access to British markets for French agricultural products, benefits to French industry from the efficiency gains made through competition with British products, and the belief that there were actually fewer people in France anyway who could afford to buy British manufactures than there were those in Britain who could afford to consume French agricultural products.[23] There was also the question, from the perspective of the French ministry, of making the terms of the treaty sufficiently attractive for the British to both want to accept and adhere to it. For its French critics, however, the treaty was viewed as an unmitigated disaster. Though historians in the twentieth century have disputed or thrown doubt on such claims, it nonetheless became the widespread belief in France that the treaty had been a strongly contributing factor, if not the signal cause, of a sharp economic downturn. The French ministry was flooded with petitions condemning the treaty, bodies such as the Normandy Chamber of Commerce publishing an angry critique of the treaty and its alleged consequences on French manufacturing and the economy in general.[24]

Opinion on the value of this treaty was also divided within the government. Boyetet, Dupont's fellow head at the Bureau de la Balance du Commerce, led the charge against a freer trade policy, defending the previous policy of protectionism as more appropriate to the French economy and its development. For Boyetet, the proposed benefits of the treaty were illusory. As he told Calonne before final negotiations on it had even begun, this treaty threatened to severely retard French manufacturing and industry at the very point when it was working

---

[23] See Dupont, 'Observations sur les motifs particuliers qui peuvent déterminer le traité de commerce', ff. 3-24; see also, Murphy, 'Dupont de Nemours', *passim.*; Adhémar to Montmorin, 27 February 1787, AAE-CP-Angleterre-559, f. 185.

[24] W.O. Henderson, 'The Anglo-French Commercial Treaty of 1786', *Economic History Review*, 10:1 (August 1957), pp. 109-112; Henri Sée, 'The Normandy Chamber of Commerce and the Commercial Treaty of 1786', *Economic History Review*, 2 (1929-1930): pp. 308-13, *passim*; The writer Bergasse commented, in a work written in 1788, that this Treaty indeed seemed only part of a general English assault upon French trade, stating that "notre commerce menace ruine de toutes parts; notre Traité de Commerce avec l'Angleterre a porté, dans le premier moment, un coup funeste à nos Manufactures; le Traité d'Alliance de l'Angleterre avec la Hollande, n'a pour objet que de nous chasser de l'Inde, & puis de nous en fermer l'entrée; les troubles du Levant, secrètement fomentés par nos ennemis naturels, peuvent finir par nous priver de la branche la plus riche de nos exportations & de nos importations". N. Bergasse, *Considérations sur la liberté du commerce; ouvrage où l'on examine s'il est avantageux ou nuisible au commerce, que le transport des denrées et des marchandises soit réduit en privilege exclusif* (London, 1788).

toward becoming more competitive, and, furthermore, to jeopardise the commercial advantages gained through the loss to Britain of its American colonies.[25] France, he urged, needed to complete rather than to stall this process of industrial development: "il est question, non seulement de conserver à la France l'industrie dont elle est en possession, & que ce traité écrasera & lui enlevera, mais de lui procurer tous les genres qui lui manquent, & de mettre La Nation en état de se suffire à elle-même". This could be done, he suggested, through such things as the importation of more advanced English machinery and manufacturing techniques, giving impetus to the development of France's superior natural economic resources.[26]

There was even some disagreement over this issue among the French diplomats in London. While Adhémar, the previous ambassador, had adhered to the ministerial line by anticipating ultimate benefits to France from the treaty, his *chargé d'affaires* Barthélemy was far less convinced. Throughout 1787 he made reference in his despatches to the growing economic might of England, and the greater advantages it could now exploit in competition with France. It was not merely that Britain possessed superior economic infrastructure and maritime strength that accounted for the relative intensity of her industrial activity, he argued, but also the *nature* of her industrial output. The fact that British production was geared in large part to the production of items of common consumption and utility, rather than 'luxury' goods, gave her wider and stronger markets than those of France. According to Barthélemy, that "une nation inquiète, jalouse" should hold such economic and commercial advantages over France was dangerous, an imbalance that needed correction. France's future as a great power, he implied, was dependent on such an inbalance being contested. In this "combat d'industrie", he wrote to Montmorin, the development of French industry was no less important to France than the development of her army and navy. "Notre intérêt", he argued, "nous oblige de chercher tous les moyens d'établir l'équilibre".[27]

In response to these criticisms of the commercial treaty, the Ministry moved to defend the free trade policy, Dupont de Nemours publishing a detailed rejoinder to the claims of the Normandy Chamber

---

[25] 'Reflexions sur le Traité du Commerce avec Angleterre', in Boyetet, *Recueil des divers mémoires, relatifs au traité de commerce avec l'Angleterre* (Versailles, 1789), Vol. 1, pp. 58-62.

[26] *Ibid.*, Vol. 2, pp. 77-80.

[27] Barthélemy to Montmorin, 22 May 1787, AAE-CP-Angleterre-560, f. 94; 3 July 1787, *Ibid.*, ff. 260-261; 31 July 1787, *Ibid.*, ff. 400-401; 14 August 1787, AAE-CP-Angleterre-561, f. 56; 11 September 1787, *Ibid.*, ff. 180-182.

of Commerce.[28] Meanwhile, in order to maximise the supposed benefits of the treaty (and hopefully, to reverse France's economic recession), the Ministry also instructed its representatives in London to press the British government for full reciprocity, to little avail.[29] Not only would the Ministry continue to be, over the following months, frustrated in these demands, but domestic grievances over the treaty would also only add to growing popular discontent with the royal government.

The Deterioration in French Internal Affairs

Throughout 1787 and 1788 French diplomats in London continued to urge the royal government to resolve its domestic and financial embarrassments, citing the damaging effect these problems were having on France's international standing. For them, the sorry outcomes of the Dutch Crisis only confirmed the ever greater imperative of the French Crown to restore and strengthen its financial position and quell internal dissent.[30] Despite such urgings, however, in both those dimensions the French internal situation was to worsen, leading the country in the middle of 1788 to a dangerous growth of civil disorder, and the desperate financial situation of its government.

The tenure of Brienne from May 1787, first as Head of the Royal Council of Finances, then also as Principal Minister, had begun promisingly enough. Following the disclosure to the Notables that the deficit was actually far in excess of what had been initially conjectured,

---

[28] Dupont de Nemours, *Lettre à la Chambre du Commerce de Normandie sur la Mémoire qu'elle a publié relativement au Traité de Commerce avec l'Angleterre* (Rouen and Paris, 1788).

[29] See Donaghay, 'Castries and the Anglo-French Commercial Negotiations', p. 312; The Government was in fact well aware that in the first year of commercial treaty's introduction, the Anglo-French balance of trade involved an official net disadvantage to France amounting to more than nine hundred thousand livres' worth of goods. See Lambert to Montmorin, 'Tableau Général du Commerce entre la France et la Grande Bretagne depuis l'Epoque du Traité jusqu'au 31 Décembre 1787', 19 April 1788, AAE-CP-Angleterre-565, ff. 86-87.

[30] Aside from the question of the actual constraints this financial situation may have placed on French military action, there was, as Adhémar and Barthélemy had noted, also the no less damaging public *perception* in foreign courts of French incapability. See Adhémar to Montmorin, 24 April 1787, AAE-CP-Angleterre-559, ff. 342-348, Barthélemy to Montmorin, 11 September 1787, *Ibid.*, ff. 180-182. In the game of international brinkmanship, this perception alone had immeasurably strengthened the diplomatic position of France's current or potential opponents, by allowing them, with reasonable confidence, to call the French bluff in the Dutch crisis.

Brienne instituted a series of stringent economies, particularly in the Royal Household. These economies, as Jean Egret has argued, had been inspired by the Notables and hence met with their strong approval.[31] Brienne's reputation as an able administrator, and his initial high standing within the Assembly, had even enabled him to float a substantial loan in order to feed the government's desperate need for cash. However, when Brienne sought to reinstitute the reforms of Calonne, he was met in the Assembly with the same resistance that had defeated the former Contrôleur-Général. Even a significant concession with regard to the form of the land-tax failed to appease the Notables, who began to insist that the only body capable of giving consent to new taxes was the Estates-General, the body supposedly most representative of the full spectrum of French corporate life, but which had not been called for nearly two hundred years.[32]

In frustration, Brienne dissolved the Assembly of Notables before the end of May 1787, and determined to press ahead with the modified reforms. The subsequent transference of resistance to tax reform from the Notables to the Parlements, however, only inaugurated a period of growing rancour in French domestic politics. The Parlements had over the preceding decades become a major source of periodic élite resistance to royal absolutism, claiming a 'constitutional' right to a quasi-legislative role through the refusal to register certain royal decrees. During August 1787, with the Dutch crisis gathering momentum, the crown had moved to force urgent registration of the decrees concerning the land-tax and stamp duty through the traditional recourse of a *lit de justice*. It then exiled the Parlement of Paris to Troyes for disputing the legality of this measure.

This action failed to have the desired effect, for the Parlements were only confirmed in their intransigence by widespread public support. The crown's determination to institute major new taxes was thus met by an equally determined and politically motivated resistance. Promoted at the time as a campaign against royal 'despotism', this resistance has since been interpreted either as a simple defence of aristocratic privilege, or as an attempt by the combined noble and bourgeois landowning élite (the 'Notables') to press 'liberal' claims for political representation. At any rate, the opposition to the Crown certainly demanded that the royal government be opened up to regular public

---

[31] Jean Egret, *The French Prerevolution*, p. 58.
[32] Goodwin, 'Notables and the "Révolte Nobiliaire"', pp. 366-373; Doyle, *Origins*, pp. 103-105.

scrutiny. This was a proposition that Louis XVI, sensitive to the traditions of absolutism, continued to find totally unacceptable.

After an attempt at compromise on the tax issue had foundered at the Royal Session of 19 November 1787, the Parlements entered 1788 with a renewed resolve to challenge royal authority. As the confrontational clamour increased, the government, which had responded by the imprisonment of leading magistrates, prepared to move decisively against the *parlementaire* opposition, finally launching its assault in early May. Henceforth, it decreed, royal legislation would be registered by a newly created Plenary Court, thereby side-stepping the Parlements altogether. This was met in turn by a wave of protest that swept the country, including the 'Day of Tiles' revolt in Grenoble.

Whether the government would have been able to weather this storm of protest is an open question. However, the government was prevented from capitalising on its judicial offensive by the sudden and irrevocable collapse of government finances at the beginning of August. This amounted to state bankruptcy. The royal government, effectively paralysed, had then no choice but to accede to the convocation of the Estates-General for May of 1789, and to reverse its offensive against the Parlements. Brienne—denounced by élites and popularly reviled—resigned, and with him, many historians would believe, went the last hopes of the absolute monarchy.

Military Reform, and the Rationalisation of French Global Power

The accession of Brienne in August 1787 to the long-lapsed position of Principal Minister had been an indication of the singular and urgent priority given by the French crown to the addressing of its financial problems and debt management. If tackling the problem of France's strangulated finances was foremost among the concerns of Brienne, and of Louis XVI himself, this was not an issue simply of alleviating the financial constrictions on the royal government, and hence of reducing the domestic political pressures to which such constrictions gave rise. The Dutch crisis had shown just how vulnerable France had become in international affairs on account of its internal financial embarrassments, a matter that continued to be of imperative concern to the French crown. As the King and his ministers understood, the effecting of general economies in the royal expenditure, especially those relating to France's army and navy, was critical to the recovery both to France's reputation and capability as a great power, in that it would allow a more effective allocation of available resources. Even Brienne, though he himself had emphatically ruled out intervention in Holland, had nonetheless been mindful of such an object. To the Swedish ambassador, Baron de Staël, he commented in September 1787 that once France's financial health had been properly restored, he hoped "to have France play the role that becomes her".[33]

The goal of military reforms and economies throughout 1787—88 was thus not merely to effect a substantial cut in overall military expenditure, but also to offset these economies by an increase in the efficiency and capability of France's armed forces. The primary instruments for these reforms were the Conseil de Guerre and Conseil de la Marine, formed by Louis XVI in late 1787 and charged with the task of forming proposals for rationalising the army and navy. Of the two services the army was in greatest need of reform and rationalisation. In its hierarchy and organisational structure it was extraordinarily top-heavy, with an excessive number of supernumerary colonels and general officers, all of which was extremely expensive to the Crown. By contrast, the common soldiery was perceived to be underpaid, often suffering from very poor conditions that diminished their morale and military efficiency. The Conseil de Guerre under the comte de Guibert thus recommended a substantial cut in the number of general officers and purely ceremonial troops, the elimination of numerous 'abuses', and an improvement in pay and conditions for ordinary soldiers. It also took the opportunity to advocate a variety of innovations regarding organisation, discipline and tactical operations, all of which were designed to enhance the army's fighting effectiveness.[34]

The French navy was in many respects in better shape than the army by 1788, having, after the American War, already undergone a series of reforms instituted by Castries in order to modernise it and increase its operational effectiveness.[35] Consequently, although the naval budget had continued to rise in previous years, the Conseil de la Marine could only

---

[33] Jean Egret, *The French Prerevolution*, p. 42.

[34] Even the recommendation of the *Conseil* to restrict officer recruitment to the 'older' nobility, which would only have the effect of reinforcing the traditional and caste-bound nature of the army, would, it was thought, also improve the capability of the army, by encouraging greater professionalism among the officer corps. *Ibid.*, pp. 47-53.

[35] Castries' reforms, including the 'Code de Castries' governing the officer corps, are generally regarded by historians as constituting one of the most significant programs of reform for French naval administration under the old regime. See William Cormack, *Revolution and Political Conflict in the French Navy 1789-1794*, Cambridge, 1995, pp. 43-47.

find, through the elimination of existing 'abuses', economies that were clearly regarded as insufficient by the king, given the depth and urgency of the current financial crisis. Indeed, it appeared that the projected naval budget for 1788—89 would remain no less high than in previous years, or might even increase owing to the demands made on the navy as a result of recent circumstances.[36] This put the comte de La Luzerne in a difficult position. As the Naval Minister explained in a lengthy *mémoire* to the king in late 1788, it would not be possible to make drastic cuts to the naval budget merely through the elimination of some 'abuses', without affecting or significantly compromising the navy's present operational capacity at the level the king had earlier decreed. The need, La Luzerne said plainly, was to establish economies compatible with the maintenance of adequate maritime and colonial defences, telling Louis that:

> C'est à votre sagesse à peser jusqu'à quel point il convient de se départir des projets adoptés dans des temps plus heureux pour assurer à ce royaume une Marine de plus en plus formidable. Mon devoir est de rechercher les moyens de la conserver sur un pied qui la fasse encore respecter lorsqu'une guerre surviendra et qui puisse accorder protection efficace soit à notre commerce, soit à nos possessions éloignées, sans excéder jusqu'à cette époque les bornes de la dépense que V.M. entend y assigner.[37]

La Luzerne's recommendations in this *mémoire* were marked by a determination to maintain at least the material existence of the French navy. Although this involved no repudiation of Castries' programme of naval expansion, it was clear that current financial circumstances precluded the fulfillment of this programme, at least for the time being.[38] In any case, as La Luzerne noted, Louis had already decided to

---

[36] These circumstances included the naval preparations required by the war in the Levant and the Baltic, and the expenses incurred as a result of recent hurricane damage on Martinique and Saint-Domingue. See the comte de La Luzerne, 14 December 1788, 'Mémoire sur le réduction des dépenses ordinaires du Département de la Marine et sur la somme annuelle à la quelle on peut les fixer', BN-NAF-9434, ff. 172-174.

[37] *Ibid.*, f. 175.

[38] According to La Luzerne, France had in advance stockpiled the materials necessary for the construction of another 18 vessels and as many frigates (in line with the decree under Castries that the number of ships-of-the-line and frigates would grow to a total each of 81). Construction of these ships, he asserted, however, could not now proceed without the required increase in naval funds, a prospect unrealisable given the current budgetry restrictions. BN-NAF-9434, f. 177.

hold in reserve any vessels exceeding the more traditional complement of sixty-three-sixty-four. These were to be fitted out and brought into action only if circumstances absolutely required it. Meanwhile, the Naval Minister assured the king that France could continue to count on the availability of the traditional number of sixty-three vessels, and as many frigates, for sending to all points around the globe. Moreover, if peace lasted for another year, France might even have enough ships for six or seven vessels, and a matching number of frigates, to be stationed at Cherbourg. If such a detachment was kept there in reserve, La Luzerne conjectured, this would have the effect of giving France a relative increase in its global maritime strength by forcing Britain to retain a far greater proportion of its fleet constantly in home waters.

Given the scale of cuts demanded by the king, it might be thought that assuring him of the potential availability of even the traditional number of French warships was in itself a tall order. Late the previous year Dorset had amended his previous view of the French navy, commenting now on the poor state of readiness of the French fleet at Brest, and describing much of the fleet as being in "a deplorable state".[39] This was a situation that was, with the worsening of the domestic and financial situation across that year, unlikely to have changed by the end of 1788.[40]

To maximise the potential availability of the existing fleet, La Luzerne therefore recommended to the king a severe paring down of the navy's operational costs and peacetime activity, concluding that even officer training could be conducted far less expensively.[41] But this was not all. In his capacity both as naval and colonial minister, La Luzerne concluded that the task of preserving the respectable footing of the French navy in the face of financial penury had required above all a review and rationalisation of France's maritime and colonial commitments.

---

[39] Dorset to Carmarthen, 25 Oct 1787, *Despatches from Paris*, Vol. 1, p. 260.

[40] During this period, long-term structural problems in the French navy, such as limitations on available personnel for the manning of the fleet, and chronic financial problems, would be compounded by shorter-term problems, such as the rising discontent among sailors and dockyard workers, which would later develop into mutinous sentiment. See Cormack, *Revolution and Political Conflict*, p. 24, Ch 3-4, *passim*.

[41] "On a fort multiplié", wrote La Luzerne, "les armements depuis la paix. Des circonstances impérieuses en ont été la principale cause, mais je crois que l'Etat habituel en était porté trop haut; qu'on pourrait former et exercer les officiers et les élèves de la Marine royale à moins de frais", BN-NAF-9343, f. 177.

The Minister presented this review to the king in the form of a survey of French colonial establishments. La Luzerne noted that these colonies were "sources intarissables d'opulence pour l'Etat", but that they were also very costly to defend. Searching for possible cutbacks and economies, he examined each establishment according to its existing and potential economic value relative to its defensive costs and circumstances. It was clear that France could no longer afford to support colonial establishments without a regime now of stringent cost-effectiveness. Turning first to France's colonies in the western hemisphere, the Minister concluded that there were few possibilities there to make substantial economies, as, he said:

> il a déjà fait depuis la paix de fortes réductions sur les frais qu'occasionnaient les Colonies occidentales. On a introduit une sage économie dans les diverses branches de leur administration civile; et leur proximité de l'Europe, la manière dont elles sont (si j'ose m'exprimer ainsi) entrelacées avec des Colonies Anglaises, rendraient selon moi très dangereuses la diminution des Troupes et des moyens de défense militaire qu'on y a affectées.[42]

This was an assessment that, as a recent governor in the region, La Luzerne was no doubt well placed to make. With regard to the islands of St. Pierre and Miquelon off Newfoundland, he recommended that the permanent naval station there could perhaps be removed, protection being henceforth provided by seasonal detachments sent from the Antilles. Yet, alive to the strategic as well as economic value of these islands, he counselled that the modest costs of their internal defense ought not otherwise be reduced, arguing that the fishing industry facilitated by these islands was not only "fort lucrative pour l'Etat, mais on peut la regarder comme la meilleure et presque comme la seule école qui nous forme une foule d'excellents matelots", this being a precious resource that in itself France could not afford to jeopardise.[43]

Although costly to defend, La Luzerne asserted that France's West Indian colonies were similarly (with the exception of the recent acquisition of Tobago) too valuable to endanger them through any further reduction in the funds provided for their defence. The colony of St. Domingue was by far the most valuable of France's overseas possessions, providing a range of profitable commodities, that when brought to France and then re-exported to the rest of Europe, was a

---

[42] La Luzerne, 'Mémoire de réduction des dépense ordinaires ...', BN-NAF-9434, f. 180.
[43] Ibid., ff. 178, 180-181.

significant contributor to France's balance of trade and an important source of national income. The islands of Guadeloupe, Martinique and St. Lucie, though as yet less fecund than St. Domingue, made up for this, the Minister pointed out, by their strategic usefulness, as shown during the last war where they were instrumental in the successes gained in the region against the British. "Il serait trop dispendieux de renoncer à ce qu'on a obtenu", he thus concluded. Even French Guyana, the despair of many a colonial minister, ought, he argued, to be preserved, on the similar grounds that it would be unreasonable to sacrifice a long-term investment when, as he alleged, it was finally due to bear fruit.[44]

La Luzerne could not, or would not, apply such arguments to France's 'eastern' colonies, by which he meant those in Africa, the Indian Ocean and in India itself. It was here that the minister intended to make the bulk of his colonial economies. This was based primarily on his conviction that these colonies were by no means comparable in value to those of the western hemisphere. "Peut-être", he said,

> n'a-t-on pas jusqu'à ce jour assez réfléchi que l'objet de ces derniers établissements ne ressemble nullement à celui des colonies occidentales, que l'utilité qu'en retire l'Etat est d'un tout autre genre. Nous n'avons en aucun temps recueilli, nous ne devons jamais espérer du sol de nos possessions en Afrique et en Asie une moisson annuelle et abondante de Caffé, de coton, d'indigo de sucre. Elles ne consomment point comme les Antilles une grande quantité de productions du royaume ou des ouvrages qui y sont manufacturés. Nous devons donc les considérer seulement comme les entrepôts d'un commerce étranger que nous voulons partager avec les autres nations de l'Europe, ou comme des points destinés à le protéger et à servir d'asile pendant les guerres futures à nos forces navales.[45]

Secondly, and following on from this classic mercantilist assessment, was what the Minister regarded as a realistic view of the actual defensibility of many of these 'eastern' colonies. Economies could thus be made, he asserted, by scaling down the defences of Sénégal on the west coast of Africa, since this colony would, in any case, always likely to be easy prey to any concerted attack by France's rivals.[46]

It was beyond the Cape of Good Hope, however, as La Luzerne noted, that the focus of these future economies would be found. In a major shift in policy, La Luzerne concluded that the time had come finally to withdraw French military forces from India, and re-station

---

[44] *Ibid.*, f. 184.
[45] *Ibid.*, f. 185.
[46] *Ibid*, ff. 185-186.

them on the Ile de France. France's scattered colonies in India had always, he argued, been costly to fortify, yet appeared no more defensible for all that effort, given the time it took to send reinforcements from Europe or from more secure settlements elsewhere. This included the chief-place, Pondichéry, which, surrounded by vast provinces belonging to France's "natural enemy" (Britain), had repeatedly succumbed when besieged in recent wars:

> Ouvrons enfin les yeux, que le flambeau de la Raison et celui de l'expérience nous éclairent. Pondichéry a opposé la plus vigoureuse résistance en 1778 et a été mal attaqué. En est-il moins tombé au pouvoir des Anglais aussi que toutes nos possessions Indiennes? C'est à Ile de France qu'il a fallu renvoyer d'Europe les forces navales et les troupes ... [It is this Island, he argued] que la nature et l'intérêt de la France destinent à être le receptacle de nos flottes et l'arsenal de nos armes, lorsque nous voudrons porter la guerre dans les extrémités orientales de l'univers ...[47]

Although this move to the Ile de France would initially carry some cost, said La Luzerne, this would nonetheless lead to a substantial reduction in general costs over the next few years. Henceforth, France would only possess simple trading posts in India, with the minimum forces necessary to police them. She would, however, possess a more secure platform in the Indian Ocean from which she could launch assaults against any prospective European enemy.[48]

It was somewhat ironic that the comte de La Luzerne, an apparent *protégé* of Castries, should have been the architect of such a policy of comprehensive military withdrawal from India, for this policy flatly contradicted that of his protector.[49] Only the previous year Castries had had the Irish-born comte de Conway appointed Commander of French establishments in India, with orders to prepare the groundwork for an eventual assault on British power.[50] Despite the positive gloss put by La

---

[47] Ibid., ff. 187-188.

[48] Ibid., f. 188. Orders for the French military withdrawal from Pondichéry were sent out as early as May 1788, the withdrawal being justified on the grounds that with Dutch crisis, and the loss hence of Trincomalee, strategic circumstances had changed in Asia. See La Luzerne to Conway, 28 May 1788, AN-FC-C4-82, f. 25.

[49] When Castries resigned, he had strongly urged that La Luzerne be chosen as his successor. See duc de Castries, *Le Maréchal de Castries*, p. 150.

[50] "En général", Conway had been told, "le but que le Roy se propose dans ce moment est de tâcher de se conserver les Princes de l'Inde dans un grand état de tranquilité jusqu'à ce qu'il soit en mesure de les secourir; et comme nous parviendrons sans doute à combiner un jour nos forces avec celle de hollande, il

Luzerne on the concentration of military resources on Ile de France, such a withdrawal was an obvious and humiliating admission of French weakness.

One might argue that this withdrawal was prompted, in the first instance, less by studied mercantilist calculations than by a simple recognition of France's apparent inability to compete in any military or territorial sense with Britain on the Indian sub-continent. This conclusion is supported by the instructions sent out from France to the India Command, for when first informing Conway, as early as May 1788, of the king's intention to withdraw his forces from India, La Luzerne had specifically mentioned the loss of Trincomalee as the critical factor in changing the strategic equation in the region against France.[51] In a subsequent *mémoire* to the Conseil d'Etat, the Naval and Colonial Minister detailed the circumstances that had led to the change in policy in India, including the increasing strength and territorial power there of the British and the superiority of their manipulation of internal Indian politics. "Le tems n'est plus", wrote La Luzerne in this *mémoire*,

> où nous devions regarder dans l'Inde les Anglois que comme les rivaux de notre commerce. Les vastes Provinces qu'ils ont envahies, les forces militaires qu'ils entretiennent dans cette partie de l'univers les ont rendu redoutables non seulement aux peuples Européennes, mais aux Souverains les plus puissants de l'Indoustan.[52]

Such were the vicissitudes of Indian politics, he argued furthermore, that it was almost too much to hope that any anti-British coalition would form, fortuitously, at the precise moment when war might break out again between Britain and France. "Sans ce concours fortuit des circonstances", he commented,

> il est évident que nos possessions incapable d'opposer aucune résistance telle que Chandernagor, Tauron, Karikal, ainsi que plusieurs Comptoirs situés dans de villes où nous n'avons pas d'autre propriété, seraient envahis facilement dès le commencement des hostilités, & que tout ce que nous y aurons renfermé de

---

      faut attendre que ces dispositions soient arrêtées pour pouvoir peser quelque base de sûreté avec cette puissance". in 'Mémoire du Roy, pour servir d'instruction particulière à M. le comte de Conway, Commandant des troupes et des Etablissements françois dans l'Inde.' 15 March 1787, AN-FC-C2-180, f. 6.

[51] La Luzerne to Conway, 28 May 1787, f. 24.
[52] Comte de La Luzerne, 'Mémoire au Conseil d'état', 21 September 1788, AN-FC-C4-85, f. 99. This was to be contrasted, of course, with the relative, and endemic, financial and military weaknesses long suffered by the French establishments in India.

Troupes, de munitions, & d'artillerie deviendra aussitôt la proïe de nos enemmis.[53]

Time and tide had thus made it far more difficult to manage, protect and exploit these distant and vulnerable Indian possessions than it had the island colonies France held in the eastern and western hemispheres. Unless France was able and prepared to play a more aggressive role in Indian politics, in order to make impregnable its otherwise precarious possessions on the sub-continent, it could only but yield to the present superiority of the British whose power, by contrast, appeared to be increasingly entrenched there.

In summary, the decision to withdraw French forces from India may be seen as a palpable demonstration of the widening gulf between French global ambitions in the last years of the Old Regime, and the means they had of achieving them. These ambitions—whether they took the form of Vergennes' goal of containment, or Castries' of ultimate confrontation—had been hamstrung by the problems inherent in French finances. In the face of these severe financial difficulties, La Luzerne—as one might expect of a naval minister and *protégé* of Castries—endeavoured to maintain at least the material integrity of the French navy, and to maintain as strong a presence in the Indian ocean region as could effectively be managed, despite the French withdrawal from India. Indeed, underlying these measures would seem to be an expectation of a future resumption and even increase in French strength at some future point, once France's financial problems had finally been addressed and resolved. Thus, while the military withdrawal from India certainly highlighted the internal structural problems with which France had long been burdened, by no means did it indicate an abandonment by France of a substantial future role in the eastern hemisphere. There was obviously an assumption by the Ministry that, in spite of current constrictions, the underlying fundamentals of French power remained solid and would in due course be more effectively harnessed.

France and the Cochinchina Project

No episode was better illustrative of the extreme difficulties France faced as a great power during this period than that of the Cochinchina project considered by the French Ministry. Insofar as it was seriously considered by the royal government, the project began in late 1787 as a

---

[53] *Ibid.*, f. 100.

way of compensating for the loss of the Dutch alliance; its abandonment a year later would be a dramatic demonstration of the paralysis of French overseas power.

The Cochinchina project had its origins in the struggle between an exiled king of Cochinchina, Prince Nguyen-Anh, and usurpers from an adjacent northern kingdom. At the behest of a French Catholic missionary named Pigneau de Behaine, otherwise known as the Bishop of Adran, Nguyen-Anh sought outside help to reclaim his throne not from Britain, Spain, Holland or Portugal, but from the king of France. In return for this help the exiled king of Cochinchina promised to accord the French exclusive commercial privileges in his country. By the mid-1780s, the French Naval and Colonial Minister Castries had begun to show interest in this project, influenced no doubt by *mémoires* and reports, such as that by Solminihac de Lamothe in early 1786, outlining the various benefits of a French trading establishment placed so strategically on the South China Sea.[54] The minister promptly sent orders to the Commander of Pondichéry to organise a reconnaissance mission to bring back information about the suitability of sites on the Cochinchinese coast. Soon after these instructions had been issued, the Bishop of Adran himself, accompanied by Nguyen-Anh's son, the Crown Prince Canh, arrived in France to press the case for French help.[55]

The subsequent crisis in Holland and the resignation of Castries, although it certainly slowed consideration of the Cochinchinese project, did not, however, ruin the chances for its acceptance by the royal government. On the contrary, the outcome of the Dutch crisis only gave impetus to the government to seriously consider the Prince's request; for with the United Provinces and its overseas establishments expected to return to the British orbit, France, it was deemed, would now need some kind of strategic counter-weight in the eastern hemisphere.[56] It was patently obvious that the French establishments in

---

[54] The comte de Solminihac de la Mothe, 'Mémoire sur la Révolution arrivée à la Cochinchine en 1785', 26 January 1786, in Henri Cordier (Ed.), 'La Correspondance générale de la Cochinchine', *T'oung Pao*, 7 (1906), pp. 559-561.

[55] See Cordier, 'La Correspondance générale', pp. 564-576; see also Lokke, *France and the Colonial Question*, pp. 102-103; Nicole-Dominique Lê, *Les Missions-Etrangères et la pénétration française au Viêt-nam* (Paris, 1975), pp. 22-29.

[56] As Louis subsequently wrote to Conway, "La révolution qui vient de se faire en Hollande, change considérablement nos combinaisons politiques dans l'Inde, et ne nous permet plus guère de regarder le Cap de Bonne Espérance, ou l'Isle de Ceylan, comme un point d'appui ou de refuge. Cette considération fair pencher

India could no longer provide such a counter-weight. Thus, not long after the Dutch affair had concluded in November 1787, Montmorin—as both now Foreign Minister and caretaker for the Navy and Colonies—recommended to Louis that an expedition to aid Nguyen-Anh be organised forthwith, and under the utmost secrecy.[57] A treaty to this effect was formally signed by Louis on 28 November, 1787. It followed the basic terms proposed by the Bishop of Adran: the French king would provide, from his existing forces on the Ile de France and from Pondichéry, a little over a thousand French and native troops and cannoniers, with munitions and the appropriate number of vessels; for his part, the Prince undertook, when successfully reinstalled as king of Cochinchina, to cede to France the port of Touran, and the islands of Hainan and Pulo-Condor situated in the South China Sea.[58]

As one among many *mémoires* presented to the French Ministry on this issue stated, the advantages to be drawn from this project, if successful, were manifold, and more than worth the costs entailed in assisting the 'legitimate' king of Cochinchina. First of all, the possession of the proposed establishment at Touran would not only allow the French easy access to the rich trade which abounded in the region, but it would also allow them to "dominer dans les mers de Chine et dans tout son archipel et de se rendre maître de tout le commerce de cette partie". Secondly, this port would give France a secure shelter for its ships in time of war, with dockyard and even construction facilities. Thirdly, the French would be able to procure there a plentiful supply of basic foodstuffs both for its naval squadrons and its colonies further afield. Fourthly, this proposed establishment would place France in a superior position to the British in regard to direct and indirect trade with China.[59]

No less compelling were the perceived advantages in relation to India. An establishment in Cochinchina would, the *mémoire* alleged,

---

le gouvernement vers le parti de porter ses principales forces, ses moyens et son attention sur l'Isle de France et sur un établissement nouveau, qui mette plus de distance entre le siège de la puissance anglaise et nous", 'Copie de la lettre écrite à M. de Conway', 2 December 1787, Cordier, 'La Correspondance générale', p. 647.

[57] Cordier, 'La Correspondance générale', pp. 633-638; C. Lokke, *France and the Colonial Question*, New York, 1932, p. 104; see also a ministerial *mémoire* of September 1787, AAE-MD-Asie-19, f. 111.

[58] See A. Clercq (Ed.), *Recueil des traités de la France*, 22 Vols., Paris, 1880-1904, Vol. 1, pp. 193-195; see also the 'Conventions relatives à l'Expédition de la Cochinchine', September 1787, Cordier, pp. 602-603.

[59] 'Déliberation du Conseil Royal de Cochinchine; Avantages d'un Etablissement à la Cochinchine', 26 Sept 1787, AAE-MD-Asie-19, f. 103.

give France a means of counter-balancing the great influence of the British with all the native governments of India, "en y paroissant avec des ressources plus assurées et des secours moins éloignés que ceux qu'on [derives] d'Europe". It would, furthermore, provide a "moyen efficace d'arrêter les Anglais dans les projets qu'ils ont de nous chasser de l'Inde et d'étendre leurs Etablissements dans toute la Côte de l'Est", and, even, a "moyen éloigné mais sûr, de faire trembler les Anglais dans le Bengale, siege de leur puissance dans l'Inde".[60] The Cochinchina establishment could thus prove to be a decisive asset in the competition between Britain and France in the eastern hemisphere.

For all this support, the project also had its trenchant critics, chief among whom was Conway, the French Commander at Pondichéry, who doubted both the project's chances for success, and the value of the benefits it promised. As Lê notes, even before the treaty with Nguyen-Anh was signed, sufficient doubts had been raised about the project that when in early December 1787 Louis sent instructions to Conway to proceed with preparations for the expedition to Cochinchina, he also sent a parallel secret dispatch advising Conway that the expedition should proceed only at the Commander's discretion.[61] The chief and immediate concern of the Government was the cost of the whole entreprise, estimated by the ministry at around 1,840,000 livres.[62] The Government's desperate anxieties about a potential blow-out in costs would continue to dog the project. Moreover, the provision of such a considerable outlay, particularly at a time of real financial distress, made the Government all the more sensitive to the question of cost: would the projected benefits and likelihood of success justify such a sizable expenditure?

Nearly a year would elapse before the responses to the Government's instructions regarding the Cochinchina project reached Versailles from Pondichéry and the Ile de France. During that time, the financial situation in France had deteriorated. Brienne had resigned, and with the virtual bankruptcy that had precipitated that resignation, the absolute monarchy had effectively become a hostage to its deficit. This placed the royal government in a most difficult position in regard to its domestic political crisis. At the Estates-General proposed for May 1789, discontented élites could endeavour to play on the Crown's financial distress in order to extract major political concessions to

---

[60] *Ibid.*
[61] Lê, *Les Mission Etrangères*, pp. 30-31.
[62] 'Aperçu de dépenses pour l'Expédition', Cordier (ed.), *Correspondance générale*, p. 650.

which, in other circumstances, Louis would have steadfastly opposed. It was in this context—the imperative need for economies—that the comte de La Luzerne instituted, in mid-to-late 1788, the rationalisation of French naval activity and the withdrawal of military forces from India.

In this climate the receipt in late 1788 of negative reports from Conway, Moracin and the reconnaissance mission ordered earlier by Castries,[63] had a telling effect on the Government's resolve in relation to the Cochinchina expedition. Such were the great potential advantages promoted by Adran that, if the financial situation of the royal government had been any more secure, it may have persisted with the plans for an expedition in spite of the criticisms levelled at the project. It is also possible that in the absence of severe financial constrictions, and the threat to the viability of French establishments in India, criticisms such as those from Conway may not have surfaced or have been pressed with such insistence. As it was, La Luzerne, who had not been party to the conception of the Cochinchina project, besought Louis on 14 November 1788 to cancel the expedition and hence to allow the full evacuation of French forces to the Ile de France. In view of these criticisms, and the financial plight of the monarchy, the king agreed.[64] For all he knew, in the following year the French Empire could find itself subject to attack by Britain, in which case it was imperative that French military resources be concentrated on the Ile de France.

The Cochinchina project had, at least in theory, seemed to offer Louis' Government all that it could have wanted in regard to the extention of French influence in the Asia-Pacific region: a strategically placed location with access to a thriving commerce, a safe harbour with dockyard facilities, ample provisioning and the co-operation of a friendly local power. For those, in particular, of a more liberal or

---

[63] On 28 June 1788, Conway penned a dispatch to the Minister, wherein he presented a point by point critique of the Cochinchina project, stating that the actual costs of the expedition would likely be at least three times that alleged by Adran, that the Dutch control of the Malaccan straits would mean the isolation of Cochinchina in times of war, and that the territorial resources of the proposed establissement had in any case been greatly oversold. Conway to Minister, 18 June 1788, AN-FC-C1-4, ff. 166-173; see also the 'Réponse secrète au ministre par M. d'Entrecasteaux', 18 April 1788, *Ibid.*, ff. 101-102. The fact that around this time the colony of Pondichéry also announced the exhaustion of its finances would only have added to the financial pressures of the Royal Government back in Versailles, see Moracin to Minister, 20 July 1788, *Ibid.*, f. 174.

[64] 'Mémoire du roi, de la main du ministre, M. de La Luzerne, rendant compte de la lecture faite au conseil d'état', 14 November 1788, AN-FC-C1-4, f. 200.

Christian disposition in Louis' court, the fact that the French were being *invited* in to form a naval and trading establishment by the 'legitimate' rulers of Cochinchina, would have doubtless been an attractive feature of the project, since this concession would be gained neither through armed force or the suppression of native peoples.[65] Moreover, this establishment would surely have served as an invaluable platform for the further expansion of French influence and navigation, enabling France to compete effectively with Britain as a great power in the region.

In summary, the Cochinchina project had offered enormous economic and strategic benefits to France as a great power, with little apparent risk other than that pertaining to the initial financial outlay. It also involved few of the morally questionable methods usually associated with European colonisation. Yet, despite all these apparent benefits, by mid to late 1788 France had been forced to abandon this project, so desperate was its financial situation. The cancelling of the Cochinchina project in late 1788 may thus be considered to mark, outside of Europe, the humiliating low point to which French power had now sunk.

Beyond Europe, the French 'retreat' thus involved the considered reaction of the royal government to its new strategic, and above all, financial realities. It entailed not merely the rationalisation of French naval activity and the proposed withdrawal of French military forces from India, but also the deferring if not outright abandonment of otherwise welcome opportunities for the further expansion of French trade and influence in the eastern hemisphere. This was surely a most regrettable and dismal outcome for a state that up to then had had aspirations to be the preeminent global power.

---

[65] As Lokke notes, "there is reason to believe that ethical principles as well as expediency moved the royal government to consider Cochin China rather than Egypt as the place to found a new colony. Going to the aid of a dispossessed prince could be regarded as an honourable act, an act of justice". Lokke, *France and the Colonial Question*, p. 111.

PART TWO
THE NATIONAL CONSTITUENT ASSEMBLY

Preface

The successful transformation, over the summer of 1789, of the Estates-General into the National Constituent Assembly can be attributed to a combination of factors. Firstly, of course, was the determined push for an undivided representative assembly with real powers by a mixture of deputies from the Third Estate and from the more liberal elements of the clergy and nobility. This determination was symbolised by Mirabeau's famous oath of defiance, at the end of the Royal Session on the 23 June, that the deputies would not be removed from their task "except by the force of bayonets".[1] Secondly, was the sudden and irrevocable collapse of royal authority in the face of popular revolt, most notably, in Paris on 14 July, and thereafter throughout the French provincial capitals and countryside. The Revolution, beginning in Versailles and Paris in June and July, thus quickly spread to the rest of France.

The founding of the National Assembly was seen as a triumph of the so-called 'Patriots' over the reactionaries and conservatives of the French court. Thereafter, the struggle between proponents and opponents of revolutionary change was carried on in a variety of ways, not merely within the Assembly itself, but also in the formation of political clubs and the explosive outpouring of both revolutionary and anti-revolutionary journalism. This struggle was understood as one between those who defended royal power and those who sought, on the principle of popular sovereignty, to assert the effective supremacy of an independent national legislature. It also began a process of polarisation within revolutionary politics that would ultimately undermine and ruin any initial hopes for a broad or workable consensus across French society regarding the nature and limits of revolutionary change.[2]

Political conflict would not, however, be confined to the ongoing struggle between revolutionaries and their opponents. Within the Patriot camp itself, leading personalities and rival factions emerged across the period of the Constituent Assembly, each aiming at the effective leadership of revolutionary and popular opinion. The prime contestants in this bitter struggle were, in this early phase of the Revolution, Mirabeau, Lafayette, and the leftist triumvirate of Barnave, Duport and Lameth. Though they were hardly separated by any

---

[1] Barbara Luttrell, *Mirabeau* (Hemel Hempstead, 1990), p. 128.
[2] See William Doyle, *The Oxford History of the French Revolution* (Oxford, 1990), Ch. 6, *passim*.

insurmountable ideological differences, their respective ambitions and rivalries would nonetheless prevent their forming an effective united front that might have been capable of stabilising both the Revolution and the Constitutional Monarchy. Beyond these figures were of course the radicals of the extreme Left, the so-called 'thirty-voices', a fringe element in the Assembly whose inflammatory rhetoric and agitation would ultimately be matched by a growing power and influence within popular revolutionary opinion.

The express purpose of the National Constituent Assembly was, as its name indicates, to provide France with its first written constitution. Yet it had also early on assumed the role of national legislature, responsible for the making of laws that would drive the work of national regeneration. As events unfolded, it became clear that this regeneration would not merely be constitutional, involving the provision simply of new constitutional principles for a new governing apparatus. It would also be both material in character and 'panoramic' in scope. It was not to be forgotten, after all, that the French state was still in the grip of profound financial and economic crisis, the general disarray now greatly compounded by the collapse of royal authority and hence the paralysis of its existing administrative apparatus. For this reason, there developed during the life of the Constituent Assembly, alongside its basic work on the constitution, an on-going proliferation of various committees and sub-committees charged with the task of reforming and overhauling many of the structures of old regime state and society.[3]

That the Assembly would, through such committees, quickly become the *de facto* centre of government in France, was partly a function of the vacuum left by the collapse of royal authority throughout the country.[4] Yet it was also, no less significantly, a function of the Assembly's own fundamental constitutional reframing of the policy process. Under the old regime the ministers, at the direction of the king, were responsible for all manner of executive and legislative policy. The Assembly, however, in applying the principle of the separation of powers, claimed for itself, as the legislative power, an exclusive role in the formation of policy. The ministers, as part of the executive power,

---

[3] There were by mid-1790 25 permanent standing Committees in the Assembly. These included, aside from the Committee on the Constitution, and those concerned with specific procedural matters, Committees on Agriculture and Commerce, on the Colonies, on Finance, Taxation, the Judiciary, the Army, Navy, police, and the Church. See Timothy Tackett, *Becoming a Revolutionary: The Deputies of the French National Assembly and the Emergence of a Revolutionary Culture (1789-90)* (Princeton 1996), pp. 220-226.

[4] *Ibid.*, p. 225.

would be deemed merely 'executors' of the nation's will, responsible in no way for the determination of policy. According to the 'Decree on the Fundamental Principles of Government' of 1 October 1789, the executive power—the king and his ministers—were prohibited not merely from making laws, but even from proposing them. The king could only "invite the Assembly to take a matter under consideration", leaving the legislature both to propose and deliberate upon any legislative response.[5] It is no surprise then that Ministers often found themselves subsequently powerless to act without the direction and close supervision of the Assembly's committees.

All this had profound implications for French foreign policy under the Constituent Assembly. Ultimately, the constitution promulgated by the deputies in September 1791 would, in defining the powers constitutionally appertaining to the executive, confirm the king's traditional role as supreme head of the army and navy, and accord him thereby also the sole responsibility for on-going management of France's external security and diplomatic apparatus. However, by the conclusion of the Constituent Assembly, events would conspire nonetheless to bring about a severe circumscription of the king's former powers over foreign policy and a corresponding expansion of the Assembly's own legislative control over it. In this sense the area of foreign policy would not escape the relentless push for 'nationalisation', both in terms of control and content, that elsewhere had characterised the creation of the new French state.

---

[5] J. Stewart (Ed.), *A Documentary Survey of the French Revolution* (New York 1951), p. 116.

4 The 'Revolutionising' of French Foreign Policy

Almost as soon as it was accepted by the National Assembly on 26 August 1789, the 'Declaration of the Rights of Man and Citizen' became the founding document of the French Revolution. It provided many of the core principles—civil liberty, legal equality, accountable government, the separation of powers, and of course, national sovereignty—that would subsequently shape the French Constitution, finally completed in 1791. These principles, and consciousness of universal natural rights, so permeated the discourse of the revolutionaries, and infused the legislative policies of the deputies to the National Assembly, that it would have been surprising had they not also eventually extended to the question of foreign policy and international relations. What specific principles would, however, the deputies employ in their eventual consideration of foreign policy and external diplomacy, and how would they apply them? What were the deputies' apparent understandings of international relations, and the nature of the international system? Were there major divisions of opinion on this matter in the Assembly, and on what did these divisions appear to be based? How would the royal government continue, meanwhile, to address issues of foreign policy, and what were its goals?

Foreign Affairs in 1789: the View from the Ministry

While French public attention in 1789 was consumed by the feverish activity that preceded the opening of the Estates-General, and the dramatic events that followed it, the French Foreign Ministry was mostly then preoccupied with the continued and deepening prostration of France within the international system, and the resulting nullification of its influence in Europe. The crippling of French finances in 1787—88 and the implosion of Vergennes' 'system' that accompanied it, had left France, in diplomatic terms, with very little room to manoeuvre. What is more, it had become obvious that Britain had, as a result, once again supplanted France as the effective arbiter of European affairs.[1]

Needless to say, this latter development was extremely unwelcome to the royal government. Vergennes' hopes for closer relations with Britain had been founded on the assumption that France would be the arbiter of Europe, so that it would be dealing with Britain from a position of strength. Now, with France effectively paralysed, both by its finances and by its foreign policy dilemmas, the situation had entirely changed. Although, as Montmorin noted, France shared British hopes for a negotiated resolution of the Eastern War, any Anglo-French diplomatic collusion to broker such a peace would be dangerous for France, and profitable only to Britain: "Cette cour nous jalouse, et nous hait", stated Montmorin, "si nous nous raprochons d'elle, elle voudra nous dominer". France, he repeatedly instructed the French Ambassador to London, would thus be the victim of any confidence placed in the British Court. If France accepted Pitt's offer of co-mediation, it would only sacrifice its relations with the Imperial powers for the sake of a transitory alliance with its most dangerous and unscrupulous rival.[2] Hence, while both Britain and France earnestly desired peace in Europe, even on much the same terms, their other differences prevented any unified action in this respect.

French anxieties regarding the Eastern War were hardly alleviated by secret negotiations undertaken with the Russian court at the behest of France's Ambassador, the comte de Ségur. From as early as 1787, Ségur had endeavoured to convince Montmorin of the benefits not merely of a formal defensive pact with Russia, but also of a Quadruple Alliance of Austria, Russia, Spain and France, which, he argued, would foil Britain's

---

[1] Late the previous year Barthélemy wrote to Montmorin from London of "la déplorable perte de notre considération et dans l'opinion publique et dans l'exercise de cette influence dont nous nous sommes pendant longtems servis pour le bonheur du monde". Reflecting traditional French suspicion of British motives, he then asserted that "elle n'en fera pas un aussi bon usage: elle ne s'en servira que pour nous nuire constamment pendant la paix et nous faire une affreuse guerre quand les circonstances lui paraitront favorables", Barthélemy to Montmorin, 21 October 1788, AAE-CP-Angleterre-563, f. 182.

[2] Montmorin to the marquis de La Luzerne, 8 February, 1789, AAE-CP-Angleterre-568, f. 136, 10 May 1789, AAE-CP-Angleterre-569, f. 223. Already the French had had the galling experience of being forced to look on while Britain not-so-secretly courted France's traditional client Sweden (financially supporting the Swedes in their war-effort against Russia in the North). There remained the possibility also that the British could capitalise on current circumstances to increase their influence down in the Levant, to the great and long-term detriment there of French commercial and strategic interests.

intrigues, preserve peace, and immeasurably strengthen the French position in Europe.[3] In November, a cautious Montmorin had given the go-ahead for secret discussions with the Russians to take place. However, he instructed Ségur that a Russian treaty was likely to prove unpopular in France—linked as they were to Austria—unless it was patently advantageous to French security; namely, Russia would be required to abandon its previous 'Armed Neutrality' and to agree to assist France in the event of war with Britain.[4] By the following March, however, things had changed; Montmorin informed Ségur that with the Estates-General imminent, and in the general climate of uncertainty, it was best that France postpone any new treaty commitments until such time as its domestic problems—namely, "la nécessité de faire disparaître la différence qui se trouve entre les revenues et les dépenses nécessaires de l'Etat"—could be resolved. Montmorin told Ségur that he had no doubt that upon such a resolution, "la France reprendra toute sa force et toute sa puissance", and become an imposing power again in European affairs.[5] Until then, however, France seemed to have little real option but to continue on alone in its crippled 'neutrality'.[6]

---

[3] Ségur to Montmorin, 19 Sept 1788, in *Recueil des Instructions données aux Ambassadeurs et Ministres de France depuis les Traités de Westphalie jusqu'a la Revolution Française* (Paris, 1884), Vol. 9, pp. 443-444; Ségur to the Prince of Nassau, 31 Jan 1789, p. 459.

[4] Montmorin to Ségur - 23 Nov 1788, *Recueil des Instructions*, p. 445. That Montmorin intended this alliance to reinforce the diplomatic system built up by Vergennes is evidenced by his insistence that both Sweden and Turkey—French clients—be excluded from the mutual assistance provisions.

[5] Montmorin to Ségur, 19 March 1789, *Recueil des Instructions*, p. 463. Barthélemy wrote to Montmorin that "il n'est ... que trop vrai que nos malheurs intérieurs entrent beaucoup dans [British] calculs. Je ne puis pas douter que les Ministres anglaises ne se flattent constamment que M. Necker trouvera des obstacles insurmontables pour rétablir les finances du Roi et que cette principale partie de l'administration restant dans le désordre, toute autre réparation deviendra impossible à effectuer. Ils seroient effrayés de la force que la France pourroit tirer d'une assemblée nationale bien organisé ...". He then stated that he would not be surprised if the British government endeavoured to sow disorder and intrigue into the upcoming Estates-General. Barthélemy to Montmorin, 7 Oct 1788, AAE-CP-Angleterre-563, f. 176.

[6] While avoiding any close co-operation with Britain in bringing the Eastern War to a negotiated conclusion, the French at the same time greatly resented that such a negotiated peace would be engineered by the British. As Montmorin remarked in early April 1790, "les choses ne sont que trop bien disposées en faveur de ce système; nous n'avons pas un seul moïen pour le contrecarrer; et il ne nous reste que dévorer en silence notre humiliation, au moins pour le moment". Montmorin to the marquis de la Luzerne, 8 April 1790, AAE-CP-Angleterre-572, f. 373.

Some foreign observers were also sufficiently farsighted to note that, while for the time-being France was unable to exert any real power or influence in Europe, a 'regeneration' or 'revolution' in French internal affairs might soon reverse her effective paralysis. This was clearly a source of anxiety among British diplomats and some members of the British government. As early as April 1788 the British diplomat Hailes had written from Paris that the 'shame' of the Dutch debacle had become the spur to a renewed desire in France to eliminate the various ills and oppressions in their own government. "In such a point of view", he warned,

> there appears without doubt much ground of apprehension for the interests of Great Britain, for it may be reasonably asked, if France, with all the vices of her Government, has been for so many ages in a situation to act often so brilliant and always so formidable a part in the affairs of Europe, what may not be expected from her when those vices shall have been eradicated, and when she shall be in possession of a constitution (as it is pretended she may) similar to that of her neighbour and Rival?[7]

Though the British government was reassured somewhat by the growing state of disorder within France, the reaction to the prospect of French recovery may be gauged in some degree by the considerable expenditures made on their military establishment throughout this period. These had been justified by Pitt, as noted by the marquis de La Luzerne in London, as "nécéssaire pour que l'angleterre reprit au déhors la prépondérance qu'elle doit avoir".[8] The British military build-up was intended to prepare for all eventualities, among which was thus not merely to prepare for possible intervention in the Eastern War, but also to galvanise themselves against any renewed French vigour.

---

[7] "So strong is the sense of present disgrace and difficulties", Hailes continued, "that it seems to have precluded all ideas of the possibility that a change should prove disadvantageous: an entire revolution in the form of Government is therefore looked forward to with the greatest eagerness". Hailes to Carmarthen, 17 April 1788, *Despatches from Paris*, Vol. 2, p. 31. See also André Fugier, *Histoire des relations internationales*, Vol. 4 (Paris, 1954), p. 20.

[8] The British were prompted to make such expenditures, thought La Luzerne, by their understanding that once French credit was re-established, her deployable resources would be much superior to those of Britain. Marquis de la Luzerne to Montmorin, 16 Juin 1789, AAE-CP-Angleterre-569, f. 356. Indeed, as La Luzerne reported to Montmorin early the following year, the British minister Landsdowne remarked to him that if the French succeeded in their revolution, they would be strong enough to dictate to all Europe. Marquis de la Luzerne to Montmorin, 15 January 1790, AAE-CP-Angleterre-572, f. 65.

In the meantime, however, the descent into 'anarchy' in France that accompanied the events at Versailles from May through to October was of grave concern to Montmorin and his ministry. They worried not merely about the fate of the French crown and its prerogatives, but also about the immediate dangers such internal disorder would bring *externally*, specifically from Britain. In the previous year there had been speculation as to whether the British would seek, in some clandestine fashion, to subvert the Estates-General and encourage public agitation, but by mid-to-late 1789 there developed a deepening fear among French diplomats in London, and within the Conseil d'état at Versailles, that the British might thwart renewed French power by a pre-emptive assault on the French colonial Empire. As La Luzerne commented, the time now seemed particularly propitious for Britain to launch a war of revenge against France.[9]

This fear may have been unfounded, but it merely reflected the diplomats' understanding of how states traditionally operated in the strategic balance of power. In view of the French situation and the prevailing uncertainties in continental affairs, it was thus hardly surprising that the French government should have responded so nervously, for the British had certainly continued to reinforce and fortify their many colonial and overseas possessions.[10] To the marquis de La Luzerne's reports of alleged British plots to seize France's West Indian colonies, Montmorin did, however, show some skepticism. He agreed on the certainty of British ill-will and on the need to keep the French navy on a respectable footing, but nonetheless averred that the British still needed some plausible pretext, not yet forthcoming, for launching such an offensive. As he had earlier written to the marquis, "le remède le plus efficace pour contenir nos ennemis seroit la cessation de nos troubles intérieurs", but, such were the current state of things, he now confided sadly, "il m'est impossible de prévoir cette heureuse époque".[11]

---

[9] Marquis de la Luzerne to Montmorin, 25 August 1789, AAE-CP-Angleterre-570, ff. 301-302, 1 September 1789, *Ibid.*, ff. 331-338.

[10] See Black, *British Foreign Policy*, pp. 147-148.

[11] Montmorin to the marquis de la Luzerne, 7 September 1789, AAE-CP-Angleterre-570, f. 347, Marquis de la Luzerne to Montmorin, 29 September 1789, AAE-CP-Angleterre-571, ff. 32-34, Montmorin to the Marquis de la Luzerne, 4 October 1789, *Ibid.*, f. 42. In March 1790 La Luzerne warned Montmorin that "si nos malheureuses affaires prenoient quelque solidité; si nos finances se rétabliseroient; si l'on en venoit au point de calmer notre intérieur, et d'avoir un pouvoir exécutif organisé, je crois bien la jalousie se ranimaroit; car au fait, la france dégagée de toutes les entraves qu'elle avoit; aïant un crédit national fondé sur les mêmes principes que celui d'angleterre;

There was hence, for Montmorin, nothing that France could do now except lay low in international affairs, and hope not to become somehow embroiled in the conflicts presently gripping Europe. She could not afford to do so: not only had France lost her role as arbiter, but with the onset of Revolution, her domestic paralysis only seemed to deepen, political and financial crisis being joined by popular anarchy and the breakdown of the royal administration. In such a situation, furthermore, it was not just French security and long-term strategic interests that were at stake, but also the very future of the French Monarchy, and the monarch to whom Montmorin was so personally attached. As all the court knew, after the turbulence of the October days, the personal safety of Louis XVI and his family could no longer even be guaranteed. Installed in the Tuileries Palace in Paris, they now believed themselves to be hostages to the Revolution.

France and the Belgian Revolt

From the very beginnings of the Revolution in May 1789, the French public had shown a marked ambivalence in feeling towards Britain and its government, which appeared to reflect traditional elements in French society of Anglophilia and Anglophobia.[12] Dorset, the British Ambassador to France, reported during July 1789 that rumours were being "industriously propogated [sic]" in Paris, and "instilled into the minds of the populace", that the British Government had been

---

aïans moins de dettes; une population beaucoup plus considérable, et un territoire trois fois plus étendu et meilleur, de viendroit un Ennemi bien formidable pour la grande Bretagne". However, in amending his previous view, the Ambassador then opined that as long as France remained in its present state of political 'nullity', she was probably safe from an assault by Britain. Marquis de La Luzerne to Montmorin, 19 March 1790, AAE-CP-Angleterre-572, ff. 251-252.

[12] See Frances Acomb, *Anglophobia in France 1763-1789: an essay in the history of constitutionalism and nationalism*, Durham, NC, 1950. The vehemence of some expressions of French anglophobia may be seen in a curious document found in the archives of the French Foreign Ministry, datable between 1789 and 1792. Entitled "L'Anglo-manie ou La Conspiration du Ministère Britannique, contre les droits du l'homme, le droit des Gens pour s'emparent du Commerce universel et des Richesses des deux Mondes", the anonymous author accused Britain, which he labelled "the new Carthage", of the crime of unjust aggression, greed and "lèse humanité", in its use of naval power in Europe and beyond, believing that they intended to provoke a general war in Europe so as to seize greater control of global commerce. See AAE-MD-Angleterre-74, ff. 227-233.

"actively instrumental in fomenting disorders" or that it had even been preparing a naval attack on Brest.[13] So concerned was Dorset about these rumours that he issued, via Montmorin, a statement denying the allegations.

The French government was hardly convinced by such assurances. At the time of the October days, the presence of a British naval squadron in the Channel fuelled the belief in government circles that a British attack on French ports might be imminent.[14] Although this scare soon passed, suspicions remained. After October, the French government's general anxiety in relation to British foreign policy became focused less on direct naval attack than on the issue of Belgium, with the outbreak there of an anti-Hapsburg revolt during the months of September and October 1789.

This revolt began as a popular reaction against an attempt by the aggressive reformer Joseph II to override local privileges in the name of imperial uniformity, and led by December 1789 to successful uprisings in the Belgian provinces against Austrian forces. Assembling in Brussels, representatives of the Belgian Estates formed then a 'National Congress', which on 10 January declared itself an independent confederation, "the United States of Belgium".[15] This pursuit of independence received the support of Britain, the United Provinces and Prussia, the latter power quickly sending troops into Liège to protect that territory's independence, thus effectively hindering the reconquest by Austrian troops of the provinces further west.

---

[13] Dorset to the Duke of Leeds, 27 July 1789, *Despatches from Paris*, Vol. 2, pp. 250-251.

[14] In August the Naval minister, the comte de la Luzerne, presented a mémoire to the Conseil d'Etat, on the subject of an English squadron of unknown destination in the Channel, reporting that even the authorities at Brest seemed anxious about a possible attack from the British Navy. "Il parait en résulter", the Naval minister wrote, "que l'Escadre Anglaise à croisé pendant plusieurs jours à l'ouvert de la Manche; mais il serait possible que ce fut pour attendre des vivres qu'on lui aurait apportés et pour se rendre ensuite à une destination ultérieure. J'ai déjà mille fois exposé que les Anglais nous trouveront faibles partout. La disette de finances a empêché que V.M. ne se déterminât à faire armer de son côté des vaisseaux, seul moyen de protéger nos possessions éloignées". At the end of this *mémoire* it was noted: "Il a été decidé que vu l'impuissance d'armer il fallait se borner aux mesures antérieurement arrêtées". Le comte de la Luzerne, 'Mémoire au Conseil d'Etat', 12 August 1789, BN-NAF-9434, ff. 213-214.

[15] Sorel, *L'Europe et la Révolution Française: les nouveaux principes*, Book One, p. 52; Louis Gottschalk and Margaret Maddox, *Lafayette in the French Revolution*, Chicago (1973), p. 277.

As with the Dutch crisis, this revolt in Belgium threatened to bring about a dramatic change in the European status quo. In so doing, it also threatened to widen the war then raging among the Northern and Eastern powers. Prussia seemed eager to exploit its archrival Austria's distraction in the Balkans, and to extend its own influence and territory in an area so far from the main body of the Hapsburg Empire. Britain, for its part, though reluctant to get embroiled in any present European conflicts, was concerned to extend its influence further into the Low Countries or at the very least prevent the French from doing so. The area of the Austrian Netherlands was for the British of major, if not vital, geostrategic importance, chiefly for its position on the English channel and below that of its new ally, the United Provinces.[16]

The Belgian revolt was to precipitate the first major foreign policy crisis of the Revolution, and one that would now also have serious domestic implications. This was not least because news of the Belgian revolt was welcomed by many people in France, particularly the revolutionaries. As Albert Sorel noted in his *L'Europe et la Révolution Française*, not only had France long coveted a preponderant influence over this area, but both the Hapsburgs and France's Austrian alliance of 1756 were loathed and deeply resented in France. Perhaps most importantly, there was also now the question of revolutionary principle. The Belgian revolt was immediately, and Sorel argues uncritically, accepted by revolutionary propagandists as the first, among their continental neighbours, of what they anticipated in their enthusiasm as similar or parallel 'revolutions' to that in France, those promoting not merely 'national' but indeed 'popular' sovereignty, entailing the political emancipation of once 'subject' peoples. Such 'revolutions' were hence depicted as fraternal struggles, and as a way in which France could now resurrect its once great influence in Europe, by exerting, as the first and largest of the 'revolutionised' powers, its leadership among the peoples of 'free' nations. Such a role for France was promoted most notably by Camille Desmoulins in his journal *Les Révolutions de France et de Brabant*, and by the Commander of the National Guard, Lafayette. Already keen to be known as the "Hero of two Worlds", the General in his vanity liked now to consider himself as the 'godfather' of like

---

[16] For the British response to the crisis in the Austrian Netherlands, see Black, *British Foreign Policy*, pp 203-215.

revolutions elsewhere, and as the veritable avatar of liberty and orderly republicanism everywhere.[17]

For the royal government, however, the Belgian revolt presented more grave dangers than it did opportunities. Montmorin knew well the dangers, both strategic and commercial, that an independent pro-French Belgium could pose to Britain and a pro-British Holland, and what could be anticipated from these latter powers to prevent such a development. From his experience in the Dutch crisis, the foreign minister certainly had few illusions about the willingness of the British to mobilise their now immense naval resources for the purposes at least of intimidation, particularly with France now so consumed and paralysed by its continuing internal troubles.

If, on one side, British action was to be feared, then the motives of Prussia, Britain's ally, were to be distrusted in equal measure. As Sorel recounts, Montmorin sensed in Prussian diplomatic soundings over Belgium the workings of a trap. Franco-Prussian collusion with regard to an independent Belgium would, first of all, likely result in the rupture of France's alliance with Austria. This would inevitably result in war, at least between Austria and Prussia, and probably also between Austria and France. Who was to say that the price of any subsequent conciliation between the German powers would not actually be then at the expense of France? "L'Empereur", wrote Montmorin,

> se croirait peut-être alors autorisé à s'entendre momentanément avec le roi de Prusse pour nous faire rentrer dans nos anciennes limites, c'est-à-dire dans celles que nous avions avant la paix de Westphalie. Les circonstances dans lequelles se trouve la France ne rendraient malheureusement que trop facile le succès d'un semblable projet. Nous devons donc éviter, au moins par notre conduite politique, de donner aucune prise sur nous.[18]

Given such fears, the foreign minister concluded that the best course for France clearly lay in retention of the status quo in Belgium, at least on the issue of sovereignty. There was thus to be no change to France's present alliance system. As a result, when late in 1789 the Belgian Congress sent dispatches to the French authorities announcing their independence, Montmorin refused even to open them (a refusal which

---

[17] Sorel, *L'Europe et la Révolution Française: les nouveaux principes*, Book One, pp. 53-54. Gottschalk and Maddox, *Lafayette in the French Revolution*, Ch. 13, *passim*.

[18] Sorel, *L'Europe et la Révolution Française: les nouveaux principes*, Book One, pp. 55-56.

diplomatic protocol in any case demanded), and requested that the Assembly do likewise with any similar communications.[19]

Such a position was anathema to many in the revolutionary camp, particularly those openly hostile to Austria and the Austrian alliance. They pressed for France to recognise and protect an independent Belgium. On 10 March 1790, the former French diplomat Charles de Peyssonnel, then renowned as the author of a work which strongly condemned the Franco-Austrian alliance, addressed the Jacobin Club on this issue of Belgium.[20] This speech is notable for several reasons. It presented, first of all, an interesting contrast to most other contemporary revolutionary outpourings on this issue, in that the warnings it contained about the machinations of various foreign powers seemed to stem less from any fears of their alleged reactionary or counter-revolutionary intent, but rather more simply from their presumed strategic ambitions and *raison d'état*. Secondly, Peyssonnel's speech was also noteworthy for its attempt to marry the perceived strategic needs of France, and its earlier traditions of foreign policy and *raison d'état*, with what he believed to be the new ideological imperatives of the Revolution (rather than supposedly deriving the former from the latter, as would soon become customary in revolutionary rhetoric). It was notable, finally, for its particularly 'global' view of French foreign policy, that is, for its close integration of 'Atlantic' and continental theatres of French geostrategic interests.

---

[19] AP, Vol. 10, p. 493. Montmorin, with the outcome of Austro-Belgian reconciliation in mind, also gave his cautious approval, in early February 1790, to Lafayette's initative in the sending of secret personal envoys to Belgium, with a plan for French mediation of the crisis, in which Hapsburg sovereignty would be readmitted in exchange for a recognition by the Emperor of effective Belgian autonomy and the provision there of a liberal constitution. The death not long after of Joseph II, and the accession of the reputedly 'enlightened', liberal-minded but rather more adroit Leopold, could only have strengthened these hopes for a French mediated reconciliation. Gottshalk and Maddox, *Lafayette in the French Revolution*, pp. 276-78.

[20] F. A. Aulard (Ed), *Histoire des Jacobins; Receuil des documents pour l'histoire du Club des Jacobins de Paris*, Vol. 1 (Paris, 1889-97), p. 17. This title of this work was self-explanatory: *Situation politique de la France et ses rapports actuels avec toutes les puissances de l'Europe, ouvrage dont l'objet est de démontrer, par les faits historiques et les principes de la saine politique, tous les maux qu'a causés à la France l'alliance autrichienne et toutes les fautes que le ministère français a commise depuis l'époque des traités de versailles de 1756, 57 et 58 jusqu'à nos jours.* Neuchâtel et Paris, 1789, 2 Vol. Another work by Peyssönnel entitled *Tableau Politique de la Situation de la France* was reportedly presented to National Assembly on 28 August 1789. see Henri Plon (Ed) *Réimpression de l'ancien Moniteur* (Paris, 1858-63), Vol. 1, p. 395.

For Peyssonnel, both these strategic and ideological aspects were focused in the problem of Belgium. Regarding this region as of vital strategic importance to France, he argued that the continued domination of this country by foreign powers would always present a threat to French security, and be harmful to France's wider interests.[21] In some respects, however, his analysis of the dangers offered by the current Belgian crisis strongly echoed that of Montmorin and the Ministry. The manouvering of foreign powers in relation to Belgium presented, for Peyssonnel, two equally threatening possibilities. The first was of a British-Prussian accord to submit the Belgian provinces to the rule of the Dutch stadtholder, thus creating

> une monarchie formidable, qui pourrait balancer les forces de terre de la France, et lui laisser à elle, Angleterre, la faculté d'attaquer au besoin cette puissance avec toute la supériorité de ses forces maritimes.

The second was of a Prussian accord with those whom Peyssonnel identified as France's natural enemies, the Austrians, which could soon result in attacks on France and the possible loss of Alsace and Lorraine.[22] This too would only help Britain in its maritime and colonial rivalry with France, by absorbing French military resources.

What separated Peyssonnel, however, from Montmorin were his recommendations, which were indeed profound, bold and radical. In order to forestall either of the above "catastrophies", Peyssonnel declared that the National Assembly ought to recognise immediately the independence of the Belgian provinces, and become their protector. Not only that,

> elle doit cimenter une alliance perpétuelle, indissoluble, exclusive, avec cette nouvelle république qui deviendra la gardienne naturelle et nécessaire de ses frontières, annoncer à toute l'Europe qu'elle lui accordera le plus ferme et le plus constant appui contre toutes les puissances qui voudraient tenter de lui donner des fers ...

This 'nurturing' of a French sponsored and fraternally allied buffer-state in Belgium should, he went further, naturally herald what would only have been an inevitable change in French foreign policy anyway: the reversal of the former alliance with Austria and the necessary

---

[21] Aulard, *Histoire des Jacobins*, p. 21.
[22] *Ibid.*, p. 26.

resumption of France's former alliance with Prussia.[23] If, as he alleged, the Austrian alliance had proven over the past thirty years to have been the primary cause behind France's international misfortunes, then this prospective switch of alliances would be of enormous benefit to France, helping to restore its fortunes on the international stage. All in all, supporting Belgium and switching alliances could conceivably create, at one stroke, an imposing strategic edifice on land and sea, that even Britain would find difficult to match. As such it might then provide the basis for a future expansion of French global power and prestige, at the expense of its primary global rival, Britain.[24]

Peyssonnel then concluded this speech with an impassioned plea to the National Assembly to give its most serious and urgent attention to foreign affairs. The Revolution and the security of France were, he argued, together at stake, and not to act now would imperil both. In a statement that raised the old issue of France's 'natural frontiers', he proclaimed that

---

[23] *Ibid.* Not only would a switch to a Prussian alliance be far more consonant to the remainder of France's alliance-system (especially with Turkey), but it would indirectly assist in improving France's prospects in her maritime rivalry with England. As Jean Favier had argued thirty years before, and the recent Balkans war amply demonstrated, committments to mutual defence with Austria were contradictory to France's long-standing and important relationship with Turkey. It had weakened this relationship with Turkey while in itself holding few compensating benefits. Removing that contradiction could now perhaps allow France to thwart recent British attempts to supplant it as a primary ally and major trading partner with Turkey, thus protecting France's valuable Levant trade. Furthermore, detaching Prussia from Britain might also allow France to regain its recent alliance with Holland, which, together with Spain, would greatly bolster France's position in the maritime and colonial balance of power. Jean Favier, *Observations de Favier, sur la maison d'Autriche, et particulièrement sur le Traité de Versailles, du premier Mai 1756; Entre le Roi et l'Imperatrice Reine de Hongrie*, New Edition, Paris, 1792, p. 27.

[24] Favier had himself advocated a French dominance of the Low-Countries, asserting the global benefits of this. "En dédommageant nos marchands pillés, l'effet de cette satisfaction auroit dû être encore de fortifier notre marine, de nous donner de nouveaux ports, ou du moins de nous rendre l'usage libre des anciens; d'étendre notre commerce, et l'assurer pour jamais contre de pareilles entreprises: d'affermir nos colonies, en reculer les bornes, ou les fixer à notre avantage, en un mot agrandir la France en augmentant et consolidant sa puissance puissance maritime. ... Il resulte donc de tout ceci que son agrandissement par terre, dans la conquête des Pays-Bas, auroit produit au moins les circonstances les plus favorables, pour son agrandissement par mer, dans le traité de paix avec l'Angleterre". Favier, *Observations*, p. 22.

la France doit, sans perdre un instant, profiter de cet respect profond, de ce religieux frémissement que la majesté de sa Constitution a imprimés à toute l'Europe, pour faire un développement formidable de ses forces, pour se mettre dans une contenance imposante, menaçante, capable de faire évanouir les projets hostiles des puissances malintentionnées; de lui faciliter, dans le cas du partage de l'Allemagne, les moyens d'étendre, sans coup férir, ses limites jusqu'au Rhin, qui est sa frontière indiquée par le nature, et d'empêcher le feu de la guerre d'embraser tout le continent.[25]

Attesting his own support for the Revolution, he then urged the formation of a committee to supervise the operations of the foreign minister, whom he criticised for appearing to follow "opiniâtrément sa marche antique et perverse".[26] Moreover, he recommended a purge of the ministries and, if necessary, of the diplomatic corps, of all those supposedly "infectés du poison de l'ancien régime". Such a purge would be, he believed, necessary for France's regeneration, for "lorsque l'on coupe dans le vif pour guérir une profonde plaie", he said, with words that would later, under the Terror, have had a more chilling connotation, "il faut tâcher de n'y pas laisser le petit point de gangrène".[27]

These various pressures, from the revolutionary camp, for vigorous support of the Belgian independence—whether for ideological or supposedly strategic reasons—placed the French ministry in a very difficult position. On one hand, Montmorin and Louis XVI were concerned not to take any steps—military or diplomatic—that might precipitate a war that in the present circumstances could only be disastrous for France, and possibly fatal to its government. On the other hand, the government's adherence to a policy of non-intervention in Belgium also had serious domestic consequences, in that it brought the government into a dangerous collision with revolutionary opinion, a collision which threatened to throw open the whole issue of the executive control of foreign policy. If the revolutionaries felt they had cause to distrust Louis XVI's handling of foreign affairs, because they suspected him of being both antagonistic to the Revolution, and supportive of its domestic and external enemies, then measures would most likely be taken by the National Assembly to remove the Crown's exclusive control and management of French diplomacy and foreign

---

[25] *Ibid.*, p. 27.
[26] *Ibid.*
[27] *Ibid.*, p. 28.

policy.[28] This was an outcome that the royal government was concerned to prevent.

By early 1790, this issue of constitutional authority and diplomatic control became connected, in the National Assembly, to the question of correspondence with the rebellious Belgian Congress. By this time, it had become apparent to many in France and to the Foreign Ministry that the Belgian rebels were now divided into two opposing factions. This was an important point that Peyssonnel had failed to mention in his address to the Jacobins. By far the strongest of these factions in the Belgian Congress, and the one most adamant about independence, were not the Belgian liberals, led by Vonck, but in fact the 'Statists', the representatives of aristocratic and clerical dominated estates. When in March 1790 the now aristocrat-dominated Belgian Congress issued direct pleas both to the French government and to the National Assembly to recognise Belgian independence, the Belgian liberals besought Lafayette to oppose this plea "as coming from a body who have usurped the sovereignty of their country in violation of the rights of the people".[29] This in turn allowed the government, and Lafayette in the Assembly, to reject the Congress' plea for a recognition of Belgian independence, on the grounds that the Congress did not draw its authority from the sovereignty of the people.[30]

These circumstances thus enabled the royal government, fortuitously, to ward off challenges to the executive control of French diplomacy and foreign policy, and to thwart proponents of an aggressive forward policy with regard to Belgium. This would prove to be, however, little more than a partial victory for the Ministry, and a temporary one at that. The Belgian situation had hardly been resolved.

---

[28] Gottschalk and Maddox, *Lafayette in the French Revolution*, pp. 201. The Royal Ministry, largely unchanged since the 'Ministry of 100 hours' of 11-16 July 1789, and still mostly comprised of highly ranked courtiers, was repeatedly denounced in and outside the Assembly for its links to the court, which the revolutionaries regarded not unreasonably as a bastion of aristocratic conservatism and as a continuing focal point for reaction. Notwithstanding this palpable lack of confidence in the king's ministry, calls for their dismissal would go unheeded for most of 1790.

[29] *Ibid.*, p. 283. This highly conservative group were naturally less than sympathetic with the principles already espoused by the French Revolution, turning to Britain and Prussia most particularly for support. Thus, when Leopold II upon his succession overturned his predecessor's decrees, and made considerable concessions to the rebellious Belgians that accorded them effective autonomy, it were the 'Statists' that proved most intransigent, rejecting such concessions as falling short of full independence.

[30] AP, 17 March 1790, Vol. 12, pp. 205-6.

Although willing to conciliate the Austrians, the Belgian liberals still preferred independence, and there were many in France, Dumouriez perhaps most prominent among them, who still wished to see an independent and pro-French Belgium.[31] The failure of France to give active support in 1790 to the Vonckists in their pursuit of independence, would hence only give rise to a deepening resentment in France against supposed Austrian influence at the French Court and hasten an ongoing decline in the popularity of the monarchy among the Parisian crowds.

The Nootka Sound Affair and the Debate of May 1790

If by March 1790 the royal government had hoped also to have forestalled legislative incursions into the foreign policy domain, then this hope was shortlived. Another foreign policy crisis, one whose origins lay outside Europe, would soon eclipse that relating to Belgium, and propel the National Assembly into a close examination not only of foreign affairs, but also of the constitutional powers pertaining to war, peace and external diplomacy.

In July 1789 ships of the Spanish Navy seized several English trading vessels anchored in Nootka Sound, on the North Pacific coast of America, and forcibly dispersed the natives there with whom the English had been trading, all on the grounds that the English presence at Nootka Sound had contravened Spanish sovereignty. When news of this incident filtered through to London in early 1790, the British government expressed its outrage. Emboldened by the evident weakness of Spain's ally France, the British Cabinet resolved to take a tough line with the Spanish Government. They demanded not only satisfaction and restitution for the insult suffered at Nootka, but also that Spain renounce its traditional claims to sovereignty in the unoccupied territories of America. Pitt, it seemed, was determined to force a showdown with the Spanish government, in order to assert the right of Britons to expand their trade and fisheries into the North and South Pacific. Thus, when the Spanish (already aggravated by the alleged incursions of British traders and smugglers into their South American empire) moved to defend their blanket claims of sovereignty by

---

[31] See Gottshalk and Maddox, *Lafayette in the French Revolution*, pp. 475-476.

mobilising their navy, the British, in late April and early May, responded in kind.[32]

For Montmorin and his ambassador to London, the prospect of an Anglo-Spanish war at this juncture was doubly dangerous. British high-handedness in regard to Spain seemed, first of all, to confirm suspicions that the British intended to profit from France's present weakness. Furthermore, though British hostility was ostensibly directed at Spain, the Foreign Minister immediately assumed that this hostility ultimately had France as its object. At the very least, he believed, this 'crisis' was merely a pretext for an attempt to break the Franco-Spanish alliance: expecting that the French, owing to their current impotence, would refuse to help Spain in this dispute, the British would thus hope to see France completedly isolated.[33] There was then the further possibility that if the British were intending to isolate and attack Spain, this might also be a prelude to an attack on France and its colonies.[34]

Determined to counter this British 'plot', on 14 May 1790 Montmorin officially informed the National Assembly of the Nootka Sound dispute, and of the recent build-up of armaments in English ports. Though he stressed Louis' efforts to mediate in this dispute, he informed the deputies that the King had, as a precautionary measure, ordered the mobilisation of fourteen vessels in support of France's ally Spain, for which he was now requesting funds. In ordering such measures the King was, Montmorin assured them, only fulfilling his duty to safeguard the security of the state. "Lorsque l'Angleterre est armée, la France ne peut ni doit rester désarmée", he declared, stating further that "il nous importe de montrer à l'Europe que l'établissement de notre Constitution est loin d'apporter aucun obstacle au développement de nos forces".[35]

The implicit threat of war finally jolted the Assembly into closer attention to the management of French foreign affairs. If Montmorin had assumed that the Assembly would unite in a show of patriotic

---

[32] See John Norris, 'Policy of the British Cabinet in the Nootka Sound Crisis', *English Historical Review*, 70 (October 1955), pp. 562-580; Harold Evans, 'The Nootka Sound Controversy in Anglo-French Diplomacy—1790', *Journal of Modern History*, 46 (December, 1974), pp. 609-640.

[33] Montmorin to the marquis de la Luzerne, 17 May 1790, AAE-CP-Angleterre-573, ff. 117-120.

[34] Marquis de la Luzerne to Montmorin, 14 May 1790, AAE-CP-Angleterre-573, ff. 104-105.

[35] AP, Vol. 15, 14 May 1790, p. 510.

support for the King's measures, he was seriously mistaken.[36] Although the right wing of the Assembly immediately and warmly supported the royal government's actions (mostly in the hope, allegedly, that this would bolster the authority of the king and their own embattled fortunes),[37] Montmorin's assurances failed to quell the consternation of other deputies who suspected either Britain or Spain of contriving this crisis in order to harm either France or the Revolution.[38]

Nor could many deputies even be sure of the constitutional validity of the king's actions. Thus on 16 May there commenced a debate in the Assembly as to the constitutional position of such action—about the relative responsibilities of the executive and legislature over, firstly, the right to declare war, and, more broadly, over the question of foreign policy itself.[39] This quickly became, however, more than a debate over the relative power of the Executive and Legislative, and, as such, one episode in their ongoing struggle for power. Rather, it engendered over the following week an intense and sometimes heated discussion over the ultimate goals of French foreign policy (and the methods used to achieve them). As one deputy put it, what it concerned was what kind of foreign policy a 'free' people ought to have.

The various positions taken during the debate, though hardly monolithic or always coherent, nonetheless broadly reflected the ongoing divisions in the Assembly, between those deputies anxious to conserve what remained of the royal prerogative, and those deputies determined to increase the power of the legislature. All speakers in this debate agreed or conceded that ultimate sovereign power rested in the nation; the issue thus for them was to whom the 'terrible' power of war would be delegated, to the king and his ministers or to the Assembly? The Left, always highly distrustful of the executive, would be, above all,

---

[36] O. J. G. Welch, *Mirabeau: A Study of a Democratic Monarchist* (Port Washington, 1951), p. 262.

[37] This was the view, among others, of the British diplomat Fitz-Gerald, who wrote to the British foreign minister, the Duke of Leeds, that the French 'aristocratical party' were supporting the Family Compact with Spain because "they see the necessity there will be of investing the King with some degree of power and hope themselves to gain strength from the reflecting rays". Fitz-Gerald to Leeds, 14 May 1790, *Despatches from Paris*, Vol. 2, p. 314. See also: Harold Evans, 'The Nootka Sound Controversy', p. 614.

[38] *Ibid.*, Fitz-Gerald to Leeds, 14 May 1790, *Despatches from Paris*, Vol. 2, p. 314.

[39] Foreign policy was here defined as including the right to declare war, negotiate peace and make or exact therein whatever concessions deemed appropriate or necessary, conclude both strategic and commercial alliances and treaties, to nominate, maintain and correspond with ambassadors and other representatives abroad, and above all, to direct and control the armed forces.

determined to safeguard liberty by preventing the executive from abusing its power or threatening the gains of the Revolution. D'Aiguillion was quick to point out that war would work against the Revolution and the constitution, and warned of the dangers posed to both by a French king victorious in war.[40] The perfidy (real or potential) of ministers was a constant theme among leftist deputies. For them, the only way to protect liberty and ensure the faithful carrying out of the general will would be to give the legislature control of foreign policy, at the very least over the right to declare war. The Right, on the other hand, would appear more worried by an excess of power being held by the legislature, asserting that one of the essential features of a monarchy was indeed the control of foreign policy. They warned of the grave dangers to the security of the French state of this responsibility passing out of the King's hands. Some other, more 'centrist' deputies recognised the problem to be more of a dilemma, upon which it was necessary to balance concerns for the liberty of the nation, on one hand, with that of its security, on the other.

This is not to say, however, that the radical Left was unconcerned about the security of France. Underlying this debate over the control and content foreign policy, and the preoccupations of either side, lay very different perspectives and understandings not only about what constituted national interest in the first place, but what factors they felt were actually to condition it.[41] Though many conservative and radical deputies may have shared similar intellectual influences, they would often appear over the course of debate to hold contrary conceptions about the nature of the international system and the role France ought to play within it. Differences of opinion and outlook were not, however, to be merely confined to the extremes of left and right, for the debate would also expose significant differences within the ranks of the Patriots, between those who would emerge as radical 'unilateralists' and those of a more pragmatic or 'realist' inclination.

---

[40] The Left as a whole was, however, more or less split on the question of the king's measures, with Mirabeau and Le Chapelier in favour of their immediate approval. AP, Vol. 15, 15 May 1790, p. 519.

[41] As such, this debate of May 1790 in the National Assembly may be seen as very much part of a broader debate in the eighteenth-century on the nature and morality of international relations, particularly within the French Enlightenment. This was a debate which had pitted 'realists', the proponents of traditional *raison d'état* who saw international rivalry as an inevitability, against 'philosophes', who saw a fundamental transformation of the system of international relations, and the elimination of war, as a real possibility. See Felix Gilbert, 'The "New Diplomacy" of the Eighteenth Century', *World Politics*, 3, (April 1952), pp. 1-38.

The discussion on 15 May pitted those who wished to pursue the constitutional issue over the right to declare war, against those who wished the Assembly to address the issue at hand, the question of the king's naval measures. The attempt by Dupont de Nemours to have the constitutional issue adjourned for three weeks proved fruitless. After the duc de Biron's opening speech proposing a vote of thanks to the king for his actions in defence of the French Empire and its commerce, there followed a chorus of deputies demanding that the constitutional issue be examined first. Alexandre de Lameth asserted that, aside from the constitutional question, the Assembly could not even give its approval to the king's actions anyway, for without knowing the full details of the case, the appropriateness of the actions could not be properly judged. After all, who was to say that that the king's measures did not constitute a concerted effort to raise "la cause des rois contre les peuples"?[42]

Following Lameth's much applauded motion, Barnave similarly warned that an adjournment might be too dangerous, for France might after three weeks already be at war, a prospect which would herald grave dangers for liberty and the future of the constitution. In what would become then virtually a signature tune for the radical Left, Robespierre took the floor to ask the deputies whether they could not believe that "la guerre est un moyen de défendre un pouvoir arbitraire contre les nations"? He added that free nations should and would abjure war, resolving to live in fraternity with one another, a motion enthusiastically seconded by Rewbell, Menou and the duc de Lévis.[43] Rejecting the *Pacte de Famille* and 'ministerial wars', they declared that henceforth only justice should guide France in external affairs. It was thus necessary to determine in this particular case whether it was Spain or Britain that was in the right, not just to follow blindly the cause of one side. Thus, as Menou said to great applause, if there were to be wars they would no longer be ministerial or dynastic, but truly national, for then, as he told the deputies, "nous développerons le courage et la puissance d'une nation vraiment libre".[44] Until this

---

[42] AP, Vol. 15, 15 May 1790, p. 516.
[43] *Ibid.*, p. 516.
[44] Were Spain to be proven to be the wrongful party in this affair, said Menou, then France should mediate accordingly. If, however, it so happened that England were in the wrong, and refused mediation, then, he affirmed, to the approval of the Assembly, "nous devons armer, non quatre vaisseaux, mais toutes nos forces de terre et de mer... nous irons attaquer l'Angleterre en Angleterre même". AP, Vol. 15, 15 May 1790, p. 518.

happened, they asserted, a precipitate war would only serve the cause of despotism and ministerial intrigue.

The leading Patriot deputy Mirabeau played here a similar role to that of Lafayette in the Belgian crisis over the autumn and winter of 1789—90, that is, as an informal and behind-the-scenes intermediary between the royal government and the Revolutionaries. Frustrated in his ambition to become a minister, Mirabeau had sought to play nonetheless an instrumental role in French politics, as both a forceful figure among the Patriot 'party' and as a covert advisor to the French court, one concerned to preserve a strong monarchy in France.[45] As such, on 15 May Mirabeau attempted both to convince the deputies that they should first of all approve the king's measures, and refer the constitutional question to an appropriate committee for examination (thus removing it from the heated atmosphere of the Assembly hall). Sensing the mood of the Assembly, however, he quickly changed tack, managing to secure the deputies' approval of the naval armament by proposing that the Assembly should indeed take up the constitutional question the following day.[46]

The next morning, the debate on the right of war and peace began in earnest. Over the following days, the position of the Left, particularly the radical Left, would be fully elaborated. Central to their view was the alleged untrustworthiness of the king and his ministers when it came to the determining of national interest. What history demonstrated for them was that the wars that had plagued Europe for untold generations had stemmed primarily from the compulsion of crowned heads toward ever greater self-aggrandisement. According to Sillery and Pétion, war was the natural and habitual behaviour of despots, each of these despots resembling the other in their vanity, insatiability, and propensity for violence. The people of Europe had, as a result of their whims and stratagems, suffered immeasurably from dynastic wars, these "funeral suites of monarchical ambition".[47] "Ouvrez l'histoire", instructed Pétion,

> et contemplez ces nombreux forfaits politiques, tous ces crimes de lèse-humanité, commis par ces maîtres du monde. Vous verrez que chaque page est teint du sang qu'ils ont versé; vous verrez que la terre a été un théâtre perpétuel de guerres et de carnage; vous verrez que les peuples n'ont pas cessé

---

[45] Welch, *Mirabeau*, Ch. 12, *passim*.
[46] AP, Vol. 15, 15 May 1790, p. 519.
[47] *Ibid.*, 17 May, p. 533.

d'être les vils instruments et les victimes des passions et l'ambition de ces farouches despotes.[48]

Ministers were themselves here depicted as the cruel and craven lackeys of despots, often instigating wars merely to serve their own ambitions at court.[49] Neither kings nor ministers were hence depicted as having any real notion of what might be in their people's genuine interest. Louis XIV and Louis XV indeed served for several speakers as prime examples of kings whose lust for glory had proven ultimately disastrous for their subjects, though numerous other examples were also cited.

The world from which the French Revolution had emerged was thus, as Pétion described, a world rent by dynastic ambition, by hatred and rivalry, a perpetually unstable system where the least event could trigger war, and where a war begun even in the Indies could spread instantly to Europe.[50] This was a system, however, that deputies of the more radical Left believed could be changed. Since it was their underlying assumption that rivalry in the international system was directly, and entirely, caused by the vainglorious desires of crowned heads, it followed that if the moral behaviour of individual states could somehow be changed, then so could the system overall. In causal terms, the dynamics of international relations was thus considered merely the aggregate of the behaviours of individual states.

Such a fundamental transformation in the international system they believed was entirely possible, for it was also the heartfelt conviction of many deputies that 'free' peoples would not naturally be warlike. It was assumed that where justice and liberty reigned between countries, there would be no aggression. Such aggression was, as D'Aiguillon and the abbé Jallet both observed, only contrary to natural rights; that states should respect each others' rights and promote peace was the "sacred principle" of all free nations.[51] It was, moreover, up to France now to set the example, for, as Sillery asserted, a 'regenerated' nation such as France must be just, and not act against the rights of men or nations.[52] Proclaiming that "le règne de l'injustice et de la mobilité est passé pour nous", the duc de Lévis had thus proposed on 16 May that the National Assembly should solemnly decree that France renounce aggressive warfare, undertaking never to transgress the rights of other nations.[53]

---

[48] *Ibid.*, p. 539.
[49] *Ibid.*, p. 532.
[50] *Ibid.*, p. 537.
[51] *Ibid.*, 16 May, p. 526.
[52] *Ibid.*, p. 532.
[53] *Ibid.*, p. 526.

This did not mean, however, that they would abandon the defence of the state. As a number of deputies pointed out, a just defence was one of the first rights of any state; only *offensive* war would be proscribed. In a theme that would be amplified by Brissotin orators in the later Legislative Assembly, and perhaps here incongruous for its tone of martial pride, Sillery even claimed that liberty would strengthen the potential power of France;

> Les nations étrangères savent ce dont nous étions capables dans le temps où nous étions accablés sous le joug, mais ont-elles calculé l'énergie de la nation française libre et ne formant qu'un peuple de frères?[54]

What it did mean was that the interest of kings was emphatically *not* the same as their peoples', or the same as *national* interest. A declaration of war was generally regarded in the Assembly as the most serious expression of national sovereignty. As such, these leftist deputies believed that only the nation's elected representatives could have the right to declare war and control foreign policy, for only they could properly determine what was in the nation's interest. Though the king might well continue, as the head of the executive, to direct the armed forces, he could not safely be entrusted with the right to declare war, for, as Charles de Lameth, Pétion and others suggested, he would only then incite war in order to subvert the constitution and increase his own power.[55] Thus, as far as the issue of war was concerned, the king should merely be the executor of the nation's will, as expressed through the Assembly.

In this perceived new era of international relations, as the radical Rewbell stated early on, "nous ne reconnaissons plus d'alliés que les peuples justes".[56] All foreign policy engagements of the royal government would hence in this view need to be reviewed. The so-called *pacte de famille* was thereon repeatedly denounced, as were several other treaties and alliances that had been entered into by the crown. Such treaties and alliances were, Pétion declaimed, only "actes d'une souveraine injustice lorsqu'ils engagent les nations à se prêter mutuellement une aveugle assistance, à se protéger dans leurs usurpations".[57] After all, if the king had a family, said Charles de Lameth, it was his own people, not the Spanish king. He reminded the deputies that Spain had already taken steps to throw a 'cordon

---

[54] *Ibid.*, 17 May, p. 533.
[55] *Ibid.*, 16 May, p. 530.
[56] *Ibid.*, 15 May, p. 516.
[57] *Ibid.*, 17 May, p. 542.

The 'Revolutionising' of French Foreign Policy 123

sanitaire' between it and France, to prevent the spread of revolutionary ideas, a singularly unfriendly, if not ominous, gesture. Any plea for help now from them would have to be regarded with some suspicion, as some kind of mutual Bourbon trap.[58]

The many criticisms of old regime diplomacy also revealed an element of Austrophobia. Several speakers fervently denounced the treaty of 1756 with Austria and its disastrous outcomes, Pétion implying that France had been there only the victim of Austrian cunning.[59] The recent commercial treaty of 1786 with Britain he also condemned, as ruinous to French commerce and industry, attributing it in this case to the simple ignorance and incompetence of the king's ministers. He commented that the nation would never have consented to either of these humiliating and ruinous treaties, if it had then been properly able to exercise its rights.[60]

Not only foreign policy initiatives, but the entire apparatus of old regime diplomacy and decision-making would, the Left argued, be made redundant in the new scheme of things. Proclaiming that "un peuple généreux n'a pas besoin d'une politique tortueuse et embrouillée",[61] these deputies argued the necessity for lifting the traditional veil of secrecy behind which the king and his ministers had so long conducted their foreign policy and hidden their diplomatic intrigues. This secrecy was thought to be not merely unnecessary but dangerous to the liberty and well-being of peoples. Since for Menou the behaviour of states in international affairs was really a question of morality in any case, he asserted that politics was not an 'élite' science capable of being divined only by select individuals, but one known to every just heart. "La vraie politique", he said, "n'est que la disposition de la justice et de la morale entre toutes les nations".[62] Only when foreign policy issues—war, treaties, alliances—were debated and decided upon openly and publicly in the National Assembly, as any other kind of law, could it be guaranteed that justice and the national interest would truly be served. Perhaps, Menou suggested, an international tribunal could even be set up to adjudicate any differences arising between states?[63] If international affairs could be conducted justly, and with full transparency, it was thus assumed by these deputies that an enduring

---

[58] *Ibid.*, p. 530.
[59] *Ibid.*, p. 538.
[60] *Ibid.*, p. 539.
[61] *Ibid.*, 16 May, p. 526.
[62] *Ibid.*, 19 May, p. 611.
[63] *Ibid.*, p. 610.

and universal peace was a real possibility. All it would take was for France's neighbours to follow her example.

This radical stance on foreign policy was, over the course of the debate, vigorously opposed by a group of deputies consisting mostly, though not exclusively, of conservatives and moderates. Neither politically or ideologically homogenous, these deputies were nonetheless united in their opposition to legislative control and radical change in the content of foreign policy, in spite of the fears of monarchical abuse raised by the Left. This was largely because they together held an understanding of the international system and its exigencies that was diametrically opposed to that assumed by many of the leftist and more radical deputies. Whereas the radical Left presumed that the conflictual nature of the international system derived from the behaviours of its individual states, for these other deputies the situation was rather the reverse. They assumed that individual states behaved as they currently did because of the inherent nature of the international system, not the other way round. As Clermont-Tonnerre explained, the international arena did not constitute a field of action morally analogous to that of individual societies (where life was governed by common and binding rules), since there was no supranational authority powerful enough to command in the world a monopoly of the means to violence, to institute common rules and laws.[64] The contexts were hence, in this respect, entirely different.

This multipolarity of the international system meant rather that it was also by nature essentially *anarchical*—requiring each state to provide as best it could for its own security, and where each state was ultimately, and necessarily, distrustful of the other. The moral behaviour of individual states was thus immaterial to the dynamics of the system overall, for every power was uniformly compelled to defend its own autonomy and integrity, or else be taken over by others. In this situation the state's actual material interest would come before any putative 'rights', for it would only be through such a calculation of state interest, and its material means, that it could defend itself in the first place. States had, it thus seemed, only as many 'rights' as they could effectively defend. This situation constituted, for these deputies, the stark reality of international relations, to which they believed foreign policy needed to respond adequately.

The key concept for these deputies in the management of international affairs remained the traditional one of the 'balance of power', wherein a 'system' of self-interested and countervailing powers

---

[64] *Ibid.*, 18 May, p. 560.

would supposedly prevent any one state from achieving too great a degree of dominance over its rivals. This was seen as both a description of what had actually been the response, up to then, of individual states to an 'anarchical' world order, and what, in the circumstances, these deputies thought should continue to occur, for it was only through this counter-balancing system that they believed there was any real hope that peace could be maintained. To those who might claim that this 'system' had in fact regularly failed to prevent war in Europe, and, indeed, was merely a recipe for nearly continuous conflict, Malouet replied that there was no better way, realistically, of maintaining a measure of order and stability in the international system:

> Cet équilibre, si vanté et si calomnié qui balance par des alliances et souvent par des intrigues, les forces des différentes puissances, ne mérite ni l'admiration, ni le mépris qu'on lui prodigue. L'Europe eût été plus d'une fois bouleversée; on y aurait vu, comme en Asie et en Afrique, des empires détruits, des peuples exterminés, sans la surveillance réciproque de toutes les cours, sans leurs combinaisons d'attaque et de défense, que la justice ne dirige pas toujours, mais qui maintient les parties de ce grand tout dans une sorte d'harmonie.[65]

It was this conviction about the competitive nature of international politics that would undergird both the perception of these deputies of the imperative needs of the French state, and their criticisms of the Left's foreign policy proposals.

Foremost among their criticisms was that directed against the Left's proposed 'peace manifesto', a proclamation to foreign countries of France's intention to abjure offensive war and 'unjust' alliances, through which it was hoped, by the Left, that the prospects of a universal peace could be promoted. Implied in this proclamation was a complete renunciation of the existing system of diplomacy and international relations, and the withdrawal of France therefrom. Praising, however, this "désir sublime de réaliser la paix perpetuelle" as laudable and worthy of a regenerated France, Sinéti and the abbé Montesquieu nonetheless both dismissed such visions as simply impractical.[66] Others thought they were downright dangerous. Such a system of general peace, said Custine, could not suit an empire whose territory was surrounded on all sides by powerful neighbours.[67] He and a succession of other deputies—Malouet, the duc de Praslin, Clermont-

---

[65] Ibid., 17 May, p. 535.
[66] Ibid., p. 547.
[67] Ibid., 16 May, p. 529.

Tonnerre, Maury, Gallisonière, Bengy de Puyvallée—described to the Assembly the inevitable consequences of such a unilateral renunciation of 'balance of power' dynamics. Rather than promoting peace, such "philanthropic dreams" reminiscent of the old *philosophe* the abbé de Saint-Pierre would, it was argued, drastically *increase* the threat of war, by making France more vulnerable to the jealous ambitions of its neighbours. Responding to Pétion's support for the manifesto, the arch-conservative Montlosier could himself barely contain his derision, stating on 17 May that it was only by this "étalage de métaphysique", this "livre de philosophie qui l'honourable membre prétend opposer avec succès à l'intérêt, à l'ambition, à toutes les passions des peuples qui nous entourent".[68] A number of other deputies thought the idea equally absurd.

These deputies asserted, moreover, that such a 'withdrawal' from international politics would have implications for more than France's short-term security. Since many of them believed that strategic and economic power were closely interconnected, this political isolation would in their view also severely compromise the long-term bases of French economic power and prosperity. France was, after all, Malouet reminded the Assembly, a maritime empire, with international trade as its lifeblood. Without this trade, and the power that it in turn gave France, the whole edifice would quickly collapse.

> En vain, essaierions-nous de nous isoler aujourd'hui de tous ces movements politiques; le commerce a changé la face du globe, les moeurs et les lois, les besoins, les richesses, la liberté, la servitude, la guerre et la paix, tout a subi son influence, et nous ne pourrions nous séparer des autres peuples du continent, sans créer un noveau système dont les bases reposeraient sur le sable et nous placeraient sur les bords d'un précipice.[69]

Such was the inherently competitive nature of the international system, Clermont-Tonnerre further suggested, that to compromise the ultimate sources of France's power and prosperity in the world would be to increase greatly the relative power of France's rivals in both colonial and continental spheres. This would thus threaten not only the French Empire, but the very existence of France itself.

> Si vous renonciez aux traités, aux negotiations, vous ignoriez toutes les mesures de l'ennemi et l'ennemi saurait toutes les vôtres. Privés de votre commerce qui ne serait plus appuyé de votre consideration, dépouillés de vos

---

[68] *Ibid.*, 17 May, p. 545.
[69] *Ibid.*, p. 535.

colonies, qui seraient plutôt envahies que menacées ...; affaiblis par la ruine entière de vos ports qu'aucun commerce ne vivifierait plus, vous seriez bientôt effacés de cette carte géographique de l'Europe ...[70]

All states in the balance of power system, it was therefore declared, needed alliances of convenience to survive. That France was both a major colonial and continental power made alliances for France even more necessary, since she was hardly powerful enough on her own to compete effectively with her rivals in both spheres. Hence, while a number of deputies conceded in principle that offensive wars and offensive alliances were reprehensible, even a "crime", they nonetheless insisted on the absolute necessity for France of *defensive* alliances. It might be, said Dupont, that all empires would be eventually united under a similar constitution, but for the present, in a world full of predatory states, "good faith" would hardly suffice. Peace and security would only come from strength, a parity in armaments, and effective alliances.

La France n'a aucun voisin qui soit, à lui seul, redoutable pour elle; mais une confédération pourrait la mettre en danger, et si les deux puissances germaniques pouvaient s'entendre à la fois avec l'Angleterre et la Hollande, actuellement gouvernée par l'Angleterre et par la Prusse, pour attaquer notre empire, le secours de nos alliés naturels, pour établir l'équilibre sur mer et pour opérer sur terre des diversions efficaces, nous serait certainment d'une grande utilité.[71]

For those, however, such as the conservatives Maury and Montlosier, this distinction between offensive and defensive measures was, in the balance of power system, simply illusory, or "more subtle than real".[72] As the duc de Praslin pointed out, in the past rulers such as Frederick the Great and Catherine II had launched wars that while ostensibly defensive in justification, had soon become wars of conquest.[73] International politics being by nature complex, how could one then discern who was the true aggressor? The abbé de Montequieu went even further, stating that, in any case, the exigencies of global competition sometimes compelled commercial nations such as France

---

[70] *Ibid.*, 18 May, p. 563.
[71] *Ibid.*, 19 May, p. 588.
[72] *Ibid.*, 17 May, p. 547.
[73] *Ibid.*, 18 May, p. 588.

to act a little 'unjustly'. This was only the result, he suggested, of material interests being brought unavoidably into conflict.[74]

It was precisely by reason of such material necessity that these deputies insisted that France's alliance with Spain be upheld. They endeavoured thereby to emphasise the *national* character of this alliance; the abbé Montesquieu even suggested that it should be no longer be called a *pacte de famille* at all, since it could be justified without any reference to dynasticism. Spain, it was repeatedly asserted, was the natural ally of the French nation in its long-standing colonial and maritime rivalry with Britain. Few of these deputies were subsequently shy about identifying Britain as a dangerous rival and natural enemy of France, though this had caused some murmurs of protest from the Left when initially stated by Le Chapelier on 15 May.[75] Seemingly jealous of its own liberty, Britain was viewed by many in the Assembly, particularly on the Left, as a country with which France should now be fraternally linked. The depth of hostility toward Britain elsewhere in the Assembly was, however, all too clear, and felt right across the political spectrum. Britain was depicted by various deputies—Sérent, Virieu, Malouet, Châtelet—as aggressively expansionist, a constant threat to France's colonies, trade and industry, a world power that would only grow as that of France weakened. Custine even accused them of aspiring to a "universal monarchy", urging France to maintain a strong navy.[76]

Spain, by contrast, was thought to hold strategic and economic interests in common with France, which France could not now afford to jeopardise, especially given the state of its finances. Furthermore, said Malouet, it was now necessary in this current diplomatic crisis for France to demonstrate its support for Spain, otherwise Britain might be emboldened to attempt either to detach Spain from its alliance with France, or else invade its possessions.[77] Such a loyal show of support, said Maury, was only what was owed to Spain anyway.

> La France ne saurait abandonner sa plus fidèle et sa plus solide alliée, l'Espagne, qui, depuis vingt ans, a deux fois déclaré la guerre aux Anglais pour défendre notre cause; ... Notre loyauté nous oblige, autant que notre intérêts, de ne point nous séparer de cette puissance qui serait évidemment

---

[74] *Ibid.*, 19 May, p. 590.
[75] *Ibid.*, 15 May, p. 519.
[76] *Ibid.*, 16 May, p. 528.
[77] *Ibid.*, 17 May, p. 535.

compromise si elle était isolée, et dont la ruine rendrait l'Angleterre maîtresse de toutes les mers.[78]

The "deplorable" outcomes of the Dutch crisis of 1787 had, he added, already given France ample indication of the dire consequences of French inaction. As others confirmed, there could be no more dire prospect for the French Empire than if Britain were to control the high seas. Several deputies warned the Assembly of the danger that Britain might soon come to dominate the world's oceans, becoming then "la reine du monde".[79] A failure to support the Spanish would, moreover, ultimately threaten France's own empire, for an invasion by Britain of Spanish possessions would, Boisgelin warned, merely be a prelude to an attack on those of France.

These deputies accompanied this critique of the radical Left's perspective on world affairs with a defence of the king's traditional control of foreign policy, integral to which, it was argued, was the right to declare war. For several speakers, notably Maury, Montlosier and Cazalès, this challenge by the Left to the king's foreign policy role was just another example of a Revolution that had already gone too far, removing one by one from the king traditional powers that they believed were essential to the character and majesty of the monarchy. They bitterly attacked this process in the Assembly, and the 'incendiary exclamations' of the radical press, whom they believed were largely responsible for propagating the notion of some kind of sinister and pending counter-revolution, and which had only stoked a continued public atmosphere of unrest and suspicion of royal authority.[80]

It must be noted, however, that most other deputies took, in their criticism of the Left's proposals, a much less reactionary stance, many even evincing firm support for the Revolution. They basically argued that the king, given the exigencies of the international system, was in *functional* terms far better positioned to oversee and direct foreign policy than the legislature. As the executive power, he possessed what they commonly believed to be the attributes considered necessary for the promotion of France's security: the capacity for secrecy, swiftness and unity, both in action and decision-making, as well as continuity of purpose.

---

[78] *Ibid.*, 18 May, p. 565.
[79] *Ibid.*, p. 558.
[80] *Ibid.*, 17 May, p. 546.

Conversely, it was asserted that the legislature patently lacked the correct attributes either to control the direction of foreign affairs or oversee national defence. For a number of reasons it was thought highly inappropriate, or even dangerous, for it to attempt to do so. Firstly, there was the question of promptness and secrecy. It was generally conceded that commercial treaties could be openly discussed in the Assembly; strategic alliances, and the negotiations surrounding them, were, however, another matter. Many deputies argued that it would be directly counter-productive, for the success of such negotiations, for an open forum such as the Assembly to either debate or even report their progress, let alone conduct such negotiations themselves. As well as publicly revealing the innermost workings of French diplomacy to other governments (who would use that knowledge to advance their own interests at the expense of those of France), it would also be a gross betrayal of diplomatic trust that would alienate even the closest ally, and prejudice any alliances. These deputies thus insisted that effective diplomacy required that some negotiations between governments remain secret, just as it was thought equally necessary that when threatened with invasion, the king should take immediate steps to protect France's security, without having to wait for approval upon the drawn out deliberations of an assembly.

Secondly, several deputies, including Maury and Malouet, wondered whether, in the end, an assembly would actually be less or *even more* likely to resort to war than would the king. Pointing out that 'republican' governments had proven in history to be no less ambitious or warlike than monarchies had been, they thus challenged the leftist view that bellicosity was an inherent feature only of monarchs and despots, Malouet indeed telling the Assembly that "despotism and liberty have produced the same excesses".[81] The simple competency of the legislature was here also questioned, for with so many passions and local interests at play in an assembly, it was alleged that the legislature might only vacillate when urgent defence measures were required, or even lose sight of the general interest altogether.

Nor could it be guaranteed that the Assembly would not in the future be misled by the misguided oratory of particular deputies, or that it would be itself immune from corruption. A number of deputies—Sérent, Malouet, Praslin, Châtelet, Maury—referred specifically to the recent examples of Sweden and Poland, where assemblies had been allegedly corrupted by foreign governments. "En Suède", said Châtelet, "la diète est toujours remplie de gens soudoyés par la France, par l'Angleterre ou

---

[81]   *Ibid.*, p. 534.

par la Russie. Les alliances, la paix et la guerre y sont le résultat de la plus odieuse corruption...".[82] Only the king and his ministers, they concluded, had the capacity, and the degree of probity and experience necessary, to ascertain what was most clearly in the national interest. Furthermore, only they could be entrusted to act upon it swiftly and decisively.

Although also concerned to prevent any potential 'abuses' of monarchical authority, all in all it was assumed by these deputies, contrary to the views of the Left, that the interests of a 'citizen king', and that of the nation, were not merely compatible, but ultimately one and the same. Some even asserted that the legislature should not be 'confused' with the nation at all, that it was not the only organ of the nation's will. It was suggested that the king, by his constitutional right of veto, also had a significant representative role in his own right. Thus, while on one hand declaring that the right to declare war was inherent in the executive power, on the other hand, these deputies also challenged the Left's apparent assumption that the Assembly held, in any case, a monopoly to speak or legislate on behalf of the nation. That the king should be *alone* charged with the defence of the realm and the direction of foreign affairs was hence, for many of them, both a practical and a constitutional imperative. Several deputies indeed warned that too powerful a legislature would contravene the vaunted principle of the separation of powers, threatening liberty and the constitution by effectively turning France into a republic.[83]

The partisans of the Left, such as Fréteau, Rewbell, Menou and Lameth were, however, equally adamant that the right to declare war should belong only to the Assembly. This was, in their view, in the best interests of liberty and the constitution. It was, after all, only in the national interest, said Menou, and only through such means, that this liberty could be preserved.[84] On the question of safeguards they retorted that the measures proposed—ministerial responsibility, refusal of

---

[82] *Ibid.*, 18 May, p. 559.
[83] For the sake of this constitution, as for the sake of French security, they argued, therefore, that the legislature should neither control or even share in the control of defence and foreign policy. If, after all, there *needed* to be some protection against the abuse of monarchical authority in either defence or foreign affairs, one could take sufficient measures that did not threaten the constitutional order. These would include, for instance, ministerial responsibility, and the right of the legislature to refuse to vote funds for initiatives of which it disapproved. To constrict further the king's authority, they chimed, would be unnecessary, unconstitutional and impracticable. *Ibid.*, 20 May, p. 615.
[84] *Ibid.*, p. 611.

subsidies—were comprehensively inadequate for a country like France, even *if* they might have worked in Britain. Goupil de Préfeln and Le Pelletier de Saint-Fargeau drew attention to crucial differences, in this respect, between the two nations. As an island, Britain had far less need of a large standing army, and hence less to fear from the dangers to liberty which such a force was assumed naturally to pose. France, being a landed power, had greater need of such an army, and hence far more to fear. It would be therefore impossible, declared Le Pelletier, to conserve liberty in France if war and foreign policy powers were not held exclusively by the legislature, for only the latter could keep these necessary internal forces in check, and thus prevent incursions upon liberty.[85]

Mirabeau and the Decree on the Right of War and Peace

This apparent deadlock in the Assembly was finally broken by Mirabeau, the maverick Provençale deputy and now secret advisor to the Court. On 20 May, after five days of intense debate and much lofty rhetoric, and against a background also of intensifying public interest, Mirabeau, a powerful orator, delivered a speech widely acclaimed to have been his finest.[86] In what has been described as a "masterpiece of persuasion", he proposed what he believed to be a workable compromise, hoping thereby to defend what remained of the royal prerogative.[87] Employing a 'middle course', he noted that it was neither practical or constitutional that *either* the executive or the legislature hold exclusive rights over the question of war and peace; as history showed, parliamentary passions had been no less guilty than kings and despots in sparking off unjust and useless wars.

Above all, he argued, the vaunted principle of the separation of powers forbade exclusive legislative control. The problem was, however, that national defence required both an element of national will—which, Mirabeau affirmed, could only be expressed by the legislature—and of action, the sole preserve of the executive. Focusing on this technical point, Mirabeau argued, ingeniously, that the immediate response of the king to any threat to French security from

---

[85] *Ibid.*, 19 May, p. 585.
[86] AP, Vol. 15, 20 May, p. 618; Barry Rothaus, 'The War and Peace Prerogative as a Constitutional Issue during the first two years of the Revolution, 1789-91', in *Proceedings of the First Annual Meeting of the Western Society for French History* (New Mexico, 1974), p. 125.
[87] Welch, *Mirabeau*, p. 264.

outside was not properly an expression of national *will*, and therefore not actually tantamount to a declaration of war. He proposed therefore, in a draft decree, that the king and his ministers should continue to oversee defence, diplomacy and treaty negotiations, and that upon the outbreak or likely outbreak of any hostilities, it should be up to the king, after ordering initial security measures, to propose a formal declaration of war to the Assembly. The power to finally decide on war (and thus provide funds) would thus be ultimately reserved to the legislature, which could then decide on the appropriateness of the executive's actions, either declaring war or demanding peace (and perhaps punishing any ministers considered to have acted improperly).[88] By thereby co-operating, or acting "concurrently", as he put it, the separate functions of the king and Assembly could thus, in practical terms, be reconciled. This, he concluded, would have the happy outcome of maintaining both the effective defence of the country, and the integrity of the constitution as it was presently conceived.

This motion was eventually passed on 22 May, but only after a climactic contest in the Assembly between Mirabeau and Barnave, the most able orator of the Triumvirate and a leading member of the Left. Riding high on several days of impassioned and near ecstatic utopian rhetoric, Barnave had on the previous day launched an assault on Mirabeau's notion of 'concurrency', alleging that the control it gave to the Assembly on the question of war was simply illusory.[89] What was more, it would, he alleged, place the Assembly virtually in a state of "civil war" with the crown. In the end, the executive would continue to have the whip hand. He thus not only reiterated the Left's plea that the legislature should have the right to declare war, but claimed that it should also possess it *unambigiously*.[90] Only this, he claimed, would best protect and serve France's national interest.

It seemed initially that Barnave may have won a decisive victory for the Triumvirate against Mirabeau, so rapturously had his retort been received by the large crowd surrounding the Assembly.[91] However, this apparent triumph was to be shortlived, for the next day Mirabeau, ever the heavyweight, countered with a masterly rebuttal of Barnave's critique that in turn brought him acclaim in the Assembly, and this time sealed the matter. For many of the deputies, such as the moderate

---

[88] AP, Vol. 15, 20 May, p. 626.
[89] *Ibid.*, 21 May, p. 643.
[90] *Ibid.*, p. 644.
[91] Welch, pp. 267-268.

Duquesnoy, that Mirabeau's motion had drawn criticism from both the Left and Right had only demonstrated for them its true merit. No better solution had been offered, after all, to what was a very difficult constitutional dilemma. The basic provisions outlined by Mirabeau, and finalised by the Assembly, were thought at least adequate to protect both France's external security and internal liberty: while the day-to-day management of diplomacy and external defence would remain under the direction of the Crown, the Legislative body would now have, within the constitution: firstly, a power of veto over any proposal by the Crown to declare war; secondly, the power to bring to an end any outbreak of hostilities or undeclared war; thirdly, the power thereafter to punish those, including Ministers, guilty of provoking or inciting a conflict deemed to be against the national interest; and fourthly, the power to ratify future alliances or treaties. Thus, with minor amendments, and to great ovation, Mirabeau's decree on the constitutional powers relating to war and peace was adopted by the Assembly.[92]

This decree had profound implications for the control, and also the content, of French foreign policy. With its explicit renunciation of offensive war, and its reassurance that French power would henceforth never be used "against the liberty of any people", the Decree of 22 May constituted what many deputies believed to be a 'revolution' in the principles of French foreign policy-making, wherein a publicly defined, and professedly 'enlightened', concept of 'national interest' replaced dynastic *gloire* and *raison d'état* as the guiding principle of foreign policy. While the instruments of diplomacy and the day-to-day management of foreign affairs would remain in the hands of the crown, it was thus clearly accepted that all future foreign policy initiatives would be subject to the examination and approval of the national legislature.

Whether this 'revolution' in the principles of foreign policy should, however, have also logically required an immediate and retrospective review of France's *existing* alliance and treaty system was, for the deputies, another matter entirely. When on 24 May Mirabeau proposed, as an *addendum* to the Decree of 22 May, that the Assembly create a "special committee" to review all of the treaties to which France was presently a signatory, and hence determine which of them should be retained or annulled, the Assembly took fright. This, it appeared, was a can of worms which—at this point—the deputies had no wish to open.

---

[92] AP, Vol. 15, 22 May 1790, p. 662. For the full text of this important decree, see Appendix, pp. 239-240.

As Fréteau remarked, there were several treaties which would not likely survive such a review, but whose annullment might immediately provoke a war. The proposal was, as such, quickly rejected, and the matter dropped.[93]

That the very same Assembly that had been so eager to engender a 'revolution' in the principles of French foreign policy-making, should have then been so loath to investigate or even discuss the specifics of France's existing alliance system is significant, and requires explanation.[94] Perhaps the silence is telling. Far from denoting a lack of interest in concrete—as opposed to abstract—discussions of foreign policy, what it may be considered to demonstrate is an acute awareness of then current realities of French foreign affairs. Fréteau's warning most probably referred to the Anglo-French Commercial treaty, highly unpopular in France, but otherwise regarded by many deputies as the only thing preventing the British from resuming hostilities with their old rival. In the political scenario then looming in Europe anything that put a brake on British hostility toward France would be most valuable, even imperative to French security. At this time Prussia was moving ever closer to war with Austria. Though the British had wished to restrain Prussia from any outright aggression toward Austria (and hence prevent any expansion of the Eastern War into a general European conflict), an Austro-Prussian war would more than likely force them to give active support to Prussia. This would only be to forestall Prussian attempts to form an alliance alternatively with France, with a consequent resurgence of French influence in the Low Countries. If France, however, remained neutral in this conflict, while being on good terms with Britain, there could be some hope that the French could

---

[93] AP, Vol. 15, 24 May 1790, pp. 662-63.

[94] There would seem to be some historiographical neglect of this point. Eric Thompson, in his *Popular Sovereignty and the French Constituent Assembly 1789-91*, Manchester, 1952, notes (p. 145) that Mirabeau's proposal was rejected after a speech by Fréteau "in which he pointed out that the time was highly inopportune for any such revision of foreign alliances", without, however, speculating as why this might be thought the case. Sorel, Hampson and Rothaus neglect to mention Mirabeau's proposal of 24 May at all. Sorel, however, makes the general conclusion that "La France, en effet, ne déchire pas les traités, ce qui serait très-simple; elle en convertit pour ainsi dire les obligations, en transforme la cause et en modifie l'objet. Les traités souscrits par les rois ne la lient plus, car elle possède et acquiert désormais en vertu d'un droit public que les rois ne connaissaient point; mais ces traités continuent de lier les Etats étrangers, car ils vivent encore sous la même règle que du temps où les traités ont été conclus". Sorel, *L'Europe et la Révolution Française: les nouveaux principes*, Book One, Ch. 3, p. 107. See also p. 90.

avoid being drawn in to the struggle at all—on either side. France, though vulnerable and isolated, might then be free to consolidate its revolution, while the major European powers were distracted by war.

For France, however, to go to war now with Britain, for the sake of some dubious Spanish claims half a world away, would thus be—in this above scenario—a most foolhardy and even suicidal act. If, one way or another, war did break out between Britain and France, it was unlikely that France would find the necessary allies among the major land-based powers of continental Europe: Britain would most likely block any resumption of the old Franco-Prussian alliance, while the National Assembly and the revolutionary crowds would undoubtedly be opposed to any fulfillment of the now all but formally defunct Austrian alliance. Hence, war with Britain would not only involve a maritime and colonial war which France and Spain would together have little or no hope of winning, and which could even mark the end of France as a colonial power, but it would also leave France—in her current state of prostration—vulnerable to the territorial ambitions of jealous neighbours, both during the course of a general European conflict, and in any subsequent peace.

The implications, alternatively, of a formal renunciation of the much-hated Austrian alliance would be no less serious. It had always been assumed by the French public that if France was not allied to the Austrians, she would likely be at war with them. Whether it was likely or not Austria would at this time risk moving against France (while elsewhere its Empire was threatened by Prussia, and by serious internal rebellions), there remained a strong possibility that Austria would attempt to appease the land-hungry Prussians at the expense of France, by proposing a mutual invasion and seizure of certain French territories. This was more or less the scenario that Peyssonnel had warned against in his address to the Jacobins on 10 March.

The above calculations may thus explain the evident haste with which the Assembly dispensed with Mirabeau's proposal for a review of France's alliance system. The great majority of the deputies had no wish to provoke the British into declaring war on France. Nor would they have wished to provoke Austria into either declaring war, or even consorting with Prussia to launch an invasion and seizure of French territory. Rather, provided that the National Assembly's 'revolution' in foreign policy could be confined to the matter of principle, and hence not involve, at least for the time-being, major changes in the *structure* of the France's existing alliance or treaty system, the deputies may have hoped that France could avoid being drawn into foreign conflicts altogether. In following such a reasonably 'conservative' course regarding alliance committments, France might therefore be left to 'regenerate' itself more or less unhindered.

In summary, by May 1790 the deputies' 'revolutionary' break with tradition extended to foreign policy in two basic ways: firstly, declarations of war and ratification of alliances became now the responsibility of the National Assembly, and hence were no longer an exclusive royal prerogative; secondly, these same foreign policy powers were now to be infused with Enlightenment and supposedly revolutionary values, demonstrated in the constitutional provision outlawing the making of either offensive war or offensive alliances. The debates on the principles to be applied to future foreign policy also exposed deep divisions within the Assembly between those, mostly in the Patriot party, who believed themselves to be on the threshold of a new 'enlightened' era in international relations, and those, mostly from the Right, who scorned such hopes as naive and unrealisable. This clash of conviction was derived in large part from often contrasting views of the nature of the international system, and its capacity for paradigmatic change.

No less significant was the apparent split among the Patriots themselves, which seemed to indicate the presence among these deputies of two different 'languages' or applied responses to the question of foreign policy. On one side were a minority of radical unilateralists who insisted that France should now totally repudiate all the supposedly reprehensible practices of the old order, including the balance of power system, which they considered morally abhorrent. On the other side were the majority of deputies who, if they disapproved at least of the apparent amorality of the balance of power system—which had seemed to require states to be ruthless and calculating in their alliance making and breaking—nonetheless accepted that a change in the traditional practices of international politics would only come slowly, and that in the interim France should hence endeavour to protect itself through the traditional instrument of alliance diplomacy. The difference now was that the basis for their calculations of *raison d'état* would not lie in dynastic *gloire* or aggrandisement, but in the needs of territorial defense and national security.

This would seem to suggest an ambivalent attitude among many of the deputies toward the concept of the balance of power: whether or not they believed that in a 'new world order' balance of power dynamics either would or should disappear in Europe, they certainly appeared to believe that, for the time being at least, a somewhat pragmatic approach to foreign policy was not merely prudent but necessary. The decree of 22 May 1790, although it specifically prohibited the formation of offensive pacts, did not, in theory, even preclude the formation of alliances with patently autocratic and 'unregenerate' regimes, provided such alliances could contribute to French security by providing a deterrent to foreign aggression. In the meantime, it was this pragmatism, and the desire for peace, that underlay the reluctance of the deputies to repudiate either their strategic alliance with Austria, or their commercial treaty with Britain. Yet, what of the future? What course would France take, once the political situation in Europe had stabilised, and France no longer appeared quite so vulnerable or impotent? As we shall see in the following chapter, it was the belief of many deputies that a fully regenerated France should also aspire to become once again the dominant force in European politics, and that this would simply be a measure of its economic might.

5 Trade and the Regeneration of the French Economy

The economic and commercial policy of the Constituent Assembly has often been described as liberal and essentially 'Physiocratic'.[1] This is because many historical analyses have tended to focus only on the internal aspects of this policy, much of which was indeed liberal and arguably Physiocratic in inspiration. The principles espoused, and legislation enacted, by the Constituents in regard to the organisation of economic life *within* France followed, by and large, the individualist and laissez-faire principles of both Physiocracy and Adam Smith. This was exemplified in the *Declaration of the Rights of Man and Citizen*—which promoted political liberty and the 'natural right of property'—and the two pieces of legislation generally regarded as most expressive of the Constituents' apparent economic liberalism: firstly, the 'Loi d'allarde' of 2 March 1791 abolishing guilds, corporations and private monopolies, and secondly, the 'Loi Chapelier' of 17 June 1791, outlawing worker associations.

Rather less has been said by historians about the response of the Constituent Assembly to the question of external trade, and commercial relations with other states. What was the Constituents' understanding of the nature of international commerce, and commercial competition *between* states? What role did the deputies expect the Revolution to play in affecting France's own position in this international trade? What, conversely, would be the role of foreign trade in the regeneration of the French state? What factors—economic, political—were considered important in affecting commercial policy, and commercial relationships with other states?

To address these questions, this chapter will consider other legislative proposals and principal pieces of legislation (and the debates surrounding them), which together may be said to form the basic policy of the Constituent Assembly with regard to international commerce.

---

[1] See, for example, W. Bowden, M. Karpovich, A. Usher, *An Economic History of Europe since 1750* (New York, 1937), p. 221; Doyle, *The Old European Order*, pp. 362-363; J. M. Roberts, *The French Revolution* (Oxford, 1978), p. 85.

Before doing so, however, it might be useful to look briefly at the specific context of economic policy-making at the beginning of the Revolution.

The French Economy in 1789 and the Legacy of the Old Regime

Despite the sharp economic downturn of the late 1780s, France was still by 1789 a major European economic power, second only to Britain.[2] This was to be expected, given the substantial size of France and its population, its geographic position in Europe, its control of, and access to, cheap colonial produce, and the abundance of its own natural resources. Aside from a short-term dip during the Seven Years' War, the volume of its trade was reported in contemporary assessments to have continued its impressive rate of expansion over the course of the century. Moreover, it has been estimated that France continued to enjoy also a very favourable balance of trade, one that had risen in proportion to its rapid economic expansion.[3] Arnould, of the Bureau de la Balance de Commerce, was to report in 1791 that the balance of trade with Europe alone (excluding the Ottoman Empire) had risen from a figure of 36 million livres in 1715 to one of around 57 million in 1789,[4] a figure that would have been even larger if France had not needed to import sizable amounts of grain during 1788—89 on account of the temporary subsistance crisis.

Such a favourable balance of trade would have seemed on the surface a healthy indicator of France's long-term prosperity. After all, international trade was during this and the previous century regarded as the principal means of increasing the accumulated capital, and hence the wealth, of any country. Yet it was the common belief in France in

---

[2] Peter Jones, *Reform and Revolution in France*, p. 98.

[3] Trade figures for the eighteenth century seem to vary widely, depending on the source, but all seem to confirm an upward trend both in volume of trade and balance of trade, albeit a slackening one from around 1770. See François Crouzet, 'England and France in the Eighteenth Century: A Comparative Analysis of Two Economic Growths', in R. Hartwell (Ed.), *The Causes of the Industrial Revolution in England* (London, 1967), *passim*; Ralph Davis, *The Rise of the Atlantic Economies*, London 1973, Ch. 17-18, *passim*; C.-E. Labrousse, *La crise de l'économie française à la fin de l'ancien régime et au début de la révolution* (Paris 1944).

[4] A. Arnould, *La balance du commerce et des relations commerciales extérieures de la France, dans toutes les parties du globe, particulièrement à la fin du règne de Louis XIV, et au moment de la Révolution* (Paris, 1791), p. 264.

1789 that, despite this favourable balance, the country had been failing to realize anything close to its real economic potential in international trade, indeed, that the fiscal and economic structures of the old regime had for a very long time impeded, inhibited and undermined the economic progress of France. As many of the *cahiers des doléances* had revealed, there was throughout French society a shared understanding of the imperative need of France to compete effectively in international trade so as to guarantee its long-term prosperity.[5] Furthermore, many cahiers exhibited the belief that the 'regeneration' of France ought to have as a principal objective the unleashing of this potential, on the grounds that France's internal prosperity and world standing depended on it. This belief in the importance to France of international trade, and the role of the Revolution in furthering it, is well reflected in this comment of an Inspector of Manufactures in 1791:

> La prospérité du Commerce & de l'industrie doit être une suite nécessaire de la régénération de l'empire; c'est de cette prospérité qu'émane la puissance d'un peuple: ne perdons jamais de vue cette grande vérité, on règne par le commerce, on est détruit par le commerce.[6]

That economic competition had become pivotally important in the relationship between states, and should not be subordinated to other exigencies, was also a view emphasised in many *cahiers*. In an oft-quoted passage from the *cahier* of Le Havre, its merchant-authors noted that

> le commerce est maintenant la première base et le premier objet de toute administration publique bien entendue et bien dirigée; il est le lien des nations comme il est le motif de leurs rivalités. Lui seul est souvent l'objet des guerres; il détermine les alliances; il doit diriger les traités. Ce n'est plus l'Europe sauvage qui se teint de sang pour la stérile possession de marais ou de landes. C'est l'Europe commerçante et riche, qui spécule, qui négocie pour le soutien et l'accroissement d'un commerce qu'elle se dispute.
>
> Oui, Sire, l'administration politique de tous les Etats policés n'est plus que la spéculation de tout ce qui peut favoriser ou étendre leur commerce. Révolution heureuse qui prouve si bien que les souverains ne s'occupent plus que du bonheur de leurs peuples.[7]

---

[5] B. Hyslop, *French Nationalism in 1789*, pp. 168-9.
[6] J. A. Lansel, *Necessité d'un régime pour conserver et faire fleurir le commerce et les manufactures* (1791), p. 1.
[7] See Edna Lemay, 'Une minorité au sein d'une minorité: un banquier et quelques négociants à l'Assemblée constituante 1789-91', *Studies on Voltaire and the Eighteenth Century*, 217 (Oxford, 1983), pp. 56-57.

The problem with the French economy under the Old Regime—according to high officials such as Calonne and Arnould—was basically that it existed not as one single integrated economy, but rather as merely an aggregate of separate economic regions, with multifarious internal barriers that constricted the flow of internal trade. Goods transported from one part of the country to another were subject to a welter of different taxes and tolls, greatly inflating their cost and hence their price at point of sale. For the Farmers-General, who collected the customs tax, there was no distinction made between these internal barriers and those on the frontier. All of this had a number of serious consequences. Firstly, of course, it discouraged the circulation of internal trade, and the forming of mutually profitable trading relationships within France, with the high costs and vexing delays that attended the internal customs regime and its complex bureaucracy.[8] This meant that in many cases foreign goods whose transport costs were negligible by comparison, such as Britain and Holland (and whose costs were sometimes even offset by their own export subsidies), could often compete more effectively in specific internal French markets than goods produced elsewhere in France. Local industry was thus considerably disadvantaged by the artificial inflation of its prices, which lessened demand for their own products while allowing foreigners to profit better from the needs of internal consumption in spite of high external tariffs. Foreign trade and industry were thus stimulated at the expense of that of France, in a market where by rights French goods ought to have received preference, and ought to have been more competitive.

Secondly, these same high costs of internal commerce also significantly hindered the competitiveness of France's exports, adding generally between 6 and 15 per cent to their cost in markets abroad.[9] Added to the relative cheapness with which the goods of Britain and Holland were produced and transported, this proved a severe handicap to France's ability to keep pace with its economic rivals, particularly Britain, whose economic power was rapidly expanding during the second half of the eighteenth century. The arrogance and aggressiveness with which the British were perceived to conduct their trade and their growing superiority in that field were the cause of considerable resentment in France, and felt at both popular and official levels. This resentment had seemed to peak in the period following the introduction

---

[8] Goudard, AP, Vol. 18, 27 August 1790, p. 307.
[9] J. F. Bosher, *The Single Duty Project: A Study of the Movement for a French Customs Union in the Eighteenth Century*, London, 1964, p. 32.

of the 1786 trade treaty with Britain. The *cahiers* of 1789 repeated many of the bitter criticisms that had earlier been made by various corporate bodies and by officials such as Boyetet.

Thirdly, this lack of a single customs regime throughout the country had as a long-term effect a dangerous pattern of uneven economic development. Frontier provinces such as those in eastern and south-eastern France which lay outside the area of the General Farm, and which were exempt also from burdensome indirect taxes such as the *gabelle*, could trade far more profitably with foreign markets than those in the interior, on account of their position and the different rights that they enjoyed. Similarly, the 'Atlantic' provinces with their ports that serviced colonial trade, and those on the Mediterranean such as Marseille, enjoyed on account of their trading privileges, and the volume of trade which they handled, a great prosperity during the eighteenth century. As Arnould was to point out, the overall structure of the economy under the Old Regime was such that these 'peripheral' regions were favoured far above those of the interior. In his report of 1791, he estimated that out of a total of 364 million livres earned through foreign trade in 1789, 228 million of this valuable capital remained in the maritime sections of France, 77 million at the frontiers, 18 and 29 million went to Paris and Lyon respectively, and as little as 11 million flowed back to the interior.[10] What investment capital existed there was steadily drained from these interior regions by various means, but mostly through heavy taxation, all of which led to the growing impoverishment and chronic underdevelopment of the rural hinterland (a reality well attested to by Arthur Young in his famous *Travels in France*). This was a situation that the existence of internal barriers only worsened, by making it harder for the centre to attract and access capital that might otherwise have been used to improve rural infrastructure.[11]

Attempts to encourage trade within the constraints of this existing system had only seemed to accentuate the problem and its inherent inequities. That the frontier and maritime sections were accorded specific financial privileges—such as the creation of free ports—only made the royal government all the more dependent on the far less prosperous interior for much needed tax revenue. Moreover, public expenditure only worsened this inequity; out of a total expenditure of over 630 million livres in 1788, the interior received from the government only 30 million, while the frontier and maritime sections

---

[10] Arnould, *La balance du commerce*, p. 69.
[11] *Ibid.*, p. 81.

together received over 200 million livres.[12] From another angle, efforts to protect French trade and industry also proved to be ultimately counter-productive. High tariffs placed on imported goods such as textiles had only encouraged an enormous smuggling industry, which could not be effectively policed at the frontiers because customs resources had to be spread throughout the country, thus weakening the frontier barriers.[13] Not only then did French industry continue to be challenged by cheaper imports, but this illicit trade also deprived the government of further revenue.

The unification of France as an economic entity in 1789 was thus not just a mere concomitant of the political expression of French nationhood, but also the outcome of recognised economic imperatives. The notion of 'national interest' was assumed from the beginnings of the Constituent Assembly to include the economic interests of France, considered now as one single entity, and the subject thereby of coherently *national* economic objectives. The urgent need for the removal of internal barriers and the creation of a national market was unquestioned in the Assembly, not least because it would free the French people as a whole from many of the vexations and economic burdens that had for so long, and so unnecessarily, oppressed them. As a representative of the Agriculture and Commerce Committee was to declare in the Assembly, "among a free people, commerce must not be enslaved".[14] The benefits were to be both economic and political; the

---

[12] *Ibid.*, p. 78. See also, pp. 77-89: "le sort des peuples de ces sections maritimes ou frontières est donc infiniment moins désadvantageux, toutes considérations pésées, que celui des habitans des sections intérieures du royaume, continuellement tourmentés *par le besoin de faire de l'or*, soit pour satisfaire à leur cotisation de l'impôt, soit pour suffire aux subsidies extraordinaires d'une guerre dont l'objet est souvent le maintien d'une branche du commerce extérieur auquel, pour ainsi dire, ils ne participent point ... Toutes ces circonstances contribuaient donc à les appauvir de plus en plus, et à les dépouiller de leurs foibles capitaux indispensables à 'explorations de leur commerce intérieur".

[13] Bosher, *The Single Duty Project*, p. 164.

[14] AP, Vol. 18, 27 August 1790, p. 307. First coming into operation on 2 September 1789, the Agriculture and Commerce Committee was to number just over forty members, predominantly from the Left, of whom the greatest proportion became Feuillants. For a description of the broad agenda of the Committee, see the *Plan de travaux du comité d'agriculture et de commerce*, AP, Vol. 12, 8 May 1790, pp 435-437. See also, J. J. Guiffrey, 'Les Comités des assemblées révolutionnaires, 1789-1795: le comité d'agriculture et de commerce', *Revue Historique*, 1 (1876), pp. 438-483. See also F. Gerbaux & C. Schmidt (Eds), *Procès-verbaux des Comités d'Agriculture et de Commerce de la Constituante, de la Législative et de la Convention*, 5 Vols. (Paris, 1906-37).

perceived abuses and regional inequities of the old system would be swept away, the subsequent generation of internal trade promoting both national union and national prosperity. Foremost, in this vision of a 'regenerated' French economy, with the unshackling of its true potential and productive capacity, was a France better able to compete *internationally*, and thus better able to assert its national interest in the competitive environment of global commerce.

The Creation of a National Economy and the Debate on a New Tariff

On 29 August 1789, only three days after the 'Declaration of the Rights of Man and Citizen' had been promulgated by the National Assembly, the deputies took the first steps toward this 'regeneration' of the French economy by reaffirming an earlier royal decree of June 1787 freeing the grain trade in France, while also stipulating that, in view of the current subsistance crisis in France, exports of grain out of the country were to be forbidden.[15] The wider issue of trade, agriculture and the French economy was also considered important in the Assembly, and its reform a reasonably high priority, for only another couple of days later the Committee for Agriculture and Commerce was brought into being.[16] This committee (numbering just over forty members) was to be dominated by mostly middle-aged *négociants*, lawyers, and some farmer-proprietors, drawn from all around the country, and most of them from the Third Estate. In terms of political affiliation, most of the members have been identified as, at least initially, members of the Left, many being Jacobin but then subsequently mostly Feuillant in sympathy. They were, however, with the exception of Dupont de Nemours, rather minor figures in the political life of the Assembly, and were neither prominent speakers in the Assembly or in the clubs.[17]

That only a small proportion of these particular deputies served on other committees, or that few seemed to have been prominent in wider revolutionary politics is unsurprising, for the task of this committee, as outlined in the Assembly the following March, was colossal and all-consuming. In communication (and, where necessary, conjunction) with

---

[15] AP, Vol. 8, 29 August 1789, 511.
[16] Ibid., 2 September 1789, 548.
[17] The membership of the Committee also remained more or less unchanged for the entirety of the Constituent Assembly. See Edna Lemay, *Dictionnaire des Constituents, 1789-91* (Paris, 1991), passim.

other relevant committees in the Assembly, the Committee was, throughout its life, to pursue the issue of reform in a variety of areas related to commerce and agriculture. This included continuing to assist in the abolition of feudal dues and privileges, reviewing various commercial treaties and state-sanctioned monopolies, such as the East India Company's monopoly of Far Eastern trade, and considering matters such as how best to exploit France's iron and coal reserves. It also included work on a comprehensive 'Rural Code' governing the organisation of French agriculture, as well as the introduction not only of a nationally uniform system of weights and measures, but also of a new system of state administration in the area of trade and manufacturing.[18]

Of all the objectives subsequently pursued by the Constituents' Committee for Agriculture and Commerce, none was considered more important than the issue of customs and tariffs. Early on, the Committee and the Assembly at large had signalled its determination to unify the French economy and create, for the first time, a genuinely national market by removing internal barriers to trade. At this point, the pivotal question before the Assembly, and the Committee, was this: having resolved to remove such internal barriers, how then would it be best to maximise France's advantages in *external* trade, and establish a basis for durable prosperity? Ought they to re-establish a protective regime in the tradition of Colbert, or give way to the invocations of the Physiocrats and commit France to a regime of free trade?

The Committee reported back to the Assembly with a legislative project on this issue on 27 August 1790. Presented by the deputy Goudard, and the work of himself, Roussillou and Fontenay (all members of the Left), and with the contribution of a number of experts long experienced in this issue, this report outlined their policy proposals in some detail. First of all, their position on the unification of the French economy was clear. There was an imperative need, Goudard affirmed, to suppress internal customs barriers on account of their pernicious effects on French trade, industry and agriculture, and their crippling of French competitiveness. After all, Holland, Britain, Russia and the majority of other European states did not have to suffer such constrictions on their

---

[18] These tasks formed some of the myriad of often urgent tasks, beyond the simple framing of the constitution, that had been forced on the Constituent Assembly by the effective collapse of the Royal Government's administrative capacities during 1789, and which had necessitated the formation of a series of specialised policy committees. See T. Tackett, *Becoming a Revolutionary: The Deputies of the French National Assembly and the Emergence of a Revolutionary Culture (1789-1790)* (Princeton, 1996), 211-239.

internal trade, so why should France, particularly when its consequences were so serious?[19]

On the question of foreign trade, however, the Committee's position was rather more ambivalent, an ambivalence reflective of the differing pressures with which the deputies were faced. On the one hand, as already noted, there had been widespread and popular condemnation of the 1786 commercial treaty, particularly from manufacturing interests in France and their associated officialdom, most of which wished to see the treaty either repealed or substantially modified, and who were generally antagonistic to the idea of free trade.

On the other hand, political expediency increasingly demanded that this commercial treaty be left in place more on less unchanged (at least until it expired in 1797). In the early months of 1790, a deputation of the Agriculture and Commerce Committee had conferred with the Ministers Montmorin, the comte de La Luzerne, and the Controleur-Général Lambert with regard to the numerous complaints about the treaty and its supposedly disastrous effects for French manufacturing. Montmorin, in particular, warned the deputation that since Britain attached a great importance to the commercial treaty, any moves in the Assembly to abrogate it might provoke an untimely 'rupture' with that country, which would likely result in war.[20] Now, at the end of August, with the Anglo-Spanish crisis still in the balance, and with Mirabeau inveighing against any move towards a premature isolationism, the Agriculture and Commerce Committee, together with the Ministers, would have been even more careful to avoid any undue provocation of the British government, lest this increase the prospects for a devastating foreign war.

The resultant policy position of the Committee can be seen as an attempt to straddle or even reconcile these contradictory internal and external pressures. While stating that a new general tariff should in theory allow no exceptions, Goudard nonetheless made it clear that all existing commercial treaties between France and other states, such as with Switzerland, Great Britain, Russia, and the Hanseatic towns, would continue to be upheld (at least in so far as they remained extant).[21] However, Goudard also made it clear that by no means should the economic liberalism of 1786 commercial treaty with Britain serve as any guide to the formation of a new general tariff. The terms of the 1786 treaty would thus indeed be truly exceptional for, in a passage

---

[19] *Ibid.*, p. 306.
[20] Untitled Note, 25 February 1790, AAE-CP-Angleterre–572, ff. 176-77.
[21] AP, Vol. 18, 27 August 1790, p. 309.

which signalled a determined retreat from its economic liberalism, Goudard announced that it was imperative that French industry be otherwise protected from cheap foreign imports.[22] Free internal trade in France was therefore to be complemented by a policy of external protectionism, whose watchwords would henceforth be "liberty, protection and security".[23]

This protectionism, Goudard argued, was indispensible to France's economic development. As he explained, it only reflected the realities of European commerce, following in the footsteps of major powers such as Britain, Russia, Prussia and Spain. Indeed, for Britain, a rigorously enforced protectionist policy had been, he claimed, the secret of its economic success.[24] Furthermore, what development French industry had attained over the century was, in the first place, largely attributable to the introduction by Colbert of protective tariffs, a policy which Goudard praised and to which he rendered homage.[25] Colbert's frustrated vision of a nationally integrated and protected economy would now then finally be fulfilled. Patriotism and the general interest, Goudard declared, demanded such a policy.[26] To do the opposite, and unilaterally remove France's external barriers, as some were suggesting, would only advantage her rivals,[27] and thus leave France utterly vulnerable in a ruthlessly competitive world.

With the nationalisation of the customs service (from a private profit-making corporate licencee to a direct government agency), the purpose of the tariff system was deliberately transformed. Under the aegis of the farmers-general, whose responsibility extended little beyond their own profit, tariffs had been primarily a means of raising revenue. Now it was to be seen as primarily a method of economic *control* employed directly by government, allowing them a greater capacity to plan and pursue national economic objectives. The redeployment of customs resources to the frontiers would make the service far more

---

[22] Both the Agriculture and Commerce Committee and the Interior Ministry were to receive numerous submissions from various parts of France testifying, among many other complaints and exhortations, to the allegedly damaging effects on French manufacturing of the 1786 Eden Treaty. See, for example, 'A nos seigneurs de l'Assemblée Nationale', from the town of Beauvais, 9 December 1789, AN-F.12-652, No. 164. See also Gerbaux and Schmidt, *Procès-verbaux*, Vol. 1, pp. 300, 464, 738, Vol. 2, p. 136.
[23] AP, Vol. 18, 27 August 1790, p. 308.
[24] *Ibid.*, p. 314.
[25] *Ibid.*, p. 305.
[26] *Ibid.*, p. 304.
[27] *Ibid.*, p. 308.

effective in regulating the flow of trade, strengthening the actual barriers and greatly diminishing the possibilities for smuggling. Certain goods could be admitted or prohibited according to whether or not their entry was perceived to be beneficial or harmful to the development of national industry, the particular tariff being able to be adjusted whenever it was thought necessary or when changing circumstances demanded it.

It was a measure of the expectations of this policy's outcomes that the committee was happily prepared to forego the revenue that would be lost from the abolition of internal barriers, for it was anticipated that this short-term sacrifice would eventually reap enormous rewards. The limiting of imports would retain currency in France, which would be then rechannelled into a reinvigorated and sizable internal market, maximising national self-sufficiency. As Goudard asserted,

> Dans un moment où nos manufactures sont repoussées par presque toutes les nations, il est d'une sage politique de subvenir, autant que les circonstances peuvent nous le permettre, à notre propre consommation ...[28]

The expansion in national wealth that would accrue from this, and the development of national industry that it would stimulate, could, it was thus assumed, only augment the economic power of the French nation, strengthening its position vis-à-vis rival trading states.

Such proposals were not, of course, to pass without controversy, especially since their protectionism sharply contradicted the fundamentals of Physiocratic thinking, the dominant economic doctrine of the time in 'enlightened' circles. In response to Goudard's report, a Parisian merchant (and *suppléant* to the National Assembly), Jean-Joseph-Chrysostome Farçot, published a work highly critical of 'prohibitionist' policies in general, and of the Agriculture and Commerce Committee in particular.[29] Evidently a student of Adam Smith, Farçot sought to contest the presumed fundamentals of economic thinking that had in the past been the basis for 'prohibitionist' (and what Smith would have called 'Mercantilist') policies, and which had seen economic development as more or less a zero-sum affair. France was, he argued in this work, only one component of an *international* economy in which the participant

---

[28] *Ibid.*, p. 314.

[29] Joseph-Jean-Chrysostome Farçot, *Questions Constitutionelles sur le commerce et l'industrie, et projet d'un impôt direct, sur les commerçans & gens à l'industrie, en remplacement des impôts quelconques sur le commerce & l'industrie, proposés à l'Assemblée Nationale par des Négocians François* (Paris, 1790).

states, with the growing volume of trade, had become increasingly interdependent. To hope to maximise one's profit by maximising the other's loss was therefore short-sighted and ultimately self-defeating, since each state depended on the other for the money to buy its surplus goods. It would only be through, rather, a *mutual* exchange and profitability that states could prosper and expand their economies, for it was the flow of commerce itself that was crucial to prosperity, not the mere accumulation of capital. Thus, Farçot concluded,

> s'il est démontré que la prospérité des nations s'est toujours proportionnée à l'étendue qu'elles ont donnée à ce commerce, la conséquence nécessaire, évidente & incontestable, doit être qu'il faut donner à ce commerce toute l'étendue possible, & par conséquent adopter franchement, pleinement & absolument les principes de la plus entière liberté.[30]

Farçot hence regarded no form or level of protectionism as either legitimate or beneficial to the economic development of France or its neighbours, who would now share peacefully with France in the benefits of a generally increasing wealth.

The author then moved on in the same work to combat specific arguments used by Goudard to justify the protectionist measures proposed on 27 August. Attacking, firstly, the use of Britain as an example of the supposed benefits of protectionism, he praised Smith's work *The Wealth of Nations*, and put forward its argument that the dynamic rise of British commerce and industry had occurred largely in spite of mercantilist policies, rather than because of them. Secondly, he defended the 1786 commercial treaty with Britain, denying that it was in any way responsible, as some had obviously alleged, for economic crises in France that may have precipitated the Revolution. Indeed, the widespread and popular belief that the treaty had quickly opened the gates to a devastating 'flood' of British manufactured goods onto the French domestic market was, he argued, simply misplaced, or even malign. British imports during 1787 were not, he reported, as great as those coming from Austrian Flanders, nor were they any greater than in previous years (taking into account the regular importing of contraband goods). The treaty was in fact, he concluded, merely coincidental to a crisis that had had much more to do with the wider effects of the royal government's "financial embarrassments" than with the supposed ill-effects of freer trade.[31]

---

[30] *Ibid.*, p. 138.
[31] *Ibid.*, p. 154.

Finally, the author directly criticised the committee, alleging that it had been poorly informed when making pronouncements on some tariffs, and further alleging that in its ignorance it had merely followed 'blindly' its own protectionist inclinations.[32] His greatest opprobrium, however, was reserved for the *députés permanents des manufactures et du commerce de France*, a corporate body with whom the Committee had consulted on the question of the tariff. This body, he claimed, had, in supporting measures of protectionism, no authority to speak for the true interests of the nation, being dominated by private and particular interests. Only the National Assembly could legitimately represent the general interest of the nation, and which the author hoped, would now act in favour of the national interest by extending the vaunted principles of liberty to the arena of foreign trade.[33]

The committee, however, plainly rejected these criticisms. A follow-up decree and report of 30 November 1790 demonstrated their ongoing committment to a policy of strict protectionism. Presented again by Goudard, the report reiterated and reaffirmed the principal points made earlier in the decree of 27 August, and in the legislation introduced on 30-31 October. France, he declared, had indeed offered in its new constitution a great example of liberty and the rights of nations to all those peoples elsewhere subsisting under more or less despotic regimes. However, to then extend this 'complete liberty'—alone, and without reciprocity with other nations—to the area of commerce would, he insisted, be

> une fausse mesure pour une nation dont le système politique est aujourd'hui d'être une puissance purement agricole et commerçante, dont la splendeur dépend des progrès de son industrie, qui doit accroître sa population, la force de l'Etat, et assurer la prosperité de l'agriculture, qui en est la véritable richesse.[34]

---

[32] *Ibid.*, p. 163-164.

[33] *Ibid.*, p. 163, 200-202. Here Farçot was no doubt referring to the Comité des Députés Extraordinaires des Manufactures et du Commerce de France, an ad-hoc body representative of French commercial interests. The Comité had initially sought admission to the Assembly as deputies, but this was refused. Instead, they were granted admission to the Assembly's debates, and were allowed to attend the otherwise closed sessions of the Assembly's Committees, where they came to play an influential role. See J. Letaconnoux, 'Le Comité des Députés Extraordinaires des Manufactures et du Commerce de France et l'oeuvre économique de l'Assemblée Constituante (1789-1791)', *Annales Révolutionnaires*, 6 (1913), pp. 149-208.

[34] AP, Vol. 21, 30 November 1790, p. 135.

While lauding the "sublime doctrine" of unlimited free trade, Goudard nonetheless asserted that this was not at present a realistic option, that it would endanger French prosperity and economic security. If it benefitted "true cosmopolitans" like commercial speculators then this was neither here nor there—only national interest ought to be considered by the National Assembly.[35] Moreover, he reminded the deputies, the newly instituted tariffs were to be considered chiefly as protective devices, rather than as simply serving the interests of the Treasury. To this end Goudard went on to announce a series of prohibitions and prohibitive tariffs that would fulfil this objective, a policy stance that was seconded by Malouet, who declared that these measures were necessary on account of the "rivalité du commerce des nations".[36]

These measures, and the assumptions behind them, were, however, immediately challenged by Boislandry, a merchant, and leftist deputy from Paris, in what was evidently a heated debate in the Assembly.[37] Boislandry's objections were both political and economic, and strongly echoed those expressed by Farçot. While the great Physiocrats of the mid-eighteenth century—Quesnay, Mercier, Mirabeau *père*—had believed that internal free trade should be complemented by a central, authoritarian government, Boislandry, in contrast, appeared convinced, as had Farçot, of the strong connection between political liberty, economic liberty and increased prosperity.[38] There were, Boislandry argued, two types of trade policies followed in Europe, that of protectionism and free trade, and, he claimed, it was the less *politically* free nations that tended toward protectionism; the ones with greater freedoms tended toward free trade and also allegedly were the more prosperous. This protectionism was, in his view, inimical in two ways to the preservation of a French liberty so recently gained. Firstly, the rigorous customs regime proposed by Goudard's sub-committee, with its

---

[35] 'Le Comité d'agriculture et de commerce", said Goudard, with some condescension, "a admiré cette théorie, qui repose sur le liberté indéfinie; elle honore ceux qui s'en sont déclarés comme les apôtres, et qui prêchent cette sublime doctrine au monde commerçant; mais il ne lui a paru sage de s'en faire les disciplines uniques, et de donner un exemple qui ne serait point imité, parce que ce serait prononcer la destruction de notre industrie." *Ibid.*, p. 135.

[36] *Ibid.*, p. 137.

[37] Lemay (Ed.), *Dictionnaire des Constituants*, p. 108. Boislandry is described as being on the list of very active members of the left. Like many members of the Jacobin Club, he became a Feuillant in July 1791.

[38] In this sense, Boislandry may have been more influenced by the ideas of Adam Smith than those of the Physiocrats.

domiciliary visits, and all its powers of search, seizure and punishment, accustomed a nation to slavery and thus subverted its liberty.[39] Only 'arbitrary' governments or those of nations prepared to sacrifice their liberty, so as to gain some temporary advantage over their neighbours, would follow such a policy.

This led on to Boislandry's second point. Given that aggressive economic rivalry was the source of so many international conflicts, a policy of high protectionism was, he believed, inconsistent with (or even directly contradictory to) France's recent renunciation of offensive warfare and commitment to peaceful relations, a declaration which had been applauded all over Europe. The deputy thus concluded by repeating Farçot's charge that not only was a system of prohibitive tariffs "un attentat au droit des gens" ("un crime de lèze-societé" [sic], as Farçot had also asserted), but it was also tantamount to a declaration of war.[40]

For Boislandry, as for Farçot, that such a policy was imprudent was also a question of plain economics. Such a high degree of protectionism would only provoke the other major economic powers of Europe to respond in kind. The consequences of this would be disastrous: French industry would be excluded from the export markets essential to its prosperity and future growth. The whole policy of 'beggar thy neighbour' and of hoarding precious metals was thus, paradoxically, harmful to the French economy. As he commented,

L'accroissement du numéraire n'est désirable en France que parce qu'il procure les moyens d'étendre plusieurs branches d'industrie; mais il faut qu'il soit proportionné à l'accroissement du numéraire chez les autres nations, afin de ne point altérer les rapports que nous avons avec elles. Sans cette condition, l'augmentation des métaux précieux serait plus nuisible qu'utile.[41]

This was not to say that France, as one part of a system of interdependent national economies, could not, however, actually

---

[39] A.P., Vol. 21, 30 November 1790, p. 138.
[40] *Ibid.* p. 141, 143; Farçot, *Questions Constitutionelles*, p. 129. For Farçot, the positive effects on international relations of a general system of free trade was obvious: "Il ne point surprenant qu'avec des principes plus généraux, le commerce libre rende les rapports politiques, entre les nations, infiniment plus faciles, diminue les causes de guerre entre elles" . *Ibid.*, p. 130.
[41] *Ibid.*, p. 143. In attempting to counter Goudard's assertion that it was the preponderance of protectionism in Europe that necessitated a similar policy in France, Boislandry grossly overestimated the existing prospects for free trade in Europe. Europe was not quite yet the "one vast republic" that he claimed it to be, inspite of its growing economic interdependencies.

increase its *relative* economic power if protectionism was removed. Indeed, France, blessed with so many natural advantages and with its geographic position in Europe, would be, Boislandry believed, the nation best able to profit from international free trade. It would have nothing to fear from the industry of other nations, for

> Aujourd'hui que la nation française jouit de la Constitution le plus libre et le plus juste de l'univers, son industrie ne tardera pas à surpasser celle de tous les peuples du monde; mais ce serait ralentir ses progrès que d'établir des lois prohibitives qui, en excitant la jalousie et le mécontentment de nos voisins, les avertiraient de porter les mêmes lois contre nous. Vous éviterez ces dangers en laissant une libre concurrence à toutes les nations étrangères; par cette concurrence vous stimulerez le génie national, et vous donnerez aux talents une nouvelle émulation et une plus grande énergie.[42]

Boislandry was hence no less interested than Goudard in seeing a relative and substantial increase in France's economic power. Though they understood the dynamics of the international economy somewhat differently, both saw it as essentially competitive, and saw that the Revolution had a positive role in greatly improving French competitiveness. The belief in free trade here thus by no means excluded a degree of economic nationalism. Boislandry was even more explicit than Goudard in identifying who their archrival in this affair would be, namely England. This country, he claimed, had been the initial source of this policy of aggressive protectionism, and had as a partial result of this enjoyed a prosperity far in excess of what its natural resources would have otherwise allowed.[43] Hence, while Farçot had suggested that free trade would make the French and British nations together "les premières de l'univers", cementing their union and friendship, Boislandry's outlook was rather more combative. It was now time to cut England down to size, by taking back from it the share of trade that it had, he suggested, illegitimately acquired. A general policy of free trade would achieve this end, for, as he argued, "ce système noble et généreux, en augmentant la prospérité de la France, frapperait d'un coup mortel le commerce et la puissance de l'Angleterre".[44] France

---

[42] *Ibid.*, p. 142.
[43] *Ibid.*, p. 138.
[44] *Ibid.*, p. 143. In assuming the intrinsic economic superiority of France over England (particularly in the production of certain goods, such as silks, lace and fine textiles), Boislandry thus believed, as Dupont had earlier professed in mémoires to the Ministry, that the 1786 Commercial Treaty was ultimately to France's benefit. AP, Vol. 21, 30 November 1790, pp. 145-146.

would hence regain the economic supremacy destiny had owed to her and which the British had stolen long ago. As *the* predominant economic superpower, she would become once again the arbiter of nations:

> les succès de nos rivaux depuis un siècle leur ont procuré, avec la prépondérance qu'ils avaient acquise en Europe, le sceptre des modes et des usages; ils ont usé de leur supériorité avec hauteur et en despotes. Votre Constitution et la fraternité à laquelle vous avez appelé toutes les nations vous rendra ce sceptre, et vous vous en servirez en amis et en frères.[45]

To do otherwise, and thereby only imitate the British, would simply turn potential friends on the continent into enemies, enemies which France could ill-afford economically. Britain's own alienation of Europe during the war of American independence here served, in this respect, as an instructive example of what to avoid.[46]

Boislandry's connection of protectionism with arbitrary and aggressive government here was certainly controversial, and an inference that would have been fiercely contested by many deputies (Roussillou, in his report on the Levant trade, was even to suggest that French protectionism actually *followed on* from the principles of liberty and equality).[47] The campaign led by this deputy against the general introduction of prohibitive measures was, however, at least partially successful. On 1 December 1790, and more fully on 22 January 1791, Goudard announced a significant lowering of the tariff level on a wide range of imported goods.[48]

Clearly, however, this was a victory less for the advocates of free trade than for those of a moderate protectionism. Although on 1 December and 22 January Goudard declined to specify particular reasons for the revision of the committee's earlier recommendations for higher tariffs on many goods, one may surmise that the committee, when joined in its deliberations on this question by the Taxation Committee, had found itself finally persuaded by arguments that prohibitively high tariffs on a wide range of goods would prove both self-defeating in their consequences, and dangerously provocative to foreign powers. This did not mean, however, that the deputies of the Agriculture and Commerce

---

[45] *Ibid.*, p. 146.
[46] *Ibid.*, p. 138.
[47] Roussillou, *Rapport du comité d'agriculture et de commerce concernant le commerce de Levant*, AP, Vol. 28, 21 July, 1791, p. 493.
[48] AP, Vol. 21, 1 December 1790, pp. 173-175, Vol. 22, 22 January 1791, pp. 425-434.

Committee were less staunch in their opposition to a policy of 'unlimited' free trade being introduced in France. They determined, in fact, that while most locally produced goods would be protected only so far as to give them an edge in domestic and foreign markets, some foreign imports, particular coal and silks, would continue to be subject to prohibitions as the Committee had initially proposed. France's developing industries would thus be given as much, but only so much, protection as they individually required in order to make them genuinely competitive, and hence promote their continuing and long-term development.[49]

As earlier noted, economic imperatives were not always the only factors taken into account in the Assembly's discussions on external tariffs. Some sensitivity to the political and diplomatic consequences of tariff legislation was shown by the deputies, for example, in the debate on the admission of fish oil from the United States. On 24 January 1791, Dupont de Nemours defended the proposal (in a follow-up decree to that of Goudard's on 22 January) that American fish oil be exempt from a blanket prohibition on the importation of this commodity, asserting that this was important to French strategic interests. Not only would the exemption be helpful in preserving good Franco-U.S. relations, but it should also prevent, he argued, experienced American seamen from being lured to Halifax (in present-day Canada), where they could be conscripted, in time of war, into the ranks of the British navy.[50] Despite the reservations of Begouen and Malouet, the Assembly clearly agreed with this argument, voting to allow imports of fish oil

---

[49] That the Assembly ultimately opted for a more moderate tariff regime has generally, as the historian John Bosher has noted, been credited to Boislandry (who had suggested in his speech that if the deputies feared that "une trop grande liberté subitement accordée n'occasionnât à notre commerce quelques secousses toujours fâcheuses", then they should at least "proscrire pour jamais le système prohibitif et à n'admettre que des droits modéré", *Ibid.*, p. 144. As Bosher has suggested, Boislandry's own role in pegging back the proposed level of tariff protection may have been overstated, at least as it pertains to his free trade convictions. Boislandry's most significant source of advice and information was in fact Mahy de Corméré, an old regime bureaucrat, reformer, and believer in moderate protectionism (and who had acted also as an advisor to the tariff sub-committee), who had counselled a return to the moderate tariff proposals produced by a commission of the Royal Government in 1787. Bosher, *The Single Duty Project*, p. 160. See Guillaume-François de Mahy, baron de Corméré, *Situation exacte des finances à l'époque de 1er janvier 1792, ou Lettre ... à M. le président & à MM. les députés composant le comité des contributions publiques, de l'Assemblée nationale* (Nantes 1792), pp. 13-15.

[50] AP, Vol. 22, 24 January 1791, p. 473.

from the United States.[51] The deputies thus recognised that there were occasions when diplomatic or strategic imperatives clashed with national economic objectives, and when concessions had to be made in the name of overall national interest.[52]

Enhancing Competitiveness: Subsidies and Exports

If both the exponents of protectionism and free trade in the Assembly desired an expansion of French economic power, both, similarly, recognised that this required an expansion of France's exports (regardless of their different views on imports). Just how this export growth was to be achieved was a subject on which the Constituent Assembly received many suggestions. It was first of all assumed that the abolition of internal barriers would make French goods generally more price competitive in foreign markets, but what further measures could be introduced to bolster France's export trade? One way, generally accepted, in which France could strengthen its commercial competitiveness was to procure and encourage industrial mechanisation,

---

[51] *Ibid.*, p. 475. This exemption may also have been seen as necessary to offset the greater competitive edge allowed to the British through the lower tariffs on their imports to France of fish oil that had earlier been struck in the Eden Treaty of 1786. See Jefferson's letter of 6 December 1787 to Montmorin on this point, AAE-CP-Angleterre-562, ff. 175-176.

[52] The relationship between economic and strategic imperatives had also been strongly emphasised by a number of speakers during the debate on war and peace in May 1790. When the issue of the Spanish Alliance flared up once again in the Assembly in August 1790, two of the Constituent's noted specialists on economic affairs, Dupont de Nemours and Le Couteulx de Cantelau, forcefully repeated this emphasis, warning of the economic consequences to France of a failure to support Spain in her current disagreement with Britain. Noting that Spain and her colonies constituted for France a vitally important market, particularly for her textiles, Dupont reiterated the argument that to jeopardise this valuable trade would be to "ruiner nos manufactures, et réduire à la mendicité plusieurs millions de Français industrieux". For his part, Le Couteulx urged that the Diplomatic Committee (which, he noted, contained no merchants among its members), "imite cependant l'exemple des Anglais qui ne s'occupent essentiellement d'un traité que sous les rapports qui peuvent être utile à leur commerce, à leur industrie et à leur navigation et qui, par cette conduite encore plus que par le succès de leurs armes, se sont élèvés depuis un demi-siècle au plus haut degré de prosperité ...". This, he argued, was in contrast to the example of France's former government, which, he alleged (in an obvious reference to the much reviled Anglo-French commercial treaty of 1786), had disdained the views and protests of merchants even when negotiating commercial treaties. AP, Vol. 17, 3 August 1790 (annex), pp. 583-602.

particularly in industries, such as textiles, that had hitherto demonstrated some resistance to the introduction and development of new labour-saving technology. A concomitant of this was that France foster—through subsidies—the development of its own hitherto underdeveloped coal-mining industry, to provide a reliable and cheap source of fuel for domestic and industrial consumption, rather than contribute to the development of their rivals' industrial resources.[53]

Another measure on which there seemed to be general agreement was that of subsidies and encouragements to other French industries, such as that of the fisheries. Goudard, Roussillou and Delattre joined others in urging subsidies for such industries as cod fishing off Newfoundland, or for French whaling, recognising the need of the French economy, and national security, that these fleets both financially, and quite literally, remain afloat.[54] For Roussillou, it was partly through such encouragements to agriculture, industry and navigation, that England,

> dont la population est si inférieure à la nôtre, est parvenue à porter son commerce à un si haut et si étonnant degré de prospérité, et a réussi non seulement à nous écarter de tous les marchés étrangers où notre concurrence pouvait lui être nuisible, mais même à introduire en France les objets de son industrie.[55]

Even Boislandry, in his speech of 30 November, had declared his support for such subsidies (in his case, as a way of offsetting the removal of tariff protection), stating that "il assurerait à [France's]

---

[53] In opposition to those such as Boislandry who wished France to lower its import duties to negligible levels, the merchant deputy Begouen implored the Assembly to follow the example of Britain, in regard to both its commercial and industrial development: "Commence par rendre votre industrie supérieure à toutes les industries qui vous avoisinent, avant de vous proposer de faire tomber devant vous des barrières conservatrices de votre main-d'oeuvre. Encouragez, multipliez de tous côtés l'usage des machines anglaises; prodiguez les primes à l'exploitation de vos mines de charbon de terre; vous serez toujours, comme vous êtes, une nation peu industrieuse". AP, Vol. 21, 1 December 1790, p. 172.

[54] Goudard, *Rapport présenté à l'Assemblée Nationale, au nom de Comité d'Agriculture et du Commerce, sur la situation du commerce extérieur de la France pendant la Révolution, en 1789* (Paris 1791). pp. 8-9. See also the *Rapport de Vergniaud sur l'état des travaux de l'Assemblée Nationale Constituente au 30 Septembre 1791* (Paris, 1791), note xiii, p. 21.

[55] Roussillou, *Rapport du comité d'agriculture et de commerce sur les encouragements pécuniaires à accorder à l'agriculture, aux manufactures, à la navigation et au commerce,* AP, Vol. 23, 7 March 1791, pp. 712.

industrie et à son agriculture les moyens de marcher toujours d'un pas égal avec les autres nations, et même de les devancer".[56]

Another way of further improving France's balance of trade would be to develop a whole new range of industries for export. For example, a combined report of the Committees of Finance, Agriculture and Commerce urged in 1791 that the French tanning industry, which had up to then been exporting very little, should be developed to the point where it could compete effectively in foreign markets with British leathergoods, lessening the latter's market share.[57] Yet another method of increasing exports would be to explore more vigorously the opportunities for expanding French commerce into areas where previously it had been weak, such as in the Baltic, where the British and Dutch dominated.[58] Where French traders already maintained a strong presence, such as in the Levant, it was asserted that efforts should be made there to shore up their position, and to remove any impediments to trade that might have remained as a legacy of the old regime. Otherwise, argued Roussillou in a report in July 1791, the protectionist measures of the previous government ought to be continued. The policies of the new regime should even allow France to trounce its trading rivals in the Mediterrenean, diminishing considerably their share of a Levant trade which Marseille was by far the best situated to exploit, but had been hampered in this by the 'vices' of the old regime. "Heureusement", declared Roussillou,

> la nouvelle Constitution de l'Empire réparera les torts de l'ancien régime. La protection que vous voulez accorder au commerce, la liberté des opinions religieuses et des cultes, la sûreté des personnes et des propriétés garanties par vos lois, sont autant d'attraits qui vous assurent un accroissement considérable dans la part que vous avez dans le commerce que l'Europe fait avec le Levant; la nouvelle Constitution vous présente la plus douce, la plus belle perspective dans l'avenir; la France libre deviendra l'entrepôt des richesses étrangères,

---

[56] A.P., Vol. 21, 30 November 1790, p. 145.
[57] Hell, *Rapport sur l'état de la Tannerie et de la Corroirie en France, et sur les moyens de les régénérer; fait à l'Assemblée Nationale, au nom des comités d'Agriculture et du commerce et des finances* (Paris, 1791), p. 7.
[58] Here the assistance of the goverment would be crucial. Forge, *Mémoire tendant à l'extension du Commerce extérieur, à la sûreté du Commerce intérieur, et à l'accroissement de la marine militaire, présenté par M. de Forge, Chevalier, ancien Ecuyer de main du Roi*, n.d., pp. 5-7. It did not escape this writer that better access to Russian naval stores would also have significant strategic benefits. See p. 22.

l'asile des commerçants éclairés, le rendez-vous de tous les artistes, le point central de tous les commerces.[59]

A number of other writers and deputies also promoted the prospects for *entrepôt* trade in France, from which, they asserted, the country would greatly benefit. For Boislandry, this had been the principal means by which he had suggested that France destroy the commercial power of England;[60] while for another, a concerted movement of French merchants into the Baltic and northern trade could eventually see France prosper as the principal *entrepôt* between the great markets of the north and those south of Europe, a position that up to then Holland had held to some degree.[61]

Delattre and the Future of French Navigation

In the final days of the Constituent Assembly, the deputy Delattre presented a report on behalf of the Committees of the Navy and Agriculture and Commerce, on the subject of a French 'Navigation Act'. This report containing an elaborate summary of many of the themes found in the committee's earlier reports and decrees, and espoused in the Assembly at large: a staunch commitment to the protection of French agriculture and industry, a trenchant critique of 'free-trading' doctrines (in the context of external trade), and an expectation of the future expansion and greater competitiveness of the French commercial economy.

Delattre began his report with an affirmation of the as yet unrealised potential of the French economy, asserting, among all the 'precious' branches of this economy worthy of protection, the particular importance and complexity of France's maritime commerce. Exhorting the Assembly to foreswear any unbecoming "arrogance", he nonetheless insisted that neither should France continue to accept a subordinate position when it came to this trade. England, with its enormous navy and enterprising merchant fleet, had, he said, grown accustomed to believing that she held a kind of sovereignty over the world's oceans, a situation that could and ought not to go unchallenged. France was, after all, larger in population than England, richer in terms of landed resources, and surely her equal in audacity and ingenuity: "Pourquoi", he

---

[59] AP, Vol. 28, 21 July 1791, p. 492.
[60] *Ibid.*, Vol. 21, 30 November 1790, p. 143.
[61] Forge, *Mémoire tendant à l'extension du Commerce extérieur*, p. 12.

thus asked, "ne marcherions-nous pas sur la même ligne dans la carrière ouverte à l'ambition de tous les peuples?".[62]

The way was now open to learn from the success of British trade and navigation. In this, however, Delattre was quick to warn against the distractions provided by the 'dangerous' and theoretical doctrine of unlimited free trade, which, he said, had become something of a religion among certain elements of the Assembly, particularly among its Taxation Committee. While not eschewing 'theory' as such, he beseeched the Assembly to follow nonetheless the wiser counsels of "experience and practice", remarking on the necessity of the new and rigorous customs regime to the development and future prosperity of French industry.[63] In language suggestive of the competitive or even combative nature of international commerce, he described the agents of France's new "douanes nationales", this "rempart" of French trade, as no longer "les satellites du fisc qui dévorait tout, mais [...] les soldats du commerce, la sentinelle de l'industrie, les gardiens enfin de nos manufactures".[64] In the first case, he said, while unlimited free trade might be an ultimate and worthy goal to which one might aspire, French industry was as yet in certain respects insufficiently strong to withstand such a regime.

In the second case, he implored the Assembly to follow carefully the example of France's neighbours and rivals. Among these, he asserted, one should not properly count the small trading states whose prosperity did indeed derive from a large degree of free trade, but rather, those more extensive states with substantial agricultural and industrial concerns. "Jetez les yeux sur toutes les grandes nations qui vous environnent, sur ces nations agricoles, industrieuses, qui produisent et qui créent; là", he declared, "vous trouverez le régime prohibitif". Foremost among these states, he declared furthermore, was Britain, "cette île de liberté", which he said, "a peut-être porté la science du commerce au plus haut degré d'élévation qu'on puisse atteindre". This most flourishing of states, he argued, in vigorously protecting its colonies, fisheries and especially its ports from unwanted foreign incursions, was nearly "cuirassée de prohibitions". How then could the 'économistes' thus declaim that such protectionism was 'fatal', when its outcomes were so obviously and demonstrably impressive?[65]

---

[62] AP, Vol. 31, 22 September 1791, p. 203.
[63] *Ibid.*, p. 204.
[64] *Ibid.*
[65] *Ibid.*, p. 205.

Central to the success, and rapid expansion over the century, of British trade and navigation, was, Delattre then argued, the British 'Navigation Act' first enacted in 1651. To provide France with a similar Act would be, he thus proposed, "un de beaux présents que l'Assemblée nationale puisse faire à l'Empire".[66] In short, such an act would entail the exclusion of foreign or at least third-party shipping from French overseas commerce, and an exclusion moreover of all ships of foreign construction from the French navy and merchant marine.[67] This, he asserted, in encouraging the growth of French maritime resources, would remedy the current situation wherein France, providing only a portion of its own freight-carrying needs, was effectively subsidising rival maritime establishments, and thus nourishing the very same seamen that would most likely be used against France in time of war. Following the dictum already espoused by numerous other speakers in the Assembly, Delattre put it in simple terms:

> Pour posséder une marine, il faut avoir des vaisseaux et il faut les construire: il faut avoir des matelots; et, pour s'en donner, il faut se livrer à la pêche: la pêche est le berceau de toute marine; elle force à la construction, elle forme les meilleurs et les plus intrépides marins.[68]

In proposing this 'Navigation Act' Delattre did however acknowledge the reservations of certain port-towns, specifically Bordeaux, Marseille

---

[66] That Britain owed its prosperity and formidable navy to its Navigation Acts was, Delattre argued, a fact universally known and recognised, particularly among *commerçants* and especially among the British themselves, including even Adam Smith, who was otherwise famed for his detestation of commercial protectionism. *Ibid.*

[67] The general principal that all ships in the French maritime establishment should actually be built in France had already been accepted by the Assembly, proposed in a decree presented by Roussillou on behalf of the Committee on Agriculture and Commerce on 4 March 1791. AP, Vol. 23, 4 March 1791, p. 639.

[68] "Un nation commerçante," he went on, "une nation qui possède des colonies, une nation qui doit envoyer ses escadres dans toutes les mers, et porter des forces dans toutes les parties du monde, ne doit pas acheter, même à très bon marché, des navires: elle ne le doit pas, parce que la construction forme des chantiers et ses magasins, qui sont indispensables pour la guerre, parce que la construction forme des charpentiers, des forgerons, des calfats, des poulieurs, des voiliers, une infinité d'ouvriers de tout genre qu'on ne peut faire sortir de terre au moment du besoin, qu'on ne peut emprunter de ses voisins pour la guerre, qu'il faut enfin, dans ces temps malheureux, trouver chez soi pour n'être pas à la merci de ses ennemis et même de ses alliés". AP, Vol. 31, 22 September 1791, p. 207.

and La Rochelle; they feared that French merchant fleets would not suffice to carry all French trade. He insisted that any shortfall in French shipping could in the interim be provided by the trading partner with whom France was directly dealing.[69] Similarly, on the question of the sufficiency of materials for naval construction, Delattre noted that both Britain and Holland had long been dependent for the bulk of their own naval materials on overseas sources (such as the Baltic region), and that France, again, would simply have to imitate them in this regard.[70]

The second part of this report concerned how this proposal for a Navigation Act would apply to the various different aspects of French navigation and maritime trade. First of all, with regard to the French coastal trade (*cabotage*) and Atlantic fisheries, Delattre argued for the total exclusion of foreign vessels or foreign imports. Both these exclusions, in supposedly stimulating the growth of French shipping, were intended to foster an expansion in France's active seafaring population, thus finally exploiting hitherto underutilised or mismanaged manpower reserves.[71] The fisheries particularly (for which Delattre called for a threefold increase in French shipping), were to be greatly encouraged by a combination of subsidies and the new demands of a unified national market, in which free ports should henceforth be eliminated. "Nous pouvons et nous devons beaucoup augmenter nôtre pêche", the deputy preached, "nous le pouvons pour la pêche en elle-même; nous le devons pour accroître le nombre de nos matelots, et pour ranimer et vivifier notre marine".[72] The encouragement of an active seafaring population was hence regarded as vitally important to the maintenance and expansion of French maritime power.

In regard to Northern Europe, Africa and the Levant, the report was similarly optimistic in its outlining of the potential for a considerable

---

[69] *Ibid.*, p. 206.
[70] *Ibid.*, pp. 207-208. The concern of the Assembly to maintain France's own homegrown strategic resources was shown in Barrère's report on National Forests, which was presented to the Assembly on 6 August 1790. In it the future *conventionnel* and member of the Committee of Public Safety argued that the conservation of France's old growth forests was vitally important to French maritime and territorial power. See the *Rapport par Barrère relatif à la conservation des bois et forêts nationales, Ibid.*, Vol. 17, 6 August 1790, p. 630.
[71] Although France had a considerably greater population than Britain, as Cormack notes, the French seafaring population was actually smaller than that of Britain. This had caused chronic manpower shortages for the French navy throughout the eighteenth century. See Cormack, *Revolution and Political Conflict*, p. 25.
[72] AP, Vol. 31, pp. 208-209.

expansion in French trade and navigation (the report's considerations on the subject of France's West and East Indian colonies will be discussed in the following chapter). It was also noteworthy for two further reasons: firstly, although rhetorical references to liberty, equality, and revolutionary zeal had found their way into earlier reports of the Agriculture and Commerce Committee on this subject, the absence in this particular report of such prevailing ideological references among the revolutionaries gives some indication that, in terms of foreign trade, French national interest was conceived by the committee largely in 'traditional' terms (the difference being that France was now economically unified, whereas formerly it had been more or less parcelised). That is, the primary goals of foreign trade were understood to include the attaining of the most advantageous and viable balance of trade with her various trading partners (and the extraction of maximum profit for French merchants), the greatest development possible of French agriculture and industry, and, finally, the denial, where appropriate, of commercial opportunities to perceived rivals. Delattre, who had begun his report with a statement that it was better to correct the faults of the previous regime, rather than indulge in the "sad pleasure" of reproaching it, even seemed to be generally praising of the recent diplomacy of the royal government in this regard, particularly the commercial treaties recently effected and re-confirmed respectively with Russia and Sweden.[73]

Secondly, this report displays a curious selectivity in its discussion of the relationship between perceived economic and politico-strategic exigencies in French foreign relations. Particularly with regard to Turkey and Spain, there was some recognition of how strategic *means* could both protect France's economic assets and enhance her commercial opportunities. In relation to Turkey, Delattre argued that the maintenance, with that country, of France's valuable and particularly advantageous trade required not merely a degree of positive diplomatic pressure (including, he implied, bribery). "Nous devons", he said also, "montrer aux yeux des Ottomans un grand appareil de puissance", by sending French warships to cruise Ottoman waters. Similarly, the report was adamant in its support for the continuation of the Franco-Spanish alliance, reflecting that their mutual interests "sont mêlés, confondus et communs dans l'une comme dans l'autre hémisphère", particularly as the two Empires were geographically contiguous both in Europe and in France's most valuable colony, Saint-Domingue. Finally, in the report, the connection of commercial

---

[73] *Ibid.*, 22 September 1791, pp. 203, 213.

maritime activity with overall naval power, and the need to unite French naval resources with those of Spain (against those of Britain), shows some understanding of the nature and dynamics at least of the maritime balance of power, and its crucial impact overall upon French economic prosperity.

At the same time, however, the report seemed to neglect the wider demands of the balance of power, particularly as it pertained to continental Europe. That is, while the committee obviously assumed that European states would continue to compete on an economic level, there seemed to be little if any recognition of the traditional and ongoing connection in European diplomacy between economic and strategic agendas, in which the balance of power and the balance of trade were considered to be interrelated issues. Would Britain stand by and watch while the prime source of her prosperity, her command of the seas, was compromised and threatened by a resurgence of French maritime power? Or would this power, as the French ambassador to London, the marquis de La Luzerne, had earlier feared, take some political, diplomatic or military action (covert or otherwise) against France and its Revolution, to forestall such a possibility? Aside from stating that France should continue to monitor the competitive actions of its commercial rivals, the report was entirely silent on this question.

There remained, moreover, the question of political and ideological reactions of the European powers to the Revolution in France. A number of speakers during the war and peace debate of May 1790 had already warned of the great dangers of France effectively isolating herself, for ideological or any other reasons, from the alliance-system of Europe. By the middle of 1790 fears had already been raised in the Assembly about a possible coalition of European powers against the Revolution, a fear that can only have gained strength with the rapprochement around that time of Austria and Prussia (engineered by Britain), and the joint Austro-Prussian Pillnitz declaration in August the following year. What of the rest of Europe? Would otherwise profitable trading relationships with countries such as Russia and Sweden continue to be uneffected by the events in France? Would their monarchs, who had early on shown their marked distaste, if not outright hostility to the Revolution, co-operate in providing France with the vital naval supplies upon which her projected naval resurgence would doubtless depend? On this question the report was similarly unforthcoming.

There are a number of possible explanations for such a neglect. It is possible, first of all, that the committee's silence on the potential diplomatic and strategic consequences of such a measure as a Navigation Act was at least partly deliberate. Given the concerns already raised in the Assembly about the possible reactions to the Revolution of various continental powers, the committee may possibly have not wished to speculate openly on any further developments or consequences of so alarming a nature. The political situation among the powers of Europe was, after all, more rightly the concern of the Diplomatic Committee. However, if their concerns about this were of any import, then it is hard to believe that the Committees on the Marine and Agriculture and Commerce would not have also wished to join formally with the Diplomatic Committee for the purposes of deliberating on the issue of a Navigation Act, and investigating its potential consequences. As it was, being virtually at the end of their term, the Constituents elected to leave the full consideration of a Navigation Act to the following legislature.[74]

The Commercial Policy of the Constituent Assembly

From the evidence adduced in this chapter one can conclude that the regeneration of a now unified French economy was of capital importance to the deputies of the Constituent Assembly, in that they believed it would underwrite the nation's future prosperity and give substance to its enjoyment of liberty. Central, moreover, to this economic regeneration, for the deputies, was a policy that was two-fold, involving a combination of free internal trade and measured external protectionism. This policy was itself hardly 'revolutionary', at least in any universalistic sense. It may in fact be said to have derived in large part from an analysis of the dynamic commercial success over the century of France's long-time rival, Britain. The deputies thus consistently eshewed fixed ideas or 'grand speculative theories' of the type promoted by the French *économistes* in favour of a pragmatic view of the then current realities and an understanding informed by past experience. What they believed the British example had shown them was that it was indeed such a determined and focused policy of internal free trade and external protectionism, combined with an entreprising commercial instinct, that had been basically responsible for the rapid expansion of both British commercial and strategic power in the

---

[74] The French government did eventually adopt a 'Navigation Act' (21 September 1793), but only once France had gone to war with Britain. See Stewart (Ed), *A Documentary Survey of the French Revolution*, pp. 501-502.

eighteenth century. The evidence for this had seemed, for many deputies, to be irrefutable.

The further, and indeed most salient, lesson to be drawn from the British experience was one that had also been promoted by such writers as Adam Smith (and, in France, by the Physiocrats)—that the goal of economic policy ought to be the enhancement of productivity rather than the mere accumulation of capital. When considering the situation in their own country, this led the deputies to place great emphasis on the rapid expansion and development of national industry, for it was the common view that hitherto the French economy had been severely 'handicapped' by the multiple strictures of the old regime state. Although some sectors such as maritime trade had managed to prosper under this regime, other large sectors of the French economy such as agriculture, mining and some manufacturing had remained chronically underdeveloped.

This was the understanding which underlay the Constituents' transformation of France's customs barriers from more or less a fiscal resource into an instrument of economic control. The Constituents believed that French trade and industry needed to be protected in some measure by the state, at least until such time as the various sectors of the French economy attained their 'natural' level of development, and could compete effectively on their own. Though they had wished to remove most of the governmental restraints that had previously constricted internal trade, the Constituents hence still saw a vital and active role for the national government in the overseeing and 'nurturing' of French industry, and the promotion of economic growth. In this way the government would work to safeguard the national interest.

It should again be noted, furthermore, that both sides in the Assembly's debate over tariff levels—liberal and protectionist—displayed a degree of 'economic nationalism'. Far from evincing a wholly 'cosmopolitan' view of international commerce, the chief proponent of a liberal (free trade) tariff regime—Boislandry—assumed, together with protectionists such as Goudard and Roussillou, that France had the capacity to develop into the world's most dominant economic superpower, and that this would give France an imposing influence on international affairs, most specifically in Europe, but also around the world. There was also some recognition in the Assembly of the political consequences of economic policy, and of the relationship between strategic means and economic goals, particularly in the area of seapower.

It should also be noted, however, that the commercial policy of the Constituent Assembly, as a whole, was one that quite clearly rejected the kind of autarchic, or 'zero-sum' approach so reminiscent of the previous century. The goal now of French commercial policy was not to 'ruin' or crush the economies of other states, but rather, to gain, within an increasingly interdependent and expanding international economy, an eventual share of international trade that was considered only commensurate with France's intrinsic economic potential, given its geography, population, and immense physical resources. If this led to an eclipse, or even collapse, of British commercial and strategic power then this was only what many deputies would have considered to be a natural and overdue readjustment of geostrategic realities. Previously blighted by the corporate strictures of the old regime, France's homegrown industries hence would, with the help of measured protection, now be able to attain a degree of real vigour sufficient to assert France's natural superiority not only in trade, but also in the political geography of Europe. France could then not help but become once again the arbiter of the European balance of power.

6 The Question of the Colonies

The promulgation of the Declaration of the Rights of Man and Citizen in August 1789 had implications which extended far beyond metropolitan France. The Declaration, with its identification of popular sovereignty, economic and individual liberty as the "sacred, natural and inalienable rights of man", had specific implications for France's colonies, in terms both of the sovereign status of the colonies, and the civil status of their populations. It was inevitable that the question of France's colonies, and the nature of their relationship with the mother-country, would become an issue in the National Assembly, and one that demanded a legislative response.

It was also inevitable that the complex colonial question (in its various facets) should become the object of considerable controversy in the National Assembly, and the source of some of the deputies' keenest dilemmas; for, as this chapter will show, on the questions of trade, sovereignty and the civil status of individuals, the Assembly would often find its most 'sacred' principles in collision with the perceived and palpable reality of the nation's material interest. How the policy makers of the Constituent Assembly navigated their way through these dilemmas, and what this should reveal about their understanding of the role and value to France of its colonies, will be the principal focus of this chapter.

The French colonial empire as it stood in 1789 will, for the purposes of this discussion, be divided into two sections, those in the western hemisphere (in the Atlantic Ocean), and those in the eastern hemisphere (in the Indian Ocean). Amongst the widely scattered colonies of this Empire the most significant and economically valuable to France were the West Indian sugar islands, of which the most significant again was Saint-Domingue. As was affirmed by royal officials such as Arnould, the great bulk of wealth accruing from French colonial trade derived from this and a few other neighbouring islands in the Antilles, including Guadaloupe, Martinique, St. Lucie and Tobago.[1] As

---

[1] Arnould, *La balance de commerce*, p. 327; Other possessions in the Western Hemisphere included French Guyana, the tiny islands of Saint-Pierre &

well as providing the largest proportion of Europe's supply of sugar, these islands also supplied France and markets beyond with such valuable and sought after commodities as coffee, cocoa, cotton and indigo.[2]

In comparison, France's colonies in the eastern hemisphere comprised only a small proportion of its colonial trade in the late-eighteenth century. With the exception of the strategically placed Iles de France and de Bourbon (which produced coffee for export to France),[3] these colonies were primarily trading posts rather than plantation settlements. Situated mostly around the coasts of India, they included Karikal, Mahé, Trichinopoly, Chandernagor and the chief-place, Pondichéry. Together, France's Indian Ocean colonies exported, via the Ile de France, a variety of goods to the mother-country, including calico and raw silk, coffee, spices, saltpetre and porcelain.[4]

The West Indian Colonies: The Policy Context in 1789

In the 1780s, the basic attitude of the planter-colonists in the French sugar islands toward the royal government was marked, most basically, by confusion, frustration, and anxiety—the direct or indirect product, the colonists believed, of the government's existing colonial policy. There was confusion, first of all, about the 'constitutional' status of the colonies. Traditionally, colonial administration had been structured in a manner analogous to that of the French provinces, with administrative duties being shared between a Royal Governor and an Intendant. When in 1787 the royal government set up provincial assemblies in some French provinces (the *pays d'état*), this was to some extent replicated in the colonies with the setting up of colonial assemblies on two of the West Indian islands, Martinique and Guadeloupe. There was thus a

---

[2] Miquelon near Newfoundland in the North Atlantic (important as forward bases for French fishing fleets), and trading posts on the coast of Senegal, Africa.

Britain and France imported, respectively, 36.7 and 43.3 per cent of sugar exported from the West Indies to Europe in the 1780s. However, while Britain consumed most of its sugar imports, France re-exported to Europe (between 1785 and 1789) 69.4 per cent of its own imported sugar. M. Duffy, *Soldiers, Sugar and Seapower*, Oxford 1987, pp. 7-8; see also T. Doerflinger, 'The Antilles Trade of the Old Regime: A Statistical Overview', *Journal of Interdisciplinary History*, 6:3 (Winter 1976), *passim*.

[3] Herbert Priestley, *France Overseas through the Old Regime: A Study of European Expansion* (New York, 1939), pp. 211-212.

[4] J. H. Parry, *Trade and Dominion: European Overseas Empires in the Eighteenth Century* (London, 1971), pp. 92-93; Arnould, *La balance de commerce*, p. 283.

reasonable basis for the colonists to argue in 1788 that the French colonies could legally be considered as a part of France, and that, as such, they had a right to be represented in the upcoming Estates-General. This, however, the royal government flatly denied, deeming the colonies to be merely French 'possessions' with no inherent right to representation.[5]

While this exclusion from the Estates-General was certainly frustrating for the planter-colonists of the sugar islands, the principal source of their frustration, in respect at least of the royal government, concerned the traditional commercial relationship existing between France and its colonies. The system of the *exclusif*, established by Colbert in the previous century and maintained since, prohibited these colonists from trading with any country other than France, to the obvious disadvantage of the planters themselves (who could trade more profitably on the open market). Forced to trade with French merchants on terms that were always unfavourable, the planters were as a result often chronically in debt to the merchants and shipowners of the *métropole*. Thus, while various elements of French commerce reaped the colossal benefits of their trade in colonial produce, the colonists themselves understandably felt that within this prohibitive arrangement they had in return been poorly served by the mother-country. Although restrictions had in fact sometimes been relaxed on particular items (usually only then in an attempt to limit smuggling), such as through the decree of 1784, the French government of the old regime continued to resist any general relaxation of the commercial monopoly.[6]

Alongside these political and economic frustrations were the anxieties felt by the colonists about the internal situation of the colonies. In the 1780s, these islands were simmering with multiple social and racial tensions, which threatened to boil over into violence and agitation. Overshadowing colonial society, first of all, was the ever-present spectre of mass slave revolt, the plantation economy of the sugar islands being largely reliant on regular supplies of slave labour brought in from Africa.[7] For the planter-colonists, the swelling of the

---

[5] Lokke, *France and the Colonial Question*, p. 123.
[6] See F. Nussbaum, 'The French Colonial Arrêt of 1784', *South Atlantic Quarterly*, 27 (1928), pp. 62-78. See also *Avis motivé de M. Barbé de Marbois, Intendant à la Séance du 11 Mai 1789 du Conseil-Supérieur de Saint-Domingue, enregistrée sur sa demande*. In *Pièces Justificatives des faits énoncés dans le mémoire de M. Le Comte de la Luzerne, Ministre et Secrétaire de la Marine*, Marine-37-H-21, pp. 53-56.
[7] The trafficking in African slaves by French *armateurs* was a central feature of France's colonial trade, one component of a triangular trading network between

slave populations in the colonies in the later part of the century (in proportion to the numbers of white colonists), though regarded as economically necessary, was nonetheless viewed with growing disquiet, lest the slaves, in their overwhelming numbers, should rise up against the harshness and brutality with which they had long been repressed and exploited.[8] Deep resentments and conflicts of interest existed, moreover, between the various sectors of the white community, rich and poor, rural and urban, planter and merchant. This was complemented by particular ill-feeling between prosperous *gens de couleur* and poorer whites, and by the equally deep resentment of the colonists toward resident royal officials, who held themselves somewhat aloof from the rest of colonial society.[9]

The mounting frustrations over colonial trade, and the colonists' anxieties regarding the slaves, were subsequently excacerbated, in the late 1780s, by two parallel developments. One was the subsistence crisis that overtook the island colonies. Under the *exclusif* France had long reserved to itself the sole right to provide the colonies with all the grain they needed (the colonies being unable to meet their own subsistence needs), but by 1788—89 France's own grain shortages prevented a less than an adequate supply to the Antilles. In Saint-Domingue, the Governor-General Chilleau took the initiative and ordered several ports open to foreign trade for a period of five years from May 1789, through which the colonists could import grain and other foodstuffs from such sources as the United States. This action was, however, quickly overturned in France by the Minister, the comte de La Luzerne,

---

the west coast of Africa, the Antilles and the French Atlantic ports. It contributed sizably to the economic growth of several such ports, of which the most dominant in the trade were Nantes, Bordeaux, La Rochelle and Le Havre. Helped along by bounties from the Royal government, and by the monopoly of slave provision to the French Antilles enjoyed by metropolitan shipowners, the trade grew steadily across the century, reaching its highest level of activity around 1790. See Robert Stein, *The French Slave Trade in the Eighteenth Century: An Old Regime Business* (Madison, Wis., 1979); Perry Vines, 'The Slaving Interest in the Atlantic Ports, 1763-1792', *French Historical Studies*, 7:4 (1972).

[8] It has been estimated that by 1789 the population of Saint-Domingue, Martinique and Guadaloupe had risen to over 730,000, of whom slaves constituted two-thirds. See Doerflinger, 'The Antilles Trade', p. 402. The Intendant Barbé de Marbois put the figure for the population of Saint-Domingue in 1789 as 509,642 blacks, 26,666 mulattoes and 35,440 whites: see Valerie Quinney, *The Committee on Colonies of the French Constituent Assembly 1789-91*, Unpublished PhD Dissertation, University of Wisconsin, 1967, p. 7.

[9] Quinney, *The Committee on Colonies*, pp. 6-7,10.

who recalled Chilleau, and subsequently refused to consider any further opening of colonial ports beyond that decreed in 1784.[10]

The second worrying development for the colonists was the formation, in early 1788, of the Société des Amis des Noirs, founded by the *philosophes* and publicists Brissot, Sieyès and Condorcet. Inspired by the work of English abolitionists such as Wilberforce, this new pressure group gave renewed impetus to the anti-slavery cause in France, although it attracted only limited public support. For the planters and colonists, this abolitionist campaign heralded not merely a potential threat to their livelihoods but possibly to their very lives. With the threat of hunger already hovering over the colonies, such an abolitionism could be, they believed, the spark which might ignite a full scale slave revolt in the colonies, the outcomes of which would likely be both bloody and terrible for all concerned.

Revolution and Public Debate on the Colonies

Around the middle of 1789 official or informal representatives of all these groups—the Amis des Noirs, the planter-colonists and the French port merchants—gathered in Versailles, and subsequently in Paris, in order to place their respective cases before the newly founded National Assembly, and before the French public. In so doing they would be contributing to a debate on the prospective 'constitutional' bases of the French colonial Empire, and on what role the colonies might then play in the 'regeneration' of metropolitan France.

The Amis des Noirs were represented in the Assembly by a number of its more prominent *patriote* deputies, including such popular figures as Mirabeau, Lafayette, Adrien Duport and the brothers Lameth.[11] While of these deputies Mirabeau would become one of the more committed parliamentary advocates for the cause of *les noirs*, the abolitionist cause was in this early stage mainly promoted by way of pamphlets and other publications.

In their efforts to sway public opinion, the authors of many of these antislavist tracts referred to the newly declared principles of the Revolution—individual liberty, justice, natural rights—in order to further substantiate a moral case against the continuation of slavery in the colonies, and the forcible procurement of slaves from Africa.

---

[10] Lokke, *France and the Colonial Question*, p. 141.
[11] *Tableau des membres de la Société des Amis des Noirs, Année 1789* (Paris, 1789).

Slavery was denounced by some as nothing more than a criminal entreprise, and one which the Revolution could surely not allow to continue, so contrary it was to its fundamental principles of liberty and justice.[12] Yet, there was at the same time, among many of these same authors, a recognition of the fact that any abrupt abolition of slavery might result in the ruin of colonial trade, which in turn would have devastating economic (and possibly strategic) consequences both for the colonies and the *métropole*. Taking this into account, they argued the case instead for a more gradual abolition of slavery, hopefully in conjunction with other slaveholding colonial powers in the region, such as Britain.[13]

Anti-slavist tracts argued, furthermore, that the eventual abolition of slavery would in fact have positive rather than profoundly negative economic consequences, for, once freed, the black population, being no longer 'enervated' by their slave-condition, would be happier and hence far more productive as a labour force.[14] The former slaves, in advancing their conditions, could then also likely develop into a thriving market for metropolitan manufactures. In this way the former slaves, and the colonies as a whole, would thence be able to participate fully in both the moral and economic 'regeneration' instituted by the Revolution in France, to the benefit of all.

Associated, to some degree, with this antislavery campaign were those authors and advocates of free trade, such as Cassan, who otherwise argued for a revision of the traditional commercial relationship existing between France and its principal colonies.[15] Like J-J-C Farçot, Cassan

---

[12] See, for example, B-S. Frossard, *Les cause des esclaves nègres et des habitans de la Guinée, portée au tribunal de la justice, de la religion, de la politique; ou Histoire de la traite& l'esclavage des nègres, preuves de leur illégitimé, moyens de les abolir sans nuire ni aux colonies ni aux colons* (Lyon 1789); Brissot, *Mémoire sur les Noirs* (Paris, 1790); J. Lecointre-Marsillac, *Le More-Lack, ou Essai sur les moyens les plus doux & les plus équitables d'abolir la traite & l'esclavage des nègres d'Afrique, en conservant aux colonies tous les avantages d'une population agricole*, (Paris, 1789).

[13] See, for example, *L'Esclavage des nègres aboli, ou Moyens d'améliorer leur sort*, n.a. (Paris, 1789).

[14] Frossard used Cochinchina here as an example of a successful non-slave producer of sugar. According to Frossard, sugar was produced more efficiently, and in far larger quantities, in Cochinchina than in Saint-Domingue (800,000,000 livres' worth compared to 123,067,300). See Frossard, *Les cause des esclaves nègres*, p. 167.

[15] Cassan, *Considérations sure les rapports qui doivent existes entre les colonies et les métropoles, et particulièrement: Sur l'état actuel du Commerce Français dans les Antilles, relativement à celui qu'y font les Etrangers; Sur les*

denounced the Old Regime's conflation of national interest with that of the port merchants, and sought thereby a wider, more encompassing definition of national interest. In the past, he claimed, ministers had tended, wrongly, to gauge national prosperity by the 'opulence' exhibited by select commercial and manufacturing towns, rather than taking a more comprehensive view of the performance of the French economy.[16] Now, he said, with the National Assembly in charge of commercial policy, the opportunity for a massive economic and agricultural renaissance lay before France, to be made possible, in large part, by the Assembly's introduction of internal free trade. Yet this introduction should not be limited to the French domestic market, he asserted. It should, rather, mark the beginnings of a general liberalisation of foreign and colonial trade.[17] This view roughly corresponded with that of Farçot, who claimed that a general liberalisation of colonial trade would result in the mutual enrichment of France and its colonies.[18]

Generally implicit in this above argument was a desire for the transformation also of the political relationship between the *métropole* and the colonies. Pro-liberalisation pamphlets seemed naturally to assume that the French colonies would enjoy in the future a strong measure of legislative autonomy. The picture often drawn then was of a future French imperium that would resemble more of a Francophone 'commonwealth' than the highly centralised Empire that had been the rule.[19] This 'remodelling' of French imperial relations was considered by

---

avantages réciproques qui résulteront pour les nations Anglaise & Française, de l'établissement d'un commerce libre & commun à l'une & à l'autre, dans toutes leur Colonies; Sur l'administration intérieure convenable aux Colonies Françaises, & sur la nécessité de réformer quelqu'une des Loix qui les gouvernent; Sur la danger d'affranchir les Nègres dans ce moment, & sur les moyens de procurer peu-à-peu leur affranchissement, sans nuire ni à la Propriété ni au Commerce (Paris, 1790).

[16] *Ibid.*, p. 36.

[17] *Ibid.*, pp. 1, 38.

[18] "En effet", wrote Farçot, "dès que le commerce sera libre, nos Colonies, ouvertes à toutes les nations, deviendront l'entrepôt naturel de tous les produits de manufactures françoises. ... Au milieu de tant d'objets, ils distingueront bientôt les produits d'industrie française, qui, sous les auspices de la liberté, deviendroient tous les jours plus abondans, mieux fabriqués, plus finis que ceux de tous les autres peuples. De la richesse de France naître la richesse des Colonies; & de celle des Colonies s'augmentera la richesse françoise". Farçot, *Questions Constitutionelles*, pp. 103-104.

[19] This was consistent with the Physiocratic view, expressed by Turgot decades earlier, that the American colonies would, once they had 'matured', eventually

its proponents to be not merely just, but in the long-term interest of both nation and colony. Fraternally bound, the separate parts of the French Empire (or 'commonwealth') would, they alleged, continue to have common interests, and seek protection under the same (combined) military umbrella.

The representatives of the French port merchants, including both deputies in the Assembly, and the semi-official *députés éxtraordinaires du commerce et des manufactures*, were, however, no less strident than their critics in putting forward their own case, which was for the retention of France's monopoly of colonial trade (including the provision of slaves to the colonies). On 2 March, Blin, deputy from Nantes, addressed the Assembly on behalf of the commercial and manufacturing interests of all France.[20] He commenced by pointing out the great importance to France of its colonial trade, and the various benefits it brought. Not only did the colonies consume surpluses of French agricultural and industrial goods, but they provided in turn the precious commodities that formed the basis of much of their trade with Europe, and the advantages therein that France enjoyed. This kept, he said, French workers gainfully employed, but even more importantly, it kept them fed. This was a compelling point when, as all deputies were painfully aware, hunger had recently in their view helped to set rural France alight with explosive and destructive anarchy, and had the potential to do so again (particularly in the atmosphere of disorder and anxiety still prevalent in the countryside). Countering arguments that 'tropical' colonies were not worth the dangers met in keeping them, and that they only benefitted the port merchants anyway, Blin asserted that colonial commerce benefitted all classes in France and that it was, he again insisted, the primary source of general national prosperity.

Naturally, as a representative of French mercantile interests, Blin then went on to defend the *exclusif* between France and the West Indian colonies, declaring it "indispensible" to their relationship. Here the speaker seemed at pains to stress the reciprocally beneficial aspect of this provision, even referring back to the old notion of the 'pacte colonial', wherein the *métropole* was supposedly to protect the colonies in return for the economic benefits that it drew from them. Such an exclusive preference for the mother-country was after all, Blin claimed, only reasonable as a contribution of the colonies to their own defence. This had been very costly to the motherland, and something from

---

separate from their respective mother-countries. Lokke, *France and the Colonial Question*, pp. 70-71.

[20] AP, Vol. 12, 2 March, p. 7.

which the planters had of course benefitted.[21] Thus, he suggested, in serving the interests of France, the colonies were ultimately serving their own. Indeed, it was very much in their interest to increase "la puissance de la Nation avec laquelle elle s'associe".[22]

This would not however mean, he went on, that the colonies would end up being simply plundered and impoverished. Rather, the effect of the Revolution would be to remove all the restrictions that had previously inhibited the mutual economic growth of the colonies and that of France, allowing them both finally to prosper to their fullest potential, bound profitably together by their ties of mutual dependence:

> il arrivera certainement, lorsque le régime des colonies sera établi sur de meilleurs principes, et lorsque notre commerce se sera plus livré aux vexations innombrables qu'il éprouve que si, d'une part, celui-ci trouve le plus grand intérêt à deployer toutes ses ressources pour enricher les colonies et les porter au plus haut degré de perfection, les colonies, à leur tour, n'auront pas d'intérêt plus réel que celui de voir notre commerce fleurir au-dessus du commerce de toutes les autres nations, et multiplier pour elle-memes les moyens d'accroissement et de jouissance auxquels leur ambition peut prétendre.[23]

The Revolution would thus result in an improved global competitiveness for French trade that would prove a boon for both the metropole and the colonies, considered together virtually as one protected national market. As Blin told the Assembly,

> Il doit même arriver dans le nouvel ordre des choses qui se prépare, que par le commerce vous acquériez enfin le grand avantage qu'a semblé promettre de tous temps à la France la fertilité de son sol et l'industrie de ses habitants, celui de pouvoir soutenir toutes nos concurrences pour tous nos produits, dans tous les marchés de toutes les nations.[24]

Not to take advantage of this opportunity, and to even risk losing the benefits of colonial trade altogether, would be not only to rob France of its "sacred patrimony", but would prove more urgently catastrophic for France; for in endangering the livelihood of the French people, and

---

[21] *Ibid.*, p. 11. French Government expenditure on colonial defence and administration in 1789 amounted to 17 million livres, against only 7 million received from the colonies in taxes. D.K. Fieldhouse, *The Colonial Empires*, pp. 41-43.
[22] AP, Vol. 12., 2 March, p. 7.
[23] *Ibid.*
[24] *Ibid.*

ruining such a crucial source of national credit, the future health of the Revolution itself would be directly imperilled, leaving it vulnerable to a "contre-coup inévitable et funeste".[25] According to Blin, the fruits of the Revolution, which for him meant the economic expansion of France, would hence be lost before they could even be tasted.

Earlier barred by the royal government from seeking any direct representation in the Estates-General, the colonists themselves finally succeeded in gaining representation when a delegation of six 'colonial deputies' were admitted to the National Assembly on 4 July 1789. These deputies presented the National Assembly with two basic demands. First of all, they demanded that the Assembly's decree of 29 August freeing up France's domestic grain trade should also include the colonies, and that, moreover, the colonies should be allowed greater freedom to establish trading relationships with countries such as the United States, to whom they could export colonial produce such as rum and molasses. While these goods were apparently of little or no use to France, their export to the US could, however, bring in to the colonies the other thing which their economy chronically lacked aside from grain, hard currency. This, it was argued, would help to improve the colonists' position, by lessening both their reliance on metropolitan credit, and the merchants' ability to manipulate prices. For, as one colonial deputy wrote, it made no sense, from the point of view of basic political economy, that the commercial interests of the metropole should continue to benefit to so great an extent, if this would only lead to the progressive impoverishment of the colonies. Targetting these "commerçans", the author reasoned that

> s'il nous enlèvent le fruit de notre travail, en mettant à prix arbitraire nos comestibles & tous les objets qu'ils nous fournissent, il nous épuisent & nous ôtent la faculté de rendre à la culture ce qu'elle donne à nos sueurs. Les Manufactures de France même en souffriront; car nous n'achetons que de notre superflu les étoffes, les bijouteries, & tous les objets de luxe qu'on nous apporte. ... Il est de l'intérêt de la France que nous soyons riche, parce que notre richesse finit toujours par se verser dans son sein.[26]

---

[25] *Ibid.*, p. 12.

[26] A. de Thébaudières, *Vues générales sur les moyens de concilier l'intérêt de commerce national avec la prosperité des colonies* (Paris, 1789), p. 10. See also: *Réponse succincte des députés de S. Domingue, au mémoire des commerçans des ports de mer, distribué dans les bureaux de l'Assemblée nationale, le 9 octobre 1789*, (Versailles, 1789).

In appealing then for at least some further modification of the *exclusif* and opening up of colonial trade, the colonial deputies were, however, far from challenging the dominance of France, nor even repudiating their own 'supportive' role within the French Empire. They were merely arguing that a fairer, equitable and more *mutually enriching* relationship between the colonies and their mother-country was simply more sustainable, and hence more in France's national interest, than a regime of outright exploitation.

Despite these appeals, in the name supposedly of French national interest, the colonists were nonetheless quickly disappointed in their pleas for the opening up of further colonial ports to foreign trade. In the Assembly, the matter was referred without discussion to the Agriculture and Commerce Committee, whereupon the proponents for French commerce used their influence to have the request rejected, a decision that evidently had the wider support of the Assembly.[27] Stymied in this respect, the colonial deputies were then all the more determined to protect what they saw as the most vital and immediate of their interests, the institution of slavery on the island colonies. Alarmed by various initiatives of the *Amis des Noirs* and their supporters in the Assembly in support of the slaves, these colonial representatives responded by launching, through what became known as the Massiac Club, an effective and concerted campaign in and outside of the Assembly to promote the planters' sectional interests. The organisers of this campaign argued, in short, that the economic health of the West Indian colonies depended squarely on a repressive regime of slavery, and indeed could not survive without it.

The colonial deputies were also not beyond intimating the possibility of secession (and their deliverance into the hands of the British), lest their demands in this latter regard should also go unmet. In the *Tableau de la situation des colonies* presented to the National Assembly on 29 December 1789, for instance, they instructed the deputies of the rising agitation and "universal terror" that the "perfidious" views spread by the *Amis des Noirs* were already causing in the colonies. They then bluntly warned them that only the preservation of the colonists' "propriétés" (their slaves) could avert what would be a disaster for both colony and mother-country alike. Describing the Colonists' heartfelt and 'patriotic' attachment to France, their representatives nevertheless wondered that if

---

[27] See AP, Vol. 10, 11 December 1789, pp. 508, 528.

délaissés, dédaignés, repoussés, les colons, à la vue d'un pavillon étranger, cédaient au sentiment si naturel de leur conservation, à qui faudrait-il s'en prendre? Serait-ce à eux, ou aux mauvais citoyens qui auraient préparé une telle révolution favorable à nos seuls ennemis, et si fatale à la France?

All it would take to avert disaster, reassure the colonists, and restore confidence and activity to colonial commerce, would, they asserted, be a simple and frank repudiation of abolitionism on behalf of the Assembly. "Un mot, Messieurs, un seul mot", implored the *Tableau*,

> et vous permettrez aux colons d'être Français, vous leur permettrez de verser, dans le sein du royaume, des trésors qui y portent partout le mouvement et la vie; vous leur permettrez d'enrichir une patrie qu'ils aimeraient encore, même après avoir été forcé de l'abjurer.[28]

An obvious corollary to this was that the colonies could not then be internally governed under the same basic principles—the universal 'rights' of man—as the *métropole* was now supposedly to be. For the colonial deputies, this meant then that the colonies should in fact be allowed not merely to write their own more appropriate 'constitutions', but also to possess basic autonomy over their own internal affairs.[29]

Barnave, the Colonial Committee and the Decrees of March 1790

The Deputies of the National Assembly were, initially, slow to organise a supervising committee for colonial affairs, so reluctant were they to legislate on internal colonial matters. This was partly at the behest of the Massiac Club, whose agents had been promoting a 'hands off' policy for the Assembly in regard to the colonies.[30] However, circumstances in the sugar islands themselves soon began to force the pace. Already by late 1789 some deputies had expressed concern about a noticeable drop in colonial trade.[31] When in early 1790, however, the Assembly learnt that the planters of Saint-Domingue had actually launched an insurrection against the royal authorities on the island, the deputies were finally compelled, on 2 March, to form a committee devoted

---

[28] *Tableau de la situation des colonies*, AP, Vol. 11, 29 Dec 1789, p. 41.
[29] Vergniaud, *Rapport de Vergniaud sur l'état des travaux de l'Assemblée-Nationale-Constituante au 30 Septembre 1791* (Paris, 1791), Note 20, pp. 3-6.
[30] Quinney, *The Committee on Colonies*, p. 24.
[31] AP, Vol. 10, 3 December 1789, pp. 362-363.

specifically to colonial matters. That this committee of twelve members was split between deputies representing either colonial or French commercial interests gives some idea of the Assembly's priorities at this time. The *Amis des Noirs* were effectively excluded from the Committee, and hence sidelined from the policy process.[32]

Within a very few days, on 8 March, Barnave presented the general report of the Colonial Committee. This report was notable, firstly, for its general affirmation of the existence of the French colonial empire, and of the importance to France of its West Indian colonies in particular. As such, it was notable also for the way it shunted aside the whole issue of slavery, and the moral contradictions such an institution in the colonies presented to the fundamentals of revolutionary principle (as enshrined in the 'Declaration of the Rights of Man'). As historians such as Robert Forster and David Geggus have noted, the issue of slavery became, from early on in the Constituent Assembly, something of a taboo subject. In this speech of 8 March, as often in other occasions when the colonies were discussed, explicit reference to slavery or the slave trade would be studiously avoided, in favour of euphemisms such as 'colonial property' and 'colonial trade'.[33] For Barnave and the Colonial Committee, the paramount issue at stake with regard to the colonies was not the moral issue posed by slavery. As far as they defined it, it concerned instead "l'intérêt de la nation française à soutenir son commerce, à conserver ses colonies, à favoriser leur prosperité par tous les moyens compatibles avec le métropole", in other words, the French national interest (considered in material terms) rather than universal principle.[34]

This national interest, as Barnave then detailed, imperatively required the preservation of the French colonies, and the trade which they conducted with the *métropole*. To those purveyors of economic theory who might doubt the usefulness to France of its colonies, Barnave retorted that this was by no means an academic issue—it was, rather, a matter of fact that "toutes les parties de notre existence

---

[32] In 1790 the members of the Colonial Committee included, from France, the deputies Alquier, Barnave, Begouen, Champagny, Garesché, Le Chapelier, Alexandre de Lameth, Thouret. The members from Saint-Domingue included the deputies Gérard and Reynaud de Villeverd.

[33] David Geggus, 'Racial Equality, Slavery and Colonial Secession during the Constituent Assembly', *American Historical Review*, 94, (December, 1989), p. 1296; R. Forster, 'The French Revolution, People of Color, and Slavery', in Klaits & Haltzel (Eds), *The Global Ramifications of the French Revolution* (1994), p. 92.

[34] AP, Vol. 12, 8 March 1790, p. 68.

sociale sont intimement liées et combinées avec la possession d'un grand commerce, avec celle de nos colonies", and that its sudden loss would be disastrous, particularly for a Revolution whose accomplishment would be to "assure à jamais la gloire et la prospérité de la nation française".[35] The prosperity of national commerce hence could not, he argued, be separated from the possession of the colonies, these being the source in France of much of its wealth, and support for its industry. "Abandonnez les colonies au moment où vos établissements sont fondé sur leur possession", he warned, "et la langeur succède à l'activité, la misère à l'abondance".[36] Skilled workers would lose their livelihoods, and agriculture and the finances would soon face the same disasters that would have already befallen commerce and manufacturing. The flow-on effects within France of such a loss of colonial trade would thus be widespread, and certainly devastating.

Furthermore, such a loss would have, in Barnave's view, more than just grave repercussions for France's internal prosperity; it would also affect France's political and economic standing in the "systeme général des puissances européennes", in particular, by comproming its naval power.[37] This was long recognised to be the key to France's future as a global power, and here the report recognised the strategic relationship between France's commercial and maritime existence and its security on the Continent of Europe. The loss of colonial trade would, aside from bringing a massive loss of national income, also deprive France of the trained and experienced sailors that its 'neighbours' (Britain, Holland) possessed in abundance on account of their extensive coastal trade (with which Barnave claimed France could not compare). French naval power would virtually be paralysed through lack of money and lack of adequate personnel. This would not only leave it crippled in time of war, but would prevent France from competing for other sources of lucrative seaborne trade, such as in the Levant.[38] Moreover, this would allow the British an unchecked domination at sea around the world, while also weakening France's traditional ally, Spain:

> L'Espagne, qui ne peut leur résister que par l'union des forces avec les nôtres, serait bientôt, ainsi comme nous, renfermée sur son territoire; ses possessions d'Amérique deviendraient enfin, comme nos colonies, la conquête de nous rivaux. Condamnée, par sa situation géographique, à n'avoir jamais sur le

---

[35] *Ibid.*, p. 69.
[36] *Ibid.*, p. 70.
[37] *Ibid.*, p. 70.
[38] *Ibid.*

continent une grande influence par ses forces de terre, elle disparaîtrait, pour ainsi dire, du système politique de l'Europe, et son alliance ne nous présentrait plus aucune utilité.[39]

To have to depend on France's dominant rivals for the much needed commodities of other climates would be very damaging, both economically and strategically. Worse still, the subsequent and corresponding growth of British prosperity (on top of its expanded strategic power) would allow further opportunities for the humbling of France by the great influence this would give Britain in continental politics. As Barnave noted, this shift in the overall balance of power would eventually find France unable even to ply and protect its own shores, forcing them to fortify heavily their own coasts from the all-powerful presence of their maritime rivals.[40] For the sake of France's future prosperity and security, and the Revolution which was to promise both, Barnave concluded, the colonies needed to be held and their present trade regime protected, whatever the cost.

The issue for the colonial deputies was not, of course, whether or not France needed its colonies—this they hardly contested—but how the West Indian colonies would, in the short and long term, both survive and prosper.[41] The colonists and the port merchants had agreed that slavery was an essential ingredient of these colonies' on-going prosperity. Where they disagreed was on the liberalisation of colonial trade, and whether the limited opening up of colonial trade decreed in 1784 should now be closed, maintained or extended. For the colonists, these two issues—the preservation of slavery and the liberalisation of colonial commerce—were focused in their demands for effective colonial autonomy. From a position of colonial autonomy the planters such as those on Saint-Domingue would, supposedly, be able to maintain their slaveholding regime without outside interference, and be able also

---

[39] *Ibid.*

[40] This would naturally mean the end of France as a first or even second rank power, since to be such required a significant *offensive* capability.

[41] In stressing the importance of such colonies Barnave's report was in fact only responding to many of the arguments that had been mounted, respectively, by the representatives of metropolitan commerce, and by the colonial deputies themselves. In their *Tableau* of 29 December 1789, the deputies had stated that among the 'political' consequences of France's loss of colonies would be "l'extinction la la marine royale, la perte d'un numéraire immense, l'accroisement de puissance des peuples voisins et rivaux", AP, Vol. 11, 29 December 1789, p. 41.

to negotiate, as now more of an overseas ally rather than a colony *per se*, at least some further relaxation of existing trade restrictions.

Depending on one's interpretation, Barnave's response to these demands could be seen as either evasive or shrewd and statesmanlike. As Valerie Quinney, author of one of the more detailed and authoritative studies of the Colonial Committee, has noted, Barnave essentially endeavoured to 'fudge' the issue in his speech of 8 March, failing to give any clarification of the precise relationship that he proposed should henceforth exist between France and its colonies.[42] Instead, what the report offered the colonists was the makings of a rough *quid pro quo* between their demands regarding internal colonial affairs, and their demands relating to colonial commerce. On the one hand Barnave assured the colonists that though ultimately answerable both to the National Assembly and the king, they would be able, through their own local elected Assemblies, to frame a 'constitution' consonant with the particular social conditions existing in their colony.[43] In return, the colonies would have to accept that, though perhaps open to minor modifications, the *exclusif* was in principle "une condition essentielle de l'union de la métropole et des colonies", and indeed an object of their reciprocal interest.[44]

Within this *quid pro quo*, Barnave thus made it clear that, despite some vague concessions to colonial autonomy, the colonial status quo would yet continue in both its most controversial aspects, slavery and the *exclusif*, and that this was dictated by national interest. The great majority of the Assembly clearly concurred with this assessment and the measures subsequently proposed, refusing even to hear any further discussion on the subject. The decree was then passed by general acclamation.[45]

It only remained then to convince the colonies. Adopting a more cajoling tone than in the conciliatory speech of 8 March, in the subsequent Instructions to that decree (which set out on 23 March the procedures for the election of colonial assemblies) Barnave attempted to dissuade the colonies from any foolish hopes of independence from

---

[42] "The reason", comments Quinney, "that Barnave could not clearly define the relationship between mother country and colony was that the Committee had considered the colony as an ally with the rights to make its own constitution, as a province subject to the French legislature, and as a colony which existed for the commercial benefit of the mother country." Quinney, *The Committee on Colonies*, p. 204.

[43] AP, Vol. 12, 8 March, p. 72.

[44] *Ibid.*, p. 71.

[45] *Ibid.*, p. 73.

France. Obviously unable to defend themselves, who else could they trust to protect them? Certainly not the covetous British, their near neighbours in the Caribbean. Any alliances or guarantees made from them would be dangerous indeed, for as Barnave insinuated, "ne voyez-vous pas que toute protection serait pour vour le commencement d'un nouveau gouvernement arbitraire?", warning them that they could either "choississez d'être les citoyens libres d'une nation libre ou de devenir bientôt les esclaves de ceux qui s'offriraient aujourd'hui pour vos alliés!".[46] Only France offered the colonies the fraternity and proper reciprocity of interest that could ensure their well-being, for if their previous colonial government had been oppressive, they would find succour in the Revolution, that is, in the decrees and instruction of the National Assembly:

> Chaque jour nous approche de terme où, degagés des entraves, qui jusqu'ici, ont contraint toutes nos facultés, nous prendrons enfin parmi les nations qui nous fut assignée. Alors notre liberté, notre puissance, notre fortune seront le patrimonie de tous ceux qui auront partagé notre prosperité se répandra sur tous ceux qui contracteront avec nous.[47]

Thus while the deputies were prepared to go some way in placating desires for colonial autonomy (on domestic matters), they otherwise remained most reluctant to relinquish the ultimate legislative sovereignty of the National Assembly.

The Issue of Civil Rights and Racial Inequality in the Colonies

If by the decrees of March 1790 the National Assembly hoped to forestall any further push in the colonies toward more complete autonomy, or even independence, then such hopes were to be quickly frustrated. The subsequent course of events both in the colonies and back in Paris would, before too long, expose the basic weaknesses inherent in the 'quid pro quo' proposed by Barnave and the Committee, and adopted with some relief by the Assembly. The first of these weaknesses was that relating to the issue of civil rights among the free blacks and men of colour (or 'mulattoes', the descendents, usually, of white fathers and black or creole mothers). While free and often propertied, this sector of the non-slave colonial population had long

---

[46] AP, Vol. 12, 20 March, p. 316.
[47] *Ibid.*

been denied many of the same civil rights as even the lowliest member of the white community on the islands. This was a situation that by the time of the Revolution was beginning to come to the attention of reformers in France, and was certainly the subject of some agitation in the colonies.[48]

Barnave and the Colonial Committee, in complying with the white colonists' demands for the *métropole* not to interfere with the internal administration of the colonies, had in their March decrees glossed over the whole contentious issue of civil rights for free non-whites, in the hope that the colonists might themselves come to some reasonable accommodation of the mulattoes' demands. Article four of the Instructions of 23 March, pertaining, among other things, to voter eligibility for the colonial assemblies, merely stated, without mention of race, that "toutes les personnes" satisfying certain age, property and residence requirements should be allowed admission to the electoral process, in other words, to become 'active' citizens.[49]

Having already succeeded in securing support for the perpetuation of the existing status quo with regard to slavery, the white colonists and their representatives in Paris were, however, adamantly opposed to any concessions to the demands of free blacks or men of colour for political rights in the colonies. For the white planters, the very fabric of the colonial society absolutely depended on the subjection both of the slaves and the free men of colour. The issues of slavery and racial inequality were thus, from their point of view, intimately and inextricably connected, the free blacks and men of colour forming a supposedly necessary 'buffer' class between the slave population and their white overlords.

As such, on Saint-Domingue, the existing colonial assembly at Saint-Marc, representing the planters, refused point blank to admit free blacks or men of colour as either voters or candidates in new elections. In May 1790 it went on to reject unequivocally the *quid pro quo* offered in the March decrees, declaring itself fully autonomous and independent from the National Assembly. On its own authority it then proceeded, on 20 July, to declare all of Saint-Domingue's ports open to foreign trade.[50]

---

[48] Geggus, 'Racial Equality', p. 1296-97.
[49] AP, Vol. 12, 23 March 1790, p. 317.
[50] See the *Décret de l'Assemblée Générale de Saint-Domingue siégeant à Saint-Marc, ouvrant tous les ports de la partie française au commerce étranger*, 20 July 1790, in J. Saintoyant, *La Colonisation Française pendant la Révolution*, Vol. 1, pp. 456-457.

These actions of the Colonial Assembly brought with them serious consequences. Their declaration of full autonomy led, firstly, to a rift with another assembly, the so-called 'Assembly of the North', representing the northern part of French Saint-Domingue, and containing mainly merchants and lawyers. This latter assembly was more willing to comply with the 'sharing' of legislative sovereignty outlined in the March decrees, provided the National Assembly refrained from initiating legislation on colonial administration not already proposed by the colonial assemblies themselves. Determined thus to thwart their rivals at Saint-Marc, they formed a coalition with the Royal Governor, who with the military forces at his disposal moved to dissolve the Colonial Assembly at Saint-Marc at the end of July 1790, an action that was later approved by the National Assembly in Paris.[51]

The second consequence was that resulting from the refusal, now reaffirmed by the Assembly of the North, to allow men of colour the political rights implicit in the March decrees. By October 1790 the frustration this caused among mulattoes led to a revolt, led by one Vincent Ogé, who had just returned from France where he had been pleading the cause of his fellow *gens de couleur*. The white planters moved quickly to contain and suppress this revolt, and other signs of agitation, before they could develop into a more general insurrection. It also caused them to intensify their demands that the National Assembly clarify the constitutional situation, and assure the colonists that it would not seek to rule on questions of racial equality or civil status in the colonies, unless it was indeed at the behest of the colonists themselves.

In its response, the National Assembly was firm at least in its desire to hold on to these islands, requesting the king, in late 1790, to send to the West Indies an expeditionary force of 6,000 troops and four capital ships to secure the islands from the British, maintain order, and support the Assembly of the North.[52] On the question of racial equality, its response was to be more equivocal. The position of Barnave here was again pivotal. Caught between the demands of the colonial lobby within the Committee, and the demands of metropolitan commerce, Barnave was anxious to oblige the colonists on the issue of legislative initiative,

---

[51] Quinney, *The Committee on Colonies*, pp. 216-7; Priestly, *France Overseas*, p. 320.

[52] Quinney, *The Committee on Colonies*, p. 251; Saintoyant, *La colonisation française pendant la Révolution*, Vol. 1, p. 298.

and thus maintain the deal implicit in the March decrees.[53] By May 1791 the Assembly was to prove, however, somewhat less obliging. This was due to a number of factors. Firstly, in the early months of that year popular support for Barnave and the Triumvirate began seriously to wane as a result of attacks from, and the rise in popularity of, more radical Jacobins. This shift in political fortunes only intensified after the king's Flight to Varennes in June 1791. Secondly, the Amis des Noirs, having failed to sway public opinion in favour of abolitionism, had quickly, and shrewdly, refocused their attention onto the issue of civil rights for free blacks and men of colour, a cause that was then taken up by the Jacobin Club and its many affiliates throughout France. The Amis des Noirs were helped, finally, in their pursuit of public support by the widespread revulsion felt in France at the news of Vincent Ogé's torture and execution at the hands of the white planters. These factors, among others, were crucial in shifting popular support in France behind the cause for civil rights for the mulattoes. This directly undermined Barnave's ability to steer his 'non-interventionist' agenda through the Assembly.

On 15 May, after one of the most tumultuous debates of the Constituent Assembly—during which Barnave called for a 'closing' of the Revolution—this struggle in France between the opponents and supporters of non-slave racial equality in colonies culminated in a compromise decree, granting political rights only to propertied men of colour born of two free parents, a group which in fact comprised only a fraction of the non-white, non-slave population.[54] Events in the colonies and back in Paris then took a dramatic turn. Instructed by the Governor of Saint-Domingue (among others) that the May decree was unenforcable,[55] and fearful of further moves toward colonial independence (with the subsequent loss of the *métropole's* traditional colonial trade advantages), the National Assembly suffered a basic loss of nerve. In the last fews days of its existence, on 24 September 1791, and at the instigation of Barnave, it retracted the decree of 15 May, and upheld its earlier policy of non-intervention.[56] Clearly, the majority of

---

[53] See, for example, the decrees of 11-12 October 1790, which confirmed the actions of the Governor Peynier and the Assembly of the North against the rebellious Assembly of Saint-Marc, in Quinney, *The Committee on Colonies*, p. 226; Saintoyant, *La colonisation française pendant la Révolution*, Vol. 1, pp. 387-389.

[54] AP, Vol. 26, 15 May 1791, pp. 87-97; Saintoyant, *La Colonisation Française pendant la Révolution*, Vol. 1, p. 127.

[55] See AP, Vol. 30, 12 September 1791, pp. 593-596.

[56] Lokke, *France and the Colonial Question*, p. 139.

the Assembly was not about to support the cause of Mulatto rights, if this could potentially result in the loss of its precious colonial trade advantages.

The colony of Saint-Domingue had, meanwhile, seen the outbreak in August of a full-scale and combined slave and mulatto revolt (the news of which would only reach France in October). Ironically, at much that same time that the Assembly was retracting the 15 May decree, the white planters on Saint-Domingue, buffeted by mulatto victories, and vastly outnumbered by the rebellious slaves, were concluding a series of accords with the men of colour, the two groups even forming a combined army against the slave revolt. This was just the kind of accommodation that Barnave and many other deputies had been hoping for all along, but it was not to last. When the white colonists finally learned of the Assembly's retraction of the 15 May decree, the accords were broken and the struggle against both the mulattoes and the slaves resumed.

The Sugar Islands and Colonial Policy under the Constituent Assembly

The other difficult issue glossed over in the March decrees was that of colonial trade. As the above account of colonial policy shows, the preservation of the *métropole's* advantages regarding colonial trade would remain throughout the whole period of 1789—91 a key concern of the National Assembly. This, from the perspective of the Assembly, appeared to be non-negotiable. That is, while the Assembly moved in 1791 to institute a measured relaxation of its general tariff protectionism regarding foreign trade, it was clear that the deputies had otherwise no intention of relaxing the existing metropolitan monopoly of colonial trade, in spite of colonial grievances. On the contrary, there was pressure from those representing French commercial interests for the Assembly actually to strengthen, rather than merely maintain, the *métropole's* monopoly of colonial commerce. For example, Delattre, in his report of 22 September 1791 on a proposed Navigation Act for France, suggested, in direct contrast to colonial demands, that the limited relaxation of the *exclusif* introduced in 1784 be closed off altogether. This was based on the assumption that the *métropole* would now be able, following the Revolution's liberation of French agriculture and commerce, to supply all the subsistence needs of the colonists).[57]

---

[57] AP, Vol. 31, 22 September 1791, pp. 209-10.

How may one characterise the views or considerations that underlay this determination to perpetuate a traditionally exploitative relationship between France and its sugar island colonies? In other words, what was the conceptual framework within which the Assembly moved to maintain, and justify, the political and economic subordination of the colonies to the will of the mother-country? Can this colonial policy be reasonably described as "essentially mercantilistic", as Valerie Quinney has claimed?[58]

On its own, and considered purely as a model of economic exploitation—the monopolisation of colonial commerce for the purposes of helping France attain a positive balance of trade—the *exclusif* could be described as 'mercantilistic'. Considered in its broader aspect, however, the Constituents' commercial or economic policy could hardly be described in such terms. Following Physiocratic principles, the Assembly had moved to create internal free trade in France, and hence a more integrated national economy, in the expectation that this would serve the goal of maximising domestic productivity. This action was, of course, based on the view that the key to national economic growth was now to be found in an increase in the volume of productive and commercial activity, rather than in the mere accumulation of specie. Yet the Constituents did not follow Physiocratic principles to the extent of assuming that colonial trade was a 'drain' on the French economy, nor even to the extent of foregoing a belief in the importance of a positive balance of trade. Quite the opposite. As Barnave and other deputies argued, colonial trade was to play a positive role in the economic regeneration of France, one that would, in fact, complement rather than undermine the other sectors of the French national economy. It would also be, for the time being at least, a vital component of this economy, and one that France could not afford to jeopardise. Without such trade, Barnave had noted on 8 March, the consequences would be immediate and far-reaching: trade and industry would be severely and disastrously affected, and the finances ruined. As such, the Constitution, "dans laquelle vous avez placé toutes vos espérances", would then itself be threatened, the despair born of poverty and hunger inviting the return again of either despotism or "cruel anarchy".[59]

There is also the question of how one might characterise the strategic aspect of the National Assembly's commercial policy with regard to the sugar island colonies. As we have seen, these plantation-

---

[58] Quinney, *The Committee on Colonies*, p. 348.
[59] AP, Vol. 12, 8 March, p. 70.

colonies were not valued by the Assembly purely and simply as a precious economic resource. They were also considered to play a vitally important role in the maintenance of French strategic power, both in Europe and on the seas. This was the point emphasised by Barnave on 8 March, and seconded by many other deputies, such as in the debates of 1790 on the Spanish Affair and on the right of war and peace.

It is important to note also that the political and strategic power of European states was not just viewed by the deputies as merely the net 'outcome' of either economic strength, commercial gain, or maritime activity. Particularly in areas outside of Europe, it was the very *means* by which this economic strength had been initially achieved, and through which it could be then maintained and further expanded. An understanding thus of the reciprocity between commercial profit and strategic power lay at the centre of the Constituent's policy with regard to France's West Indian colonies. That is, while colonial commerce was believed to be crucial in sustaining French maritime power, this maritime power was in turn considered by the deputies to be the pivot of the whole imperial 'system'. The strategic equation by which they understood this 'system' to operate can be described as basically circular, and quite direct: from one side, the colonies contributed, through monopolised trade, to the maintenance of a maritime balance of power (and by extension, to the preservation of a continental balance of power). Yet it was only through the employment of such maritime power that France was able, in turn, to protect its colonies, and its trade.

The East India Company and Trade with India

The National Assembly having affirmed in March 1790 the importance to France of its West Indian possessions, what was then the policy stance of the deputies toward French possessions in the East Indies, that is, in India and all other areas east of the Cape of Good Hope? To what extent did they form part of a geostrategic equation similar to that in the West Indies? In other words, what ultimate goals were these scattered possessions understood to serve? What means—economic and strategic—were required, and considered appropriate, in order to fulfill these goals?

Such a general appraisal was forced upon the Constituent Assembly following the raising of two specific issues in and around the Assembly during the winter of 1789—90. The first of these two issues concerned the ongoing status of the French East India Company, resurrected by

Calonne in 1785, and which had since been the only official conduit for French commerce with India. The principal question here concerned French commercial activity: should Franco-Indian trade continue as a company monopoly or be open to all French nationals? If the latter, then what kind of tariff regime should apply specifically to Indian goods entering France? The second issue concerned French strategic activity: the decision of the royal government in 1787 to withdraw all its troops from Pondichéry and relocate them on the Ile de France. Would the Assembly endorse or reject the royal government's policy of concentrating French strategic resources in the Indian ocean on this island, or move to reverse it? Both these issues would be the subject of some controversy in French public affairs.

When debate began on the India Company in early April 1790, the Company received criticism from two directions. From one side, the company was denounced as being incompatible with the Rights of Man and the new constitution of France. Here, principle was presumed to coincide with perceived national interest. That one privileged consortium should have exclusive control of French commerce with India was not only seen as palpably unfair, particularly to other French merchants who were thus unable to participate more directly in that trade, and a vestige of traditional 'despotic' practices, but was also seen as causing serious ill-effects to the French national economy, because of perceived gross inefficiencies in its carrying trade. From another side, the company was criticised for behaving contrary to what, in fact, was *traditionally* expected of such privileged companies, by allegedly serving the interests of sheer profit above the needs of national competitiveness. The India Company was alleged by Delattre to be "dishonouring their flag", that is, profiting from their privilege in such a way as to serve the commercial interests of the British, rather than those of France.[60] The French state was said to have borne the cost of this privilege in the first place, yet appeared to receive from it inadequate returns.

Some of those who argued for the retention of this privilege, such as Duval d'Eprémesnil, asserted that it was actually 'free' trade that had made the French 'slaves' to the British in India, during the sixteen years between the initial abolition of the French monopoly and when it was reinstated anew in 1785.[61] Like Duval, the other principal defenders of

---

[60] *Ibid.*, 3 April 1790, p. 534.
[61] *Ibid.*, 2 April 1790, p. 526. Duval's position here may perhaps in some way be accounted for by the fact that he was himself born in India, in the French colony

the India Company, Maury and Le Couteulx, argued for the retention of this privilege (or, at least, against its immediate abolition) on the grounds of imperative necessity, that the conditions of Indian commerce in fact required a company monopoly to serve best the needs of national competitiveness. Maury even claimed to accept that in principle this 'privilege' was unjust, but nonetheless questioned whether privileges ought to be viewed as contrary to the new constitution, if they could be seen to be in the national interest.[62]

Le Couteulx, in a lengthy speech, argued similarly that while one might accept the abolition of all privilege in theory, in certain cases circumstances dictated that this principle be 'bent' in order better to serve French political interests, particularly with regard to its exterior commerce.[63] There could be no better example, Le Couteulx asserted, of the Assembly already having acceded to "imperious and salutary necessity" than in the case of France's Caribbean colonies. In his view the precedent was thus well established. A privilege of sorts, the *exclusif*, one clearly contrary to the Rights of Man, had been recently upheld by the Assembly, despite the particular grievances of the colonists in the Caribbean, and supposedly in the interests overall of the French Empire.[64] It was no less imperative to France, he argued, that the India Company and its monopoly be preserved, particularly given the ambitions of the British to seize that share of the trade held in India by the French.[65]

Hernoux, in an earlier report on this issue of 18 March, canvassed figures which purported to show during which period in the last few decades the India trade had flourished most, noting that these figures were subject to contestation.[66] For most of those involved in the debate on this privilege, however, the question of whether Indian trade would be best exploited by either a monopolised or an 'open' carrying trade, was largely beside the point. What, for many deputies, the issue of this

---

of Pondichéry, and, furthermore, was married to a daughter of one of the former India Company's directors.
[62] *Ibid.*, 1 April 1790, p. 514.
[63] *Ibid.*, Vol. 12, 3 April 1790, p. 532. Jean-Barthélemy Le Couteulx-Cantelau (1746-1818). A financier and magistrate in provincial France before the Revolution, he was recognised in the Assembly as a specialist on financial and commercial matters. He authored a detailed report on the English textile industry, which was presented to the Assembly on 3 April 1790. *Ibid.*, p. 537.
[64] *Ibid.*, p. 532.
[65] *Ibid.*, p. 531.
[66] *Ibid.*, 18 March, p. 225.

privilege really hinged upon was whether or not the Indian trade was actually beneficial to the French economy in the first place.

This question in itself proved highly controversial. Maury and Le Couteulx put their views in no uncertain terms. For Maury, the India trade was in fact a "scourge" to France, harmful to the growth of the French economy and the accumulation of national wealth, largely because, since there existed a substantial trade imbalance with India, it drew precious specie from France without adequate return.[67] Imported Indian goods were paid for not by exported manufactured goods from France (for which there was very low demand in India) but by specie. The more this trade flourished, Maury suggested, the more the state would be impoverished.

Here Maury echoed the traditional, mercantilistic prejudice, firstly, against the net loss of bullion, and secondly, against the importing of so-called 'luxury' goods, which, when in the form of finished products, supposedly did not contribute to the growth of French manufactures.[68] From much the same basis he also decried an alleged British 'plot' to scupper the French East India Company, and remove thereby the primary means by which France could limit the entry of both manufactured and luxury goods from India. Those in France who then demanded the abolition of the Company, these "apostles of luxury", were, he pronounced, the true enemies of the nation, since their views were contrary to its prosperity.[69]

With equal forthrightness, Le Couteulx also pointed out the dangers of this trade to the French economy. He even went so far as to assert that "le commerce de l'Europe, fait dans l'Inde, est plus préjudiciable à la France qu'à aucune autre puissance", and that Indian industry (specifically, its textile manufacturing) would be a greater rival to French industry than that of Europe, even more than that of the British.[70] Cotton manufacturers in France would be particularly threatened by the importation of finished textiles from India. In this respect Le Couteulx repeated Maury's charge that the British, already in a strong position, had ambitions to monopolise Indian commerce and, thereon, to flood French markets with cheap Indian textiles, thus ruining the French textile industry of which, he averred, the British had

---

[67] *Ibid.*, 1 April, p. 514.
[68] These 'luxury' goods included porcelain, silks and other textiles, all of which were produced in France in significant quatities.
[69] *Ibid.*, 1 April, p. 515.
[70] *Ibid.*, 3 April, p. 530.

long been jealous.[71] On this basis he counselled the Assembly not to take any imprudent steps that might jeopardise France's economic interests, concluding also that present circumstances did by no means favour an unregulated trade with India.

Nairac, Dupré and Guinebaud countered in their turn that the India trade was in fact absolutely necessary to France's prosperity. Nairac asserted that the removal of the India Company's privilege, so "oppressive" and "harmful" to France (not to mention contrary to public opinion), would soon see this trade flourish like never before. This would be beneficial to the French economy, he said, for French manufacturers had up to now been unable to meet demand on such goods.[72] Not to participate in this trade, added Dupré, meant these goods would be purchased through other countries, such as Britain and Holland,[73] thus according these countries an unnecessary profit and degree of economic influence over France.

Signalled early on in Hernoux's report of 18 March, and confirmed in Fontenay's report and draft decree of 28 June, the ultimate policy response of the Agriculture and Commerce Committee recognised the issue to be actually somewhat more of a dilemma. The declaration of the Assembly, at the end of the session on 3 April was that "le commerce de l'Inde, au delà du cap de Bonne-Espérance, est libre pour tous les Français".[74] This meant that all French traders could now participate in Indian commerce with France. However, in their policy stance, the Committee responded equally to the desire to shield French industry, particularly the as yet underdeveloped textile sector, from cheap foreign imports. Against such goods, it introduced a policy of measured protectionism. "Vous n'oublierez pas, Messieurs", said Fontenay,

---

[71] *Ibid.*, p. 531.
[72] *Ibid.*, 2 April, p. 519.
[73] *Ibid.*, 3 April, p. 529.
[74] *Ibid.*, p. 535. This decree was voted only after seven hours of passionate debate, at the end of which the Assembly had still been unable to come to a decision regarding access to trade beyond the Cape. What finally persuaded the Assembly to support the opening up of trade beyond the Cape to all French merchants was an address by the *députés extraordinaires* of Bordeaux, on behalf of five hundred merchants, who more or less offered, in return for the end of the India Company's monopoly, to underwrite future "projets de finance" adopted by the National Assembly. Letaconnoux, 'Le Comité des députés extraordinaires', p.184.

que l'expérience de ces dernières années ne nous a que trop appris combien il est imprudent de mettre l'industrie aux prises avec l'industrie étrangère, avant qu'elle soit en état de combattre aux armes égales.[75]

This had been the view also of a number of other deputies, even many of those who otherwise disdained or denounced as odious the privilege of the India Company. By implication, the Declaration of the Rights of Man and Citizen had required the abolition of this privilege, but what if this should adversely effect national industry, by making it more vulnerable to foreign competition? One of the very first speakers on this issue, Gillet de la Jacqueminière, pointed to this dilemma and made a plea for some kind of 'middle way', whereby the privilege could be abolished yet national industry remain protected from the dangers of unfettered free trade, which would thus supposedly conciliate the interests of all concerned—the home and colonial merchants, manufacturers, and the nation overall.[76]

To this end Fontenay's report of 28 June stated, on behalf of the Committee, that it would be the condition of all French commerce undertaken that imports from India should continue to be made through one port only, that of Lorient in Brittany. This continued choice of Lorient was because of its supposedly excellent facilities for warehousing, and for monitoring and controlling the passage of imports into France.[77] Heavy tariffs were placed there on goods thought to compete with those produced in France, and some Indian goods were to be prohibited altogether—accepted only into France by way of *entrepôt*.

The general effect of these stipulations was to change and sharpen the focus of debate concerning the East Indies. For with the monopoly of the French East India Company now a dead letter, the debate shifted in focus to become an issue more simply of protectionism versus free trade, one no less controversial than that of privilege. At the centre of this debate lay the Committee's proposal to continue Lorient's position as the sole official port handling imports from India. The principal speakers against this 'monopoly', Nairac and Mirabeau, addressed the Assembly on 28 June. Both speakers thought this measure to be contrary not only to revolutionary principle, but also to what they considered to be the national interest. Not accepting the contention that the India trade was harmful to France, they believed that the deliberate restriction of that trade to be unjust and unreasonable, and

---

[75] *Ibid.*, Vol. 16, 28 June 1790, p. 543.
[76] *Ibid.*, Vol. 12, 1 April 1790, p. 513.
[77] *Ibid.*, Vol. 16, 28 June 1790, p. 544.

ultimately counter-productive to its own alleged goal, since it would again only encourage smuggling.[78] From their perspective, France's future prosperity could only be guaranteed by a more complete liberty of commerce, one that encouraged rather than discouraged trade. As Nairac declared,

> L'influence de la liberté s'étendra d'ailleurs sur ce vaste empire. Notre agriculture va devenir florissante, ses productions se multiplieront; elles offriront plus de matières à l'industrie et aux arts; elles rendront les échanges plus nécessaires, et c'est à nous, Messieurs, à creuser d'avance les canaux par lequels ces sources de richesse et de puissance doivent couler.[79]

In his rather more declamatory style, Mirabeau declared similarly that since the laws of equality and liberty proscribed all types of 'exclusive regimes' (unless public interest should imperatively require the contrary), then trade restrictions such as this could only be regarded as contrary to the Rights of Man. There was only one reasonable code of commerce, he said bluntly, and that was "laissez faire, laissez passer".[80] Furthermore, as Nairac posited, in the French empire, as in an increasingly global economy, there was a "universal chain" or web of commercial and economic relationships. This constituted a kind of "equilibrium" that further protectionism would only upset, bringing with it disastrous results.[81]

Running through this rhetoric of high principle and national interest was, however, a concern to advance local interests. After fervently denouncing Lorient's monopoly of the India trade, and protectionism in general, as contrary to natural rights and destructive of international competitiveness, Mirabeau went on to imply that if there had to be a single port for the India trade, then reason dictated that this port should be Marseille, his own constituency. Given that Turkey was the greatest consumer of Indian goods, for the purposes of *entrepôt* it was preferable that the port which dealt principally and directly with Turkey should handle the India trade. Since Lorient was isolated on the Atlantic coast and hence costly to access by other French merchants, Marseille, he concluded, was in a far better position to re-export these goods, and thereby improve France's balance of trade.[82]

---

[78] *Ibid.*, p. 549.
[79] *Ibid.*
[80] *Ibid.*, p. 554.
[81] *Ibid.*, p. 549.
[82] *Ibid.*, p. 537-8.

When the debate resumed on 15 July, Malouet countered Mirabeau to the extent of proclaiming the necessity of protectionism, seeming initially to support also the monopoly of Lorient.[83] However, agreeing with Mirabeau that the Mediterranean indeed offered the best opportunities for re-exporting Indian goods, or at least, presented the only markets for Indian goods that France could effectively penetrate, he suggested that this 'monopoly' should include also a Mediterranean port. This, however, should not be an open port such as Marseille, but one that offered the same facilities for control and against smuggling as did Lorient. This port was none other than Toulon, for whom, perhaps not coincidentally, Malouet had been the Intendant in 1788.[84]

The general response here by members of the Agriculture and Commerce Committee was more or less to reiterate that the choice of Lorient was in the national interest, and to rebut the charge that this measure was in contravention of revolutionary principles. Roussillou rejoined that since all French merchants could participate in the India trade *through* Lorient this hardly contravened the principles of liberty and equality. Roederer, though not on the Committee, had also stated that since Marseille had also profited from a monopoly of sorts (vis-à-vis the Levant trade), its representatives were not themselves in a position to denounce that of others.[85] Above all, the members of the Committee, while endorsing internal free trade, nonetheless reaffirmed the great necessity of measured external protectionism. For Roussillou, as for Le Chapelier (the eventual architect of internal economic liberalism),[86] the India trade remained "onerous" to the French state.[87] While, however, Roussillou was in this case prepared to concede that this monopoly might be extended to another port, Le Chapelier

---

[83] *Ibid.*, Vol. 17, 15 July 1790, p. 91.
[84] *Ibid.*, p. 93.
[85] *Ibid.*, Vol. 16, 28 June 1790, p. 553.
[86] Isaac-René-Guillaume Le Chapelier (1754-1794). Lawyer, Member of the Third Estate and a founder of the Breton Club, he became the author of the 'Le Chapelier Law', which forbad workers' associations. He became a Feuillant in 1791 and was later guillotined during the Terror.
[87] Comparing the trade of the West and East Indies, Roussillou commented that "le commerce avec nos [Caribbean] colonies est aussi avantageaux que celui de L'Inde est nuisible à l'Etat". On Mirabeau's general proposition of "Laisser faire, laisser passer", Roussillou replied that "s'il a entendu ne parler que du régime intérieur du royaume, je suis fort de son avis ... Mais s'il a voulu appliquer la maxime: *laisser faire, laisser passer*, à l'importation libre de l'étranger, des draperies, des soieries, des toiles, des vins et eaux-de-vie, je lui déclare que mon opinion est entièrement opposée à la sienne". AP, Vol. 17, 15 July 1790, p. 95.

remained unpersuaded that the extension of this monopoly to certain other ports such as Bordeaux, Marseille, or Toulon would be at all useful to the state. Moreover, to those who found Lorient's 'monopoly' an infringement to liberty, he retorted that if 'liberty' meant the destruction of French manufacturing, agriculture and commerce, then they had better examine the consequences of their principles. After all, would they, also for the sake of 'liberty', want to stop the quarantining of goods from the Levant? Hardly. Lorient must therefore, he said, remain the sole port.[88] Once again, the fact that Le Chapelier himself came from Brittany, where Lorient was situated, may well have been significant here.

Profit, Power and Strategic Policy in the Eastern Hemisphere

Underlying this debate on the India Company, and Franco-Indian trade, was a more or less implicit debate on the relationship between commercial gain and political power. For Paul Nairac, one of the more articulate advocates of freer trade policy in the Assembly, external commerce was vital to France's international position as much in a political as in an economic sense. However, he considered that it was freer trade, rather than continued protectionism, that would in fact best contribute to an augmentation of France's wealth and power.[89] Conscious of the economic rivalry of Britain, and the power that it derived from the wealth it drew from India, Nairac stated that

> il faut avoir à la fois des manufactures florissantes et un grand commerce extérieur, et ne pas abandonner aux autres nations un commerce de plus de 60 millions que nous pouvons ajouter à celui que nous faisons déja. Jetez les yeux sur l'Angleterre: son commerce de l'Inde est immense ... Il fournit presques toutes les nations de l'Europe; il fournit à ses propres besoins, et cependant les manufactures n'y languissent pas.

Thus, he continued,

> comme l'effet du commerce est de revêtir un corps politique de toute la force qu'il est capable de recevoir, ce n'est qu'en étendant votre commerce extérieur que vous y parviendrez. [By this means] vous éléverez la France au plus haut degré de richesse, de population et de puissance.[90]

---

[88] *Ibid.*, p. 98.
[89] *Ibid.*, Vol. 16, 28 June 1790, p. 548.
[90] *Ibid.*, p. 548.

Nairac had, however, rather less to say about how this commerce should be garnered in the first place, and what might be required, in India, to make such commerce serve French interests first and foremost. For those more wary of the Indian trade, this was in fact the crux of the issue. As Maury argued, the secret of British prosperity with regard to India was not that it had brought, at least directly, an expansion of the British home economy. Aside from the fact that Britain did not itself consume but rather re-exported Indian goods to northern Europe, the real source of their success in India was, he observed, the growth of their territorial dominion on the sub-continent; this presently brought them internal Indian revenues amounting to some 320 million *livres* per annum.[91] There was thus for the British a close nexus, in India, between profit and military power, this 'extracted treasure' evidently contributing greatly to British prosperity and power both in India, and in Europe. This being the case, French activity in India should, as Maury (and Le Couteulx) then implied, have above all a political and arguably 'negative' role: to check or even reverse the expansion of British trade or dominion in India, lest this impact upon the balance of power in Europe and elsewhere.

The crucial importance to France of military and land-based power in India was also argued by those, such as Duval d'Eprémesnil, who had defended the privilege of the India Company before the National Assembly in more positive terms. That Britain had achieved such great trade advantages in India was due, in his view also, to one central factor: that it had not confined itself to a mere commercial role, but had also made itself a *landed* power there, significantly, through the instrument of "une compagnie souveraine armée".[92] This, Duval suggested to the Assembly, was the lesson that Dupleix had known, and had tried to act on so many years before. Now, he lamented, it looked as if domestic political troubles in France would, humiliatingly, prevent the French in India from profiting from this lesson, and thus from creating a proper base upon which to challenge there the power of the British. As the Abbé Bérardier had, on 2 April, also argued, "une compagnie peut seule rétablir la gloire de la France dans l'Inde"; furthermore, "il serait ignominieux de renoncer à la puissance que nous avons eue", particularly when, as he said, "nous y avons des amis puissants" (among the local princes), on whom they could presumably count for help. Even the king

---

[91] *Ibid.*, Vol. 12, 1 April 1790, p. 515.
[92] *Ibid.*, 3 April 1790, p. 527.

of Cochinchina, Bérardier concluded, was favourably disposed toward France.[93]

Given these views, it is not surprising that the royal government's decision in 1788 to relocate French troops from Pondichéry to the Ile de France should have become the subject of grave concern, even alarm, among those then attached to the India trade. For such interested parties, French activity in India held both a positive and negative dimension: they believed not only that Indian commerce was of benefit to France in positive terms, but that it was also imperative as a goal to deny the British further expansion of their seemingly commanding position in Indian trade and internal politics. As such, in late 1789, the *députés extraordinaires du commerce et des manufactures* raised, on behalf of the merchants of Lorient, objections to the withdrawal of troops from Pondichéry. They feared that this would leave this coastal position unprotected and totally vulnerable to the depradations of either the British or Indian powers.

The Minister, the comte de La Luzerne, for his part, stood firm behind the policy of withdrawal. The Ministry merely made public the calculations that had initially led in 1787 to this 'rationalisation' of strategic resources in the Indian Ocean: namely, that the re-fortification and garrisoning of Pondichéry was unnecessarily costly, and that the position had in any case proven in the past to have been indefensible, even against poorly mounted attacks. At a time when the situation in France had and still demanded stringent economies in government expenditure, France, the Minister argued, was compelled to make what he and his advisors believed to be the best use of their limited strategic resources in the eastern hemisphere. This meant leaving French possessions in India simply as trading posts, while concentrating military resources on the Ile de France. This relocation, the Minister argued, by making this island a more secure base for military operations elsewhere, particularly in India, would ensure the future of French power and influence in the region.[94]

The public justifications for this policy, however, failed to convince its critics. Rejecting the Minister's arguments, the *députés*

---

[93] *Ibid.*, 2 April 1790, p. 519.
[94] See the comte de La Luzerne's 'Eclaircissements sur le mémoire adressé à l'assemblée nationale par les habitans de Lorient relativement à l'évacuation de l'Inde', BN-NAF-9373, f. 175 (incorrectly dated 1788—the document clearly dates from 1789 or after). Secretly, of course, the Government continued to hope that, through clandestine diplomacy, the French could prevail upon Tippoo and Nizam Ali to bury their differences and combine in a stable opposition to the growth of British power in India.

extraordinaires more or less accused the government of wishful thinking, and of failing to appreciate fully the importance of France's possessions in India. According to their calculations, French commercial power and diplomatic influence on the sub-continent were interconnected, and together dependent upon a French willingness to maintain a permanent military presence there. Having thus asserted that France, in their view, had no choice but to remain as a political force within India itself, the *députés extraordinaires* then pressed the National Assembly to order the immediate restoration of the Pondichéry garrison (to the figure of 2,500 European troops with an equivalent number of sepoys).[95]

For the Pondichériens themselves, the importance of a French military presence in India itself was clear and urgent. This was especially the case, now that war appeared to be brewing between Britain and Tippoo Sultan, France's old ally in India. Thus, in this same month, March 1790, as La Luzerne was, coincidentally, formally announcing to the National Assembly the royal government's decision to demilitarise Pondichéry, the assembled 'citizens' of Pondichéry, having heard the news of the Revolution in France, themselves issued a *mémoire* addressed to the National Assembly.[96] In it they criticised the royal government's decision to downgrade Pondichéry militarily (finally effected between July and September 1789), and place it under the command of a Governor-General residing as far away as the Ile de France. In its own summary, it stated that

> les intérêts politiques de la Nation et ceux de son commerce lui font également la loi de conserver ses établissements dans l'Inde, qu'elle peut les protéger sans faire des dépenses au-dessus de ses moyens; que Pondichéry doit nécessairement être le chef-lieu de nos établissements, et que, comme tel, it doit être défendu par des fortifications et des troupes ...

To abandon the defence of Pondichéry was to them a dangerous and indeed false economy, for they asserted that

---

[95] "Sans l'appareil militaire", the députés demanded, "croit-on que les Indiens seront jaloux d'être nos alliés, lorsqu'ils nous verront sans fortresses, sans point d'appui?". *Précis sur l'Affaire de Pondichéry, ou, Réponse des Députés extraordinaires des manufactures & du Commerce de France, aux Eclairissemens fournis sur le Mémoire adressé à l'Assemblée Nationale, relativement à l'evacuation de l'Inde* (Paris, 1790), pp. 5, 16 (Marine-37-H-21).

[96] '*Mémoire de l'assemblée des citoyens*', March 1790, in *Doléances des Peuples Coloniaux à L'Assemblée National Constituante 1789-1790* (Paris, 1989). (A.N., C42, plaquette 368, pièce 9)

notre existence dans l'Inde, telle faible qu'elle soit, suffit pour arrêter les progrès de la grandeur anglaise [et] que l'économie que l'on a en vue, en évacuant Pondichéry, sert bien plutost les Anglais que la Nation française.[97]

This was not a question of wanting military conflict that might disrupt the "peaceful operation of commerce", assured the colonists. Rather, an adequate defense of Pondichéry would actually be a *guarantee* of stability, by acting as a bulwark against the ambitions of their jealous rivals, the British. "Elle nous donnerait", they said, "des alliés, elle leur ferait partager les douceurs de notre tranquillité, elle contiendrait nos enemies, elle en imposerait à nos rivaux, et elle soutiendrait l'honneur et la majesté de la Nation".[98] Moreover, it was not just the fate of Pondichéry that was at stake here, they argued, but France's position in India and in Asian commerce generally. The placing of regional command, and the concentration of military resources, far away on the Ile de France, seemed to them particularly egregious. Knowing full well the vagaries of local Indian politics, how, they asked, could France best take advantage of opportunities for extending its power and influence in India when decisions were to be made, and troops dispatched, from such a distance? Furthermore, if France's position in India was sacrificed, would not the Iles de France and de Bourbon simply become useless and a further burden on the treasury? Of only minor economic value in themselves, the primary purpose of these island colonies was to act as waystations for the sea traffic between France and the East Indies. Their military capacity to support French establishments in India or elsewhere in the region, the colonists argued, was severely limited. In short, without a proper military presence on the actual Indian sub-continent, France, it was asserted, could not hope to compete there with the British.[99] Its prospects generally in the East Indies and China would, as a result of this policy, also be bleak.

In the event, the colonists refused to comply with the orders for the completion of the military evacuation of Pondichéry, resolving to maintain its defences where they could, and thereon hope for the

---

[97] *Ibid.*, p. 142.
[98] *Ibid.*, p 134.
[99] *Ibid.*, p. 140. According to this mémoire the consequences of such an evacuation would be far-ranging. They would include, they said, "la ruine de nos établissements, l'anéantissement total de notre commerce dans l'Inde, l'accroisement terrible des Anglais en Europe, et notre avilissement aux yeux de l'Asie, et peut-être de tout l'univers...". *Ibid.*, p. 132.

best.[100] On 15 October, 1790, in the National Assembly back in Paris, Jean-Louis Monneron, the recently admitted deputy for Pondichéry, took the floor to plead the cause of the colonists, and to propose a plan of action. He addressed, first of all, the question of the economic value of France's Indian possessions, extolling the present and positive benefits to France of Indian commerce, and warning of the grave consequences to French manufacturing if prohibitive trade restrictions were put in place. France, with its new constitution, he told the deputies, was now called on to play a greater role in this trade, a source of wealth which he claimed the previous regime had only misunderstood; "les effets de notre Constitution", he said,

> doivent nous faire monter au rang que la situation physique de la France nous impose, et c'est cette heureuse position qui explique notre existence au milieu de tous les vices et de toutes les erreurs de notre ancienne administration.[101]

The general expansion of French trade in the East Indies would, Monneron asserted, carry with it a variety of further benefits that was indeed global in scope. For one thing, it would stimulate the French shipbuilding industry, which might in turn provide the vessels by which France could better penetrate markets presently dominated by British and Dutch merchant fleets (such as in the Northern trade). More important, however, were perhaps its overall global strategic benefits. He pointed out that

> L'Angleterre, par le fait seul de ses possessions et son commerce aux Indes, reçoit chaque année une augmentation de richesses de cent vingt millions, qui lui donnent une influence bien sensible et bien marquée dans le mouvement général des affaires en Europe.[102]

---

[100] See Dennis Showalter, 'Ni Tumulte, Ni Grandeur: Revolution in Pondicherry', *Journal of Indian History* (Golden Jubilee Volume, 1973), p. 578.

[101] AP, Vol. 19, 15 October 1790, p. 655. The recent affair involving Cochinchina was, for Monneron, just one example of commercial opportunities being previously mishandled. The French Governor of Pondichéry, Conway, had decided not to assist the erstwhile emperor of Cochinchina to regain his throne. If it had not then been for the Bishop of Adran, who himself helped to organise some military assistance independently (from among the citizens of Pondichéry), France, Monneron observed, may not have thus gained, as it did from this venture, some excellent opportunities for lucrative trade with Cochinchina. *Ibid.*, p. 656.

[102] *Ibid.*

This predominance that Britain enjoyed in India, and which accorded them such power in Europe, was, he stressed, by no means guaranteed. British possessions were encircled by the forces of four major Indian princes, at least one of whom, Tippoo-Sultan, was currently in conflict with them. Monneron urged that a united effort among these princes to break the stranglehold of the British in India, and confine them within six months to the coastal ports, was not impossible to engineer. Tippoo-Sultan had already amply demonstrated his amity and support for the French in Pondichéry and gave indications that he would be a faithful ally against the British.[103] The fact also that the British establishments, and their military resources, were so far spread out, only increased the precariousness of the British position, and the chances for the French to re-assert their power on the sub-continent. This alone, it was implied, would produce a significant shift in the European and global balance of power toward France, with enormous economic benefits.

For the above reasons, Monneron asserted, the military evacuation of Pondichéry ordered by the Minister could not be more "impolitic". It could even lead potentially to the loss of Ile de France itself, since, as he alleged, that island depended ultimately on the food supplies sent by the Pondichériens. If it was simply just a question of cost, he argued, then concentrating military resources on Ile de France would quickly prove far more expensive than the maintenance of Pondichéry's own defences. But this was not, he reminded the deputies, just a question of financial cost. It was also a question of the security of France and its whole empire, for this measure held serious implications not only for French possessions in India, but also for "votre tranquillité en Europe, et à la sûreté de vos colonies occidentales". In such a propitious moment, with a Revolution in the process of re-invigorating France, would they needlessly jeopardise their future in the East Indies and, moreover, their global future? As he appealed to the Assembly,

> Consenteriez-vous, Messieurs, à adopter une mesure aussi honteuse dans ses principes que désastreuse dans ses effets, l'évacuation de vos colonies de l'Inde? Voudriez-vous, dans une moment de régénération, et lorsque vous vous livrez, avec un courage qui étonne l'Europe, à transfuser des sucs nourriciers et

---

[103] Already financially supporting the French military establishment in India, Tippoo-Sultan sent emissaries to France in 1788 to offer handsome trading privileges to the French crown, if they would in turn provide troops to support him in his war against the English. Such, however, was the parlous state of the finances and the sense of domestic crisis, that the offer was not taken up by the French Government. Malouet, *Mémoires*, Vol. I, p. 206.

vivifants dans toutes les parties de l'Empire, que ses dernières ramifications déssèchent entre vos mains?[104]

Only the assurance of France's ongoing protection could prevent this, Monneron concluded, proposing a draft decree to that effect. Monneron demanded the full restoration of Pondichéry's former garrison of 2,400 European troops and 1200 sepoys, to which would now also be added 200 black troops. Overall, he estimated, the cost of this restoring this garrison, and completing Pondichéry's fortifications, would be roughly equivalent to the revenues the French government currently drew from its trade with India.[105]

Monneron had hoped for a prompt and favourable response from the National Assembly. It would, however, take ten further months for the deputies to come to any decision on the re-investment of Pondichéry. In the interim the Assembly quickly moved to refer the matter, without discussion, to the combined Marine, Colonial, Military, Commerce and Diplomatic Committees. An initial proposal also for the creation of an 'Asian Committee' was overturned, in favour of co-opting Monneron onto the Colonial Committee, for which he became a *rapporteur*.

One may assume that a major reason for this delay, and lack of open discussion, was that the Assembly became, over 1790-91, increasingly absorbed with the problems and ever worsening situation of the West Indian colonies, an issue which clearly took priority over other colonial concerns. The deputies had, initially, not even wanted to consider the question of Pondichéry at all, at least not until the problem specifically of Saint-Domingue had been satisfactorily resolved. Yet, one may surmise that this was not the only reason. One may argue that the proposals outlined by Monneron in his report were highly problematic in themselves. For the deputies, the provision of an adequate garrison for Pondichéry in order to protect French trade was one thing. Pursuing an alliance with Tippoo for the purposes of combating the British in India was, however, a different prospect altogether, and one that held enormous and troublesome implications, both in constitutional and strategic terms. Firstly, as any alliance with Tippoo would be undoubtably offensive in character, it would be patently in contradiction

---

[104] AP, Vol. 19, 15 October 1790, p. 659.
[105] *Ibid.*, p. 660. To this he appended a detailed inventory of the fortifications of Pondichéry, and the estimated costs of repairing them, so that they might withstand a siege.

with the Assembly's earlier renunciation of offensive treaties and foreign conquests.[106]

Secondly, however much the deputies may have agreed with Monneron that India would henceforth be the pivot upon which the global balance of power between Britain and France would ultimately rest, in the short-term France could in no way afford to provoke a war with Britain, in India or elsewhere. The whole episode of the Nootka Sound Crisis had exposed, for all to see, the present and undeniable strategic realities to which France was presently subject.[107] That both the Assembly and the French government had been so desperate to achieve a diplomatic solution to that crisis was largely owing to the fact of palpable French weakness, compounded now by the dissension, chaos and agitation that had, since the Revolution, overtaken France and many of its colonies.[108] By contrast, it was well known that Britain was now stronger militarily than it had ever been in either hemisphere. As a result of the Dutch crisis in 1787, the British could now also rely again on the support of the Dutch navy, and have access to the network of Dutch colonial ports, particularly at the Cape of Good Hope and in the Indian Ocean. It was doubtful whether France would receive much help from its own maritime ally, Spain, having effectively abandoned that power during the Nootka Crisis.

So concerned had the French government been not to provoke the British that they had been at pains to reassure them that reinforcements sent to their Caribbean islands were intended only to maintain order there. There was good reason for the British to accept that this was, in fact, the case. The situation with Pondichéry was somewhat different. It would have been threatening enough to the British had the former Pondichéry garrison not been withdrawn, so precarious was their position still on the sub-continent. For France, however, to *remilitarise*

---

[106] Far from approving of any military presence in India, let alone military adventures, the journalist Brissot scornfully denounced both these proposals—restoring Pondichéry's garrison, and renewing the alliance with Tippoo—as typical of the "politique tracassière" of the former government in relation to India: "L'espoir de relever la puissance françoise dans l'Inde telle qu'elle étoit au temps des Dupleix et des Bussy, est absurde et irréconciliable avec nos bases constitutionelles, puisque nous avons renoncé à toute espèce de conquêtes". See *Le Patriote François*, No. 435, 17 October 1790, pp. 1-2.

[107] See Chapters 4 and 7.

[108] The internal strife that had made Saint-Domingue and Martinique so vulnerable to attack was not even confined to the West Indies, for the Ile de France and Chandernagor experienced themselves, in 1790, a measure of popular agitation inspired by the Revolution back in France. See Monneron, AP, Vol. 22, 20 January 1791, p. 349.

Pondichéry in the strength proposed by Monneron would likely have been regarded by the British as an extremely provocative act. The British government could not have been reassured that such a reinstalment of French military power in India was not likely to be a prelude to armed intervention in Indian politics, or at least to a support of Britain's enemies. That the ultimate target, in any case, of such action would be Britain had, moreover, not even been disguised in Monneron's speech, but was explicitly spelt out.

It would have been reasonable for the deputies then to assume that a reinforcement of Pondichéry to its former strength would have provoked some form of retaliatory action from the British. It was also entirely possible that British retaliation would not be confined either to India or the Indian Ocean. Whether, in fact the British took the French threat seriously or not, the reinforcement might also have proven the excuse for Britain finally to launch, as many in France had feared, a general war of revenge against French colonial power in both western and eastern hemispheres. France would have been hardly able to withstand such a comprehensive onslaught, as the deputies well knew. Thus, one may conclude that while on the one hand the full restoration of Pondichéry's garrison may have seemed a logical response to fears, voiced even by the freetraders, about the unchecked growth of British power around the globe, on the other hand, the deputies knew that the outbreak of war with Britain could, at least for the time-being, prove cataclysmic for France, and probably lead to the destruction of their entire overseas empire.

Such general anxieties would have been sufficient reason for the Assembly to delay any immediate response to the matter of Pondichéry's defenses. Yet there were also some specific criticisms of Monneron's proposals, which somewhat clouded the whole issue of the requirements for a simple defence of Pondichéry. Firstly, the deputies representing the twin islands of Ile de France and de Bourbon, though sympathetic to the plight of the Pondichériens, took umbrage at Monneron's suggestion that the islands would actually lose all importance without Pondichéry as a fortified *point d'appui* in India, and that the loss of Pondichéry would, in turn, necessarily entail the loss of the islands themselves. These deputies argued that, regardless of Pondichéry's fate, the Ile de France could, and indeed should, continue to be held as a stronghold and base of operations for French power in the Indian ocean and beyond.[109]

---

[109] See the *Mémoire présenté à l'Assemblée Nationale, par les Habitans des Iles de France et de Bourbon, actuellement à Paris*, Paris, 1790, pp. 12-15.

Secondly, Charles Mallet de Maisonpré, the *député-suppléant* for Pondichéry, published in January 1791 a *mémoire* dissenting from the position of Monneron, and challenging his recommendations.[110] Mallet agreed that it was vital for an independent French trade in India that Pondichéry be protected militarily. He agreed also that the defence of Ile de France was linked to that of Pondichéry. Where he disagreed with Monneron was on the question of how much money, and how many troops, would be required for France to maintain an adequate military presence in India. He began by reminding the deputies that French activity on the sub-continent was presently constrained by, firstly, the Assembly's renunciation of all foreign conquests, and secondly, by the continuing terms of the 1783 peace treaty with Britain (which prohibited France from military intervention in local Indian politics). Assuming that French military resources were to be used only for *defensive* purposes, he estimated that only one thousand European troops, together with twelve hundred sepoys, would suffice to make Pondichéry defensible (at least until such time as help could arrive from elsewhere). What is more, in challenging Monneron's costings, Mallet argued that the garrison, as well the repair of Pondichéry's fortifications, could be amply funded from the revenues derived from India and the India trade, requiring a significantly smaller expense to the French government.

In the end, the deputies of the Constituent appeared to opt for caution as well as economy. Not wanting to provoke the British into any retaliatory measures, on 3 September 1791 the Assembly voted to accept the combined committees' recommendation for the provision of a European garrison at Pondichéry no more than a thousand-strong.[111] Interestingly, this garrison was to be largely made up from reinforcements sent directly from France, which would suggest that the deputies were also concerned not to reduce French forces on Ile de France, lest this impair the maintenance of order on this important island or compromise its external security.

What is interesting also is that Delattre, in later explaining the Constituents' policy with regard to the reinforcement of Pondichéry,

---

[110] Mallet had served in India for twenty years from 1753, and in various capacities—military, civil, diplomatic—before returning to France at the start of Louis XVI's reign. He seemed both surprised and pleased to be chosen by the colonists at Pondichéry to act as Député-Suppléant to Monneron and Beylié. Charles Mallet de Maisonpré, *Mémoire sur les demandes de la colonie de Pondichéry*, Paris (18 January 1791).

[111] AP, Vol. 30, 3 September 1791, pp. 472-473.

should not have made any mention whatsoever of Tippoo Sultan.[112] This seems an understandable yet striking omission. Forced finally to choose between either provoking the British, or disavowing their former ally Tippoo, the French seemed finally to withdraw into the state of armed neutrality with regard to Indian politics to which they had been officially confined in 1783. They were, for the moment, powerless to do anything else. Until such time as France could possess the capability to sustain a prolonged and global maritime war, and protect its colonies, it could not hope to play a decisive role in India.[113]

The Question of further Colonisation

The National Assembly was generally so consumed by the question of how France's existing colonial empire might be kept intact that the question of further colonial expansion received comparatively little attention. The deputies clearly made a distinction here, however, between the colonies France already possessed, particularly in the western hemisphere—the value of which was not seriously doubted—and the acquisition of further colonies. While the deputies were otherwise greatly concerned to retain France's existing colonies, on the latter question the dominant sentiment of the Assembly appeared to follow 'enlightened' opinion, which had become increasingly critical of European colonisation, for moral and economic reasons.[114] This was

---

[112] See Delattre's report on French navigation, *Ibid.*, Vol. 31, 22 September 1791, pp. 210-211.

[113] The members of the Colonial Committee during the Legislative Assembly were to be much less cautious in their approach to the question of French activity in India than that of the Constituent. The deputy Journu-Auber presented a report on 7 January 1792, on behalf of the Legislative's Colonial Committee, which condemned the former policies of the Royal Government with regard to India as weak and "déshonorante". Regarding the recent partial restoration of Pondichéry as basically inadequate, he denounced the earlier demilitarisation ordered by La Luzerne as nothing less than a shameful betrayal of their "generous ally" Tippoo. "On reconnait", he declared, "le même esprit qui présidait au ministère débile qui abandonna lâchement nos alliés, les Hollandais à l'invasion prussienne". The deputy, however, failed to speculate on the potential dangers of a more active military presence in India. *Ibid.*, Vol. 37, pp. 149-153.

[114] In the two decades preceding the Revolution, writers such as Rousseau, Montesquieu and most influential of all, Raynal, had railed either against slavery in general, or the brutality of colonial slavery in particular. Meanwhile, Physiocrats such as Mirabeau and Turgot, and writers such as Mably and Bernardin de Saint-Pierre, had argued the economic case against colonialism,

partly expressed in the Decree of 22 May 1790 abjuring foreign conquests, and promising that France would never again work against the liberty of any other people—a proscription which surely had to include aggressive colonisation. The popular orator Mirabeau summed up the 'enlightened' repugnance toward armed colonial expansion during his report on the Nootka Sound Affair, in which he explicitly condemned European efforts to subjugate native peoples.[115]

This apparent abhorrence of colonial conquest begs the question of the Cochinchina project, abandoned by the royal government in late 1788. Since the French had been effectively invited in by the local rulers, this project represented, in contrast to the traditional brutal methods of European colonisation, a far more palatable way of extending French trade and influence in an area of growing European interest and competition. The project had become public knowledge in France at least by late 1789, when *Le Moniteur* published an anonymous letter from a resident of Pondichéry announcing the project's abandonment, and bitterly lamenting the lost opportunity that this represented for French interests in the eastern hemisphere.[116] Subsequently, Monneron, in his speech of 15 October 1790, gave to the Assembly a short account of the project, and pronounced as regrettable the decision cancelling the proposed expedition to help restore the rightful ruler of Cochinchina. For the mere price of some "faible secours", he declared, this project would have given France great advantages. "Jamais", he thus concluded, "l'impéritie d'un ministre n'a frappé d'une manière plus funeste sur les intérêts commerciaux d'une nation".[117]

Notwithstanding these laments, it appears that neither the Ministry nor the Constituent Assembly were inclined to resume the Cochinchina

---

stating that it merely diverted resources away from the home economy. All of this had had a powerful effect on public opinion, which in turn tended to discourage further colonisation. See Vincent Confer, 'French Colonial Ideas before 1789', pp. 352-353; Lokke, *France and the Colonial Question*, Ch. 1, *passim*.

[115] Mirabeau, AP, 25 August 1790, Vol. 18, p. 263.

[116] As this letter argued, "cependant jamais les circonstances n'ont été si favorables pour le succès complet du rétablissement du roi détrôné, déjà en possession de cinq provinces méridionales de ses Etats, et nous manquons par cette inconstance de former un établissement solide et précieux dans un royaume qui, avant quatre à cinq ans, offrait à la nation un commerce exclusif de plus de 20 millions, et particulièrement les moyens d'exercer celui de Chine sans aller à Canton y éprouver des avanies". Letter dated 15 June 1789, in Henri Plon (Ed), *Réimpression de l'ancien moniteur*, Vol. 2, p. 507.

[117] Monneron, AP, 15 October, Vol. 19, p. 656.

project, for reasons that might be partly obvious. Firstly, the grave financial problems that had led to the cancelling of the expedition in 1788 had not markedly improved, and had certainly not been resolved, by the end of the 1791. Secondly, given the highly unsettled state—either produced or intensified by the Revolution—of the French overseas possessions, the deputies and the royal government may have preferred to concentrate their efforts on the retention of France's existing colonial empire. Less obviously, reports via Pondichéry recounting the successful progress of Nguyen-Anh in his campaign to reclaim his kingdom may have reassured the Government that the proposed expeditionary force had not even been necessary. This may have confirmed for them the wisdom of the earlier cancellation. During 1789, the Government had itself chosen to stand by and reaffirm the actions of Conway, Governor and military commander of Pondichéry, despite the complaints, protests and entreaties of the Bishop of Adran.[118] The subsequent reception in 1791 of a goodwill letter from the newly restored king of Cochinchina may have then reinforced the government's sense that it had lost nothing—in terms of future opportunities—in the expedition's cancellation, and had in fact saved a considerable outlay at a time when the state of the French finances had demanded drastic economies.[119] The government's response to Nguyen-Anh's letter indicated a continuing interest in developing at the very least a commercial relationship with Cochinchina, for it commissioned a further study on this subject from the French agent Cossigny.[120]

From the perspective of the Assembly, the evident disinclination to reconsider the Cochinchina expedition may be explained as stemming from its low priority, if only in domestic political terms. Given the far greater importance of the West Indian colonies to the affluent French port towns, the deputies would have been concerned first and foremost to placate the port merchants and the 'American' colonial deputies, rather than the far less numerous merchants residing in Pondichéry, the value of whose trade to French economic development had been doubted during the debates over the privilege of the India Company. The urgent need, counselled by Monneron and others, to protect and reinforce militarily the French trading posts in India may also have overshadowed the question of the Cochinchina venture.

---

[118] AN-FC-C1-4, ff. 202-203.
[119] 'Traduction d'une lettre de Nguyên-Anh, roi de la Cochinchine, au roi de France', 5 February 1790, *Ibid.*, ff. 206-207.
[120] 'Minute de note sur la lettre du roi de Cochinchine, lu au Conseil d'Etat', 15 April 1791, *Ibid.*, ff. 213-215.

In conclusion, while the deputies of the National Assembly explicitly rejected the idea of territorial conquest and the brutal methods long associated with European colonisation, they did not, however, repudiate the project of colonial expansion in itself, as long as it could be pursued by more acceptable means, and be considered to present worthwhile commercial opportunities. Moreover, the ostensible purpose of French colonisation would be trade rather than dominion, and would hence likely be limited in scope. Yet once France had successfully completed the process of political, social and economic regeneration, its colonies could then become a platform for the expansion of French overseas trade and influence, enabling France to compete with—and even eventually supercede—all other maritime nations. For the time being, however, the consolidation of the existing French empire was clearly, for the deputies, a more imperative goal, and one fraught with numerous difficulties and complex dilemmas.

7 Defending a 'Regenerated' France

By its decree of 22 May 1790 the Assembly vowed in principle never to pursue offensive war and territorial conquest against any other country. This decree inaugurated, many assumed, a new and more 'enlightened' era in the management of foreign affairs, in which priorities based on 'national' rather than dynastic interest, and a respect for the liberty and rights of all peoples, would guide future French foreign policy. The Assembly having thus defined in abstract terms the principles which France would henceforth follow in its foreign relations, how did those who now shared the responsibility for the determining of war, peace and alliances—the Foreign Minister and the National Assembly—respond to more practical questions of foreign policy?

The *Pacte de Famille* and Montmorin's Dilemma

For Montmorin, the decree on the Right of War and Peace only compounded the existing difficulties of his position as Foreign Minister, in that it now formally confirmed his reliance on the confidence of the Assembly—after all, ministers could now be charged with the crime of "lèse-nation" for decisions that might subsequently be condemned by the Assembly.[1] The following week the marquis de La Luzerne wrote from London that he shared Montmorin's "sorrow" at the passing of this decree, and warned him that the decree, in fact the whole debate on war and peace, had only strengthened Britain's hand in its current dispute with Spain. Indeed, by further impairing France's reliability as an ally, and hampering its diplomacy, this "miserable opposition" of the Assembly, and the circumscription of the Crown's foreign policy powers, had only confirmed the perception abroad of French impotence. With English public opinion demanding victory over Spain,

---

[1] See Appendix, pp. 240-241.

La Luzerne thus repeated earlier forebodings that a comprehensive, and anticipated, defeat of Spanish colonial and maritime power would inevitably rebound on France.[2]

As was then expected, the actual crisis between Britain and Spain continued to worsen over the following month. British demands from May to June for immediate satisfaction for the insult caused by the Nootka incident became strident and implacable. The Spanish met this British implacability with the continued mobilisation of their armed forces, and a circular, issued on 13 June to all the European powers, defending their own position and their claims to the sovereignty of Nootka Sound and the region in general. This, in turn, only confirmed the British cabinet in their determination to force their demands upon Spain, and to go to war if those demands were not met.[3] It being publicly known that Spain found these demands to be unreasonable, if not outrageous, it was assumed on all sides that war was inevitable.[4] As such, the Spanish finally sought to gain from France an assurance of its immediate and unqualified support: on 16 June Fernan-Nunez, the Spanish Ambassador to Paris, wrote to Montmorin, calling on France to confirm and fulfil its obligations under the terms of the *Pacte de Famille*.[5]

Montmorin, already in an invidious position, was thereby plunged into yet another quandary. On the one hand, it was thought vital to France's material interests that she retain Spain as an ally, a point which had hardly been challenged by the Left during the May debate. On the other hand, given the deputies unequivocal rejection of offensive war, Montmorin could hardly expect the Assembly to respond positively to a general mobilisation in favour of Spain in fulfillment of a *Pacte de Famille* that indeed contained clauses allowing for offensive warfare. There was, as the May debate had furthermore revealed, some considerable doubt in the Assembly as to the justice of the Spanish claims, and hence negligible enthusiasm for supporting their cause by force of arms. Yet, as Montmorin and others well knew, an outright refusal by the Assembly to support Spain could lose France that alliance. Fernan-Nunez's letter had indeed contained the threat that, failing

---

[2] AAE, CP Angleterre 573, La Luzerne to Montmorin, 31 May 1790, ff. 197-209.

[3] John Norris, 'The Policy of the British Cabinet in the Nootka Crisis', *English Historical Review*, 70 (October, 1955), p. 577.

[4] During May Montmorin wrote to La Luzerne in London stating that an Anglo-Spanish war now appeared inevitable. Montmorin to the marquis de La Luzerne, n.d. no. 15, AAE-CP-Angleterre-573, f. 194.

[5] Barry Rothaus, 'The War and Peace Prerogative', p. 130. See also Harold Evans, 'The Nootka Sound Controversy', p. 614.

French support, the Spanish government might be forced to seek other allies.[6] This was a catastrophe that could hardly be countenanced.

Beyond this, of course, were the dangers involved for France in being drawn into a major maritime war. Both its internal and external situations made such a venture extremely perilous, if not impossible. French finances and credit remained a shambles, and there were also growing doubts about the reliability of France's armed forces.[7] Furthermore, there remained the prospect that this war might well trigger a general European conflict, the Eastern War still being in progress. Regardless of its continental outcomes, such a conflict could lead, with Britain now supplemented by the Dutch, to the complete destruction of France as a maritime and colonial power, and a likely end to hopes for its material 'regeneration'.

Although the Assembly's attentions in June and July had focused on more domestic concerns, there continued nonetheless into August a vigorous public discussion on the 'Spanish Affair'. Dupont de Nemours, in particular, published a series of pamphlets defending the Spanish Alliance, one of which he tabled in the Assembly when the issue resurfaced there at the start of August. Where previously, on grounds of the 'balance of power', he had advocated closer relations to Britain, now on the same grounds, in these *mémoires*, he made an impassioned plea for the retention of the Spanish alliance and an unhesitating fulfilment of its obligations, forecasting irreparable damage to France, and the possible ruin of its own Empire, if this course was not followed.[8]

---

[6] See AP, Vol. 17, 2 August 1790, pp. 503-504.

[7] Growing anxieties about the collapse of order and discipline in the Royal Army were focused by August 1790 in the mutiny of the Châteauvieux regiment at Nancy, which was subsequently repressed at the beginning of September with the approval of the Assembly. Serious disturbances had also occured in various naval stations, such in Toulon in 1789. The most serious development in terms of military capability was the mutiny in Brest, the French navy's principal Atlantic port, that near paralysed naval activity for several months in late 1790-91. See Samuel Scott, *The Response of the Royal Army to the French Revolution* (Oxford, 1973); Cormack, *Revolution and Political Conflict*, Ch. 3-4, *passim*.

[8] *Le Pacte de Famille et les conventions subséquentes, entre la France & l'Espagne; avec des observations sur chaque article, par M. Dupont, Député de Nemours à l'Assemblée Nationale*, Paris, s.d. July 1790, AN-AD-XV-38, *La Pacte de Famille entre la France et l'Espagne: avec des observations sur chaque article*, AP, Vol.17, 3 August 1790 (annex) p. 586. Dupont's allegations that English agents in Paris were encouraging France to remain neutral in this affair, or even support Britain, had some truth, for at least one unofficial agent of Pitt, Miles, was indeed active in Paris clubs such as the Jacobins, endeavouring there to build support for Britain, particularly among those of the left. See Miles, *Correspondence of W.A. Miles*, Vol. 1, pp. 40-49. One

Against such pleas radical journalists such as Brissot declared, in *Le Patriote François*, that if the dispute was a question of international law and rights, then it would be unjust for the National Assembly to support Spain in this dispute, so absurd were their claims and unacceptable their behaviour in support of them.[9] As he and other journalists argued, not only was the Spanish cause unjust, but the involvement of France in a major war would most likely have deadly consequences for the progress of the Revolution and the completion of the Constitution. As such, he labelled those partisans of the *Pacte de Famille* "false patriots and enemies of the Revolution".[10]

At this point Mirabeau offered the government a possible solution to the question of the Spanish alliance. In his secret advice to the French court in late June, he suggested that the Ministry itself take the lead in transforming the *Pacte* into a national and specifically defensive alliance, making it incontestable when subsequently presented to the Assembly for approval.[11] However, by the time that the government elected to act on Mirabeau's advice, sending an emissary to Spain to negotiate the proposed changes to its alliance and to assure them of French support, it was all too late: on 5 July the British issued the Spanish with an abrupt ultimatum, to which, in the absence of

---

    member of the Jacobins (possibly Miles himself, or one of his French associates), published anonymously a long rejoinder to Dupont, slavishly defending the British position in the Nootka Affair, even stating that "la cause de l'Angleterre est donc ici celle de tous les peuples commerçants, celle de l'humanité entière". See *Appel aux faits, à la raison, et à l'intérêt national en faveur de la paix, ou lettre à M. Dupont, Député de Nemours à l'Assemblée Nationale. Publié par un Membre de la Societé des Amis de la Constitution* (Paris, 1790), AN-AD-XV-38, f. 284.

[9]   *Le Patriote François*, 16 June 1790, pp. 2-3.

[10]   *Ibid.*, 24 June, 1790, p. 4. Another radical journal, *Les Annales patriotiques*, was even more vehement in its opposition to French involvement in supporting Spain, when it asked that "City merchants, national confederate guards, brave soldiers of the troops of line, worthy municipal officers, and you citizens, who have formed patriotic societies, let us all unite together; let us raise one deadly voice against this treacherous plan of the ministers, against the ministers themselves. Let us drive them from the presence of a king whom they ceaselessly infect with their insolent venom. Why do we wait to hunt out these stupid and insolent beings? Have they not gone too far in wanting to involve us in a foreign war? Why do we wait to declare that we wish to be the friends of all nations, the enemies of all tyrants, and that we acknowledge no family pact other than the pacts of national families?". J. Gilchrist & W. Murray (Eds), *The Press in the French Revolution* (Melbourne, 1971), p. 206.

[11]   Rothaus, 'The War and Peace Prerogative', p. 130.

unequivocal French support, they had no choice but to accede.[12] By the time Montmorin finally forwarded to the Assembly the earlier Spanish request for French support, on 2 August, this only preceded by one day the announcement there that Spain had given in to the British demands for 'satisfaction'.[13]

Various reasons have been suggested by historians as to why the French government waited so long before either taking this action or at least informing the Assembly of the Spanish request. One interpretation points to the role of Lafayette, the initial 'strong man' of the Revolution, who pressed Montmorin to defer the consideration in the Assembly of the Spanish request until after the *Fête de la Fédération*, when it was supposed that the royal government may have recovered much of its position in the Assembly.[14] Another version holds that the diplomatic manoeuvre—the sending of an envoy to Spain—was hamstrung by incompetence, indecisiveness, and by a lack of candour between Louis XVI and his foreign minister. According to one of Mirabeau's recent biographers, the deputy had urged Louis to negotiate a change in the Spanish alliance before 14 July to forestall an expected upsurge of anti-monarchical feeling. Not only had Louis then dithered in selecting a envoy, but he had also declined to inform Montmorin of the source of this particular advice, or to involve Mirabeau in its execution. Poorly briefed, the envoy had then failed to effect any conclusive changes to the Spanish alliance, but rather only reinforced the impression at the Spanish court that the French were reluctant to fulfill their obligations and come to the aid of Spain.[15]

Each of these factors may well have played a role in the apparently unsuccessful outcome of this diplomatic manoeuvre and the dilatory actions of the royal government. Louis XVI's capacity for indecision was certainly notorious, and only seemed to worsen with the increased uncertainty in public affairs. The correspondance between Montmorin and his ambassador in London may, however, provide an alternative or additional interpretation for this delay in responding to the Spanish request. This correspondance reveals that, while the French government did not wish to jeopardise the future of the Spanish alliance, Montmorin was also keen to compel the Spanish to go to the negotiating table.[16]

---

[12] Norris, 'The Policy of the British Cabinet', pp. 578-579.
[13] AP, Vol. 17, 3 August 1790, pp. 582-583.
[14] Gottshalk & Maddox, *Lafayette in the French Revolution*, p. 467.
[15] Luttrell, *Mirabeau*, pp. 220-21.
[16] Montmorin to the marquis de la Luzerne, n.d., no. 15, AAE-CP-Angleterre-573, f. 194.

After all, according to Montmorin, it was Louis XVI's express wish that the question of satisfaction might be resolved reasonably between Britain and Spain, without France having to commit itself to supporting Spain militarily.[17] The delay in the Ministry's response may therefore be interpreted, at least in part, as a semi-deliberate hedging, the kind of tactic whereby it could simply dodge the issue (a tactic which Montmorin may have become accustomed to employing since taking office). It might therefore have been seen by Montmorin as the safest course to follow through this perilous foreign policy dilemma, and the one most synchronous with the king's timid and hesitant inclinations, not to mention his own. Assuming, rightly, that the British were prepared to go to war with Spain if their ultimatum was rejected, the government may have been concerned for the time-being to withhold French support, lest this encourage Spanish obstinacy. In this case, the Government may perhaps have known full well that its initiative of mid-July would be too late to have any telling effect.

Another factor was that the French government also suspected that it was unlikely that the British would go to war with France until they were certain of French intentions regarding the *Pacte de Famille*.[18] Understandably then, given its effective 'neutrality' on the specific issue of Nootka Sound, the Ministry was reluctant to show its hand or otherwise compel the Assembly to do so, at least until the Anglo-Spanish crisis seemed to have abated. As we shall see, only when it became clear that the Spanish would accede to the British ultimatum (effectively acknowledging their 'guilt' in the Nootka Sound affair), would Montmorin finally bring the Spanish request for a fulfilment of France's alliance obligations to the attention of the Assembly.[19]

Thus, despite the efforts of Mirabeau to infuse a more positive note into French foreign policy, Montmorin had endeavoured, in July 1790, to secure their shared aim—averting an Anglo-Spanish war—through what could aptly be described as a policy of 'creative inertia', whereby

---

[17] On 26 June Montmorin wrote to the marquis de La Luzerne that "le Roi n'a pas fixé de jour pour porter à l'Assemblée Nationale la question relative à l'Espagne; quoique cette Puissance ait réclamé de la manière la plus précise les secours stipulés par le pacte de famille, il a paru à S.M. qu'il n'y avoit pas d'inconvéniens majeurs à différer tant que l'on conserveroit des espérances fondées d'une conciliation entre l'Espagne et l'Angleterre". Montmorin to the marquis de La Luzerne, 26 June 1790, AAE-CP-Angleterre-573, f. 313.

[18] Marquis de La Luzerne to Montmorin, 13 July 1790, AAE-CP-Angleterre-574, ff. 54-55.

[19] A.P., Vol. 17, 2 August 1790, p. 504.

decisive choices to troubling dilemmas could be deliberately avoided, or at least deferred.

The Summer of 1790 and the Question of French Security

After two months of being occupied with pressing domestic issues, and despite the Decree of 22 May leaving the management of French foreign affairs to the executive power, by late July 1790 the National Assembly was once again forced to confront the vexed question of foreign policy.[20] This time, however, it was not naval and intercolonial squabbles that sparked discussion in the Assembly, but the more urgent problem of France's security on the continent of Europe. This security was called rapidly into question when, on 27 July, Dubois-Crancé reported to the Assembly the state of fear, bordering on panic, into which France's northern frontier had been suddenly propelled by the prospect of Austrian troops crossing into French territory.[21] These troops were supposedly on their way to restore Austrian authority in the Belgian provinces, which required them to pass through French territory near the frontier with Luxembourg. The populace of the French frontier regions feared, however, that this would be merely a pretext for an invasion of France by its old enemy. Although Montmorin subsequently argued that the French Government had been obliged to accede to this request on account of the reciprocal obligations laid down in the Franco-Austrian Treaty, and that this entailed no compromising of French frontier security since this area was adequately fortified and garrisoned, on 27 July Dubois-Crancé and

---

[20] Although the Assembly's time over June and July was mostly taken up with pressing domestic concerns, this was with the exception, early in July, of a letter read to the Assembly by Dupont from the "députés du commerce de France" which demanded that French naval forces be immediately dispatched to protect French maritime commerce. They warned in no uncertain terms that, with the recent sailing of the English fleet (the news of which had been announced in the Assembly the previous day) and the mobilising of the Dutch navy, "nos places maritimes sont en alarme et notre commerce en danger", suggesting also the French colonies might also be threatened. After a response by Robespierre suggesting (to the consternation of the Assembly) that this talk of threatening naval manoeuvres was merely a screen for counter-revolutionary machinations, the matter had been adjourned without decision. AP, Vol. 16, 4 July 1790, pp. 694-695.

[21] *Ibid.*, Vol 17, 27 July, pp. 379-380.

Fréteau heatedly accused the ministers of treacherous complicity in weakening French defences in order to facilitate an Austrian invasion.[22]

This development proved highly disturbing to the revolutionaries, in a number of ways. That the Austrians should be allowed to re-conquer Belgium was galling enough, for though France had remained officially neutral in this affair, many revolutionaries continued to sympathise strongly with the Belgians' efforts to secure their independence from their foreign overlords. Here, however, traditional Austrophobia coalesced with growing fears of a possible foreign counter-revolutionary intervention. The flexing of Austrian muscle in the north, Voidel and D'André both alleged, was complemented by ominous military build-ups particularly in Savoy, in the south, and by the counter-revolutionary agitation of the Rhine Princes.[23]

The majority of the Assembly were thus driven by these anxieties to name on 27 July six *commissaires* from among their ranks, whom they charged with liaising with the ministers of war and foreign affairs, both to re-examine the Austrian request and to investigate the present status of France's frontier defences.[24] Such a review was to have two initial outcomes. Firstly, on the recommendations of the *commissaires*, the Assembly voted the following day to refuse passage to the Austrians (pending further information from them on troop numbers, line of march, and so forth), on the basis that only the legislature had the right to decide on the admission of foreign troops into French territory.[25] Secondly, the Assembly resolved to step up its ongoing review of France's defences and military capability.[26]

---

[22] Ibid.

[23] Ibid., pp. 380-381.

[24] The six *commissaires* named were Fréteau, Dubois, d'André, Menou, Elbecq and Emmery. See Rothaus, 'The War and Peace Prerogative', p. 128.

[25] In support of this, they had cited the Assembly's decree of 28 Febuary 1790, which stated that no foreign troops could be introduced onto French territory without the immediate and express sanction of the National Assembly.

[26] As part of this review Alexandre de Lameth, leftist and member of the Triumvirate, presented on 29 July a report on behalf of the Military Committee which looked at the question of the size and general organisation of the French army. This report began with a short mémoire by the War Minister, La Tour-de-Pin, the Assembly having on the 22 July solicited his views on the appropriate regular peacetime footing for France's military. In this *mémoire*, dated 25 July, the Minister sought to contest what he saw as a popular misconception that an army devoted purely to defense should only be large enough to defend France's frontiers, arguing that in fact the best deterrent against aggression lay in an ability to convert defense into vigorous counter-attack, and to pursue an enemy well beyond one's own frontiers. Taking into account the nature of France's

This, however, failed to satisfy a number of the leftist and more radical deputies, such as Voidel, Robespierre and D'Aiguillon. While the *commissaires* had seemed now to imply that Montmorin and the War Minister La Tour-du-Pin had merely been mistaken in acceding to the Austrian's request, these other deputies remained convinced that the Ministers' actions were not merely treacherous and counter-revolutionary in intent, but were also now possibly part of a vast international conspiracy to threaten the Revolution. "Nous ne pouvons nous dissimuler les inquiétudes que donne l'état politique de l'Europe", declared D'Aiguillon. "S'il existe un traité secret, jamais l'Autriche n'aurait une plus belle occasion de s'emparer de nos frontiers, pour pénétrer ensuite dans l'intérieur du royaume". He alleged that a number of European powers aside from Austria, including Prussia, Britain and Spain were already in the process of forming a counter-revolutionary coalition against France.[27]

Such claims did not, of course, go unchallenged. The constitutional monarchist Rabaut Saint-Etienne argued in the Assembly against the existence of such a coalition, for, as he suggested, any plundering of French territory by Prussia or Austria would in fact constitute, for the other states of Western Europe, an unwelcome change in the European balance of power: "L'Angleterre", for example,

> cette puissance dont la politique en Europe est d'y conserver un ascendant digne d'elle, de quel oeil verrait-elle l'occident envahit par l'orient, une puissance pondérante disparaître de la terre ferme, le Hanovre entouré de voisins agrandis, et l'Ile Britannique se rapetisser et se resserrer devant les masses continentales? ... verra-t-elle de sang-froid une ligue européenne dont les progrès et le désordre ne pourraient être calculés et qui dérangerait l'équilibre actuel, si convenable à cette puissance?[28]

'amphibious' geography, its size, population and government, its existing alliances and likely enemies, as well as the needs of her colonies and empire, La Tour-du-Pin arrived at a total optimum figure of 250,000, of whom, in ordinary circumstances, only 150,000 need be placed on an active footing. This estimation was in large part accepted by Lameth in his report. AP, Vol. 17, 29 July 1790, pp. 400-411. Throughout the period of the National Constituent Assembly, thorough-going reforms to recruitment, pay, conditions and promotion would be enacted by the deputies. For a summary of these reforms, see Norman Hampson, *A Social History of the French Revolution* (London, 1963), pp. 121-123.

[27] AP, Vol. 17, 28 July 1790, p. 391.
[28] *Ibid.*, pp. 395-98.

Royalists like the Abbé Royou, in his right-wing journal *L'Ami du Roi*, went further, deriding claims that foreign powers were preparing for a counter-revolutionary intervention as baseless and hysterical. There was no evidence, Royou argued, to suggest that the present dispute between Britain and Spain was anything but genuine, or that their respective war preparations concealed secret counter-revolutionary designs. Moreover, the Austrians, he asserted, were simply too distracted by internal revolts and the threat of Prussian aggression to move against France. "In a word", Royou declared,

> despite the peaceful views of the Assembly, the writers and the incendiary clubs have done everything necessary ... to raise up against us all the European powers; but we still see nothing that indicates that they are thinking of profiting by our weakness. ... They take good care not to attack us, since we inflict on ourselves all the evils that the ambition of our cruellest enemies could wish on us.[29]

The majority of the deputies were, however, sufficiently unsettled by the prospect of foreign aggression, and fearful of royal or ministerial collusion with foreign powers, that they now effectively deemed the constitutional arrangements voted in the Decree of 22 May (for the 'sharing' of foreign policy powers between the executive and the legislature) to be inadequate to protect France and its Revolution. Athough Montmorin remained one of the more popular and trusted of the royal ministers, the *commissaire* Fréteau told the Assembly on 29 July that the preservation of national security now required a greater measure of legislative surveillance in the area of foreign affairs. He hence urged the immediate creation of a committee charged with examining the remainder of France's existing treaties and foreign committments, one empowered to make both its own examination of foreign affairs and its own recommendations as to "les moyens de pourvoir à la sûreté de l'Etat".[30] Despite protests from the Right that such a measure was an unconstitutional intrusion on the executive power, the Assembly quickly agreed. On the motion of Emmery, it voted to create a Diplomatic Committee of six members, whose task would be to "prendre connaissance des traités existants entre la France et les puissances étrangères, et des engagements respectifs qui en

---

[29] L'Abbé Royou, *L'Ami du Roi*, 30 July 1790, cited in Gilchrist and Murray (Eds), *The Press and the French Revolution*, pp. 207-8.
[30] AP, Vol. 17, 29 July 1790, p. 399.

résultent, pour en rendre compte à l'Assemblée au moment où elle le demandera".[31]

Hence, while the Assembly already possessed, by virtue of the Decree of 22 May, a decisive veto power over formal foreign policy initiatives of the royal government, the looming spectre of a foreign counter-revolutionary coalition, combined with doubts over the faithfulness of the royal government to the Revolution, compelled the deputies to create a mechanism which would soon allow them to move ever closer toward a *de facto* management of foreign affairs.

Mirabeau and the Transformation of the Spanish Alliance

The members of the newly formed Diplomatic Committee were nominated on 1 August 1790. They included, aside from Mirabeau and his rival Barnave, two prominent members of the Left, Fréteau and Menou, and two members from the Right, Châtelet and D'André. With Mirabeau, the seeming ally of the royal government, now installed on this committee, it is not surprising that Montmorin should have chosen this moment finally to pass on to the Assembly the Spanish request for support, for it was, as the Minister requested, immediately referred to the Committee for examination. Louis and his Minister no doubt assumed that wiser counsels would prevail there than in the more easily inflamed atmosphere of the Assembly hall.

The installation of Mirabeau on the Diplomatic Committee indeed inaugurated what might be considered a virtual partnership between the deputy and Montmorin over the general direction of foreign affairs. Their shared aim, in the short-term, was the pursuit of a dual objective: firstly, the preservation of the Spanish alliance, and secondly, peace with Britain. It was Mirabeau, however, who clearly played the leading role in this informal partnership. As Welch notes, Mirabeau, the frustrated would-be minister, quickly became the dominant force on the Diplomatic Committee, and, in effect, the "de facto manager of foreign affairs". Montmorin, increasingly out of his depth and "pathetically anxious for guidance", was for his own part only too happy to co-operate with Mirabeau and the Committee, and to receive the views and guidance of its most imposing and influential member.[32]

---

[31] *Ibid.*

[32] Welch, *Mirabeau*, pp. 287-290. See also Masson, *Le département des affaires étrangères*, p. 88.

It was not until 25 August that Mirabeau, as *rapporteur*, finally presented the report of the Diplomatic Committee on the matter of the 'Spanish Affair'. It produced another of his great masterpieces of political oratory, one designed ultimately to convince the Assembly to approve the continuation of a 'revamped' Spanish Alliance. The report began with an attempt to engage leftist and radical opinion, particularly with regard to the Nootka Sound issue and French relations with Britain. In an expression of the new morality now represented in the Assembly, Mirabeau asserted that the territory around Nootka Sound belonged to neither power, but rather to the natives who presently inhabited it. Thus, he clearly repudiated the idea of active colonial expansion, if it should involve the transgression of the rights of native inhabitants. The contested territory was in any case, he added, hardly worth the shedding of blood and the colossal expenditures that would be occasioned by a war between Britain and Spain.

Declaring therefore that the apparent source of dispute between these powers was insufficient as a *causus belli*, for them as for France (whose own material circumstances in any case currently demanded peace),[33] Mirabeau then deftly separated this issue from the general question of the Franco-Spanish alliance. Though, he said, one should look confidently forward to a time when the rights of nations would prevail, and when enemies, and the need for allies, hence no longer existed, France, particularly given her geographic position and that of her overseas possessions, still had to take account of the fact that the 'old system' still prevailed in Europe, and protect herself accordingly. Simple prudence thus forbade any premature isolationism, defensive alliances being vital for the preservation of French security and prosperity, and especially the French colonies.[34]

Similarly, while Mirabeau indignantly rejected as "insidious" the idea that Britain should be regarded as the inveterate rival and enemy of France, particularly now as they together shared the same "political

---

[33] AP, Vol. 18, 25 August 1790, p. 263.

[34] "Nos possessions lointaines", asked Mirabeau, "parsemées dans les deux mondes, ne nous exposent-elles pas à des attaques que nous ne pouvons pas repousser seuls sur tous les points du globe? ... Tant que nous aurons des rivaux", he thus concluded, "la prudence nous commandera de mettre hors de toute atteinte les propriétés particulières et la fortune nationale, de surveiller l'ambition étrangère, ... Tant que nos voisins n'adopteront pas entièrement nos principes, nous serons constraints, même en suivant une politique plus franche, de ne pas renoncer aux précautions que réclame la prudence". Not to do so, he further noted, would merely encourage, and make France vulnerable to, these states' greed and ambition. *Ibid.*, Vol. 18, 25 August 1790, p. 263-264.

religion", on this matter he also beseeched the deputies to follow "the counsels of wisdom" and prudence. It might indeed be hoped, he said, that, with such a free and enlightened people, "une autre genre de rivalité, l'émulation des bonnes lois, va prendre la place de celle qui se nourrissait de politique et d'ambition". Yet, let us suppose, he cautioned,

> que l'Angleterre prévoie avec inquiétude l'accroissement qu'une Constitution libre doit un jour donner à nos forces, à notre commerce, à notre crédit; qu'elle lise dans propre histoire l'avenir de nos destinées, et que, par une fausse politique, elle veuille profiter des circonstances pour rompre une alliance formidable dont elle a souvent senti tout le poids: quelle sont les mesures qu'une telle supposition doit nous inspirer?[35]

Since the only way France could presently counter-balance the number of British warships was with the alliance of Spain, France was obliged, Mirabeau concluded, to follow her own interest in confirming that alliance. Avoiding any mention of alleged Spanish ill-will towards the Revolution, Mirabeau thus defended their long-time alliance with France, stating, as others earlier had done, that Spain had already on several occasions come to the aid of France over the last decade or so, most recently arming in support of its ally during the Dutch crisis.[36] To fail to assist Spain now, when called upon to do so, would be to break a treaty that had hence been very useful and favourable to French interests.[37]

Mirabeau then moved on to discuss and allay fears that armed support for Spain might itself actually precipitate a war, and subsequently bring a halt to France's 'regeneration'. If, as he posed, the

---

[35] *Ibid.*, p. 265.

[36] In this speech, Mirabeau also referred to the "époque honteuse" of the Dutch crisis of 1787, the 'shame' of which seems to have been felt right across the political spectrum of the Assembly, though, perhaps, for different reasons. For Mirabeau, it was not merely that it involved the abandonment of an ally (who represented, moreover, the cause of 'popular' rights against those of 'despotism'), but that it also "nous priva ainsi d'un moyen presque assuré d'être à jamais en Europe les arbitres de la paix", that is, by depriving France of the means whereby it could hold the continental balance of power. *Ibid.*, p. 264.

[37] Mirabeau more than implied here that the object of France in reaffirming the Spanish Alliance was partly to prevent a humiliating Spanish submission that might in turn be prejudicial to French interests, arguing that "s'il est certain que l'abandon de nos engagements forcerait l'Espagne à négocier plus promptement la paix avec l'Angleterre, il n'est que trop facile de prévoir quelle pourrait être dans ce cas la nature de cet accommodement, et le tort irréparable qu'une semblable négociation ferait à notre crédit, à notre commerce". *Ibid.*, p. 265.

flexing of British military muscle in this current dispute was merely a bluff, intended to intimidate Spain into humiliating concessions, then France could safely fulfill its obligations to its ally, and protect also its own interests, without fear of war. The greatest danger lay, however, in French inaction. This, Mirabeau told the Assembly, "augmenterait nos périls, au lieu de les éloigner", for if the British were so insensible to justice that they were determined in any case to attack and defeat an isolated Spain, what could France and its Empire expect in turn in the face of such insatiable ambitions? Would war not follow in either case? Only by calling this British bluff, and supporting Spain, he thus reasoned, could the Assembly best fulfill its own duty to help protect French commerce and overseas possessions.

With this speech Mirabeau thus attempted to square the 'pacific' principles already avowed by the Assembly with the exigent needs and realities of France's geography, and its position as a colonial, and indeed, global power. Idealism was to be tempered with a necessary pragmatism. Finishing with the statement that in order to "remplir vos engagements sans imprudence, à changer l'ancien système sans secousses, à éviter la guerre sans faiblesse", he thus proposed the following decree: that while all existing treaties between France and other powers would continue to be observed, at least until they were otherwise formally changed or abrogated, the king would make it known to all powers contracted to France that this would be on the basis that only defensive and commercial stipulations were to be hence recognised as valid. The king's ministers were thus to make immediate efforts to renegotiate and reaffirm the Spanish alliance on this basis. At the same time, in recognition of the general rising scale of armaments among the European powers, and the consequent security needs of France's colonies and maritime commerce, the king would be called upon to order an expansion of the navy's active footing to a total of thirty ships-of-the-line, with the proportionate number of lesser craft.

With this proposal, the push for immediate isolationism that had been espoused by some of the more radical deputies was emphatically rejected. As long as other countries harboured aggressive or expansionist aims, defensive alliances based on mutual and substantive material interest, on national rather than dynastic imperatives, would continue to be vital to the ongoing security and prosperity of France. The Spanish alliance, especially given its essentially maritime nature, could, in spite of the disagreeable character of the Spanish regime *per se*, thus fulfil the new 'positive' requirements of a national alliance—it was the mutual and palpable benefit it brought to their respective peoples that was crucial. By the same token, it was implicitly acknowledged, such was the evident nature of the international balance of power and political economy, that an entirely harmonious relationship with otherwise politically 'sympathetic' regimes such as Britain was by no means always guaranteed, contrary to what some had earlier maintained.

So persuasive seemed Mirabeau's address that the response of the Assembly to his proposals exceeded even his own and the Diplomatic Committee's expectations. For on the following day, in answer to the proposition that France should respond to the armaments of neighbouring powers, the deputy Ricard motioned that the proposed figure of thirty ships-of-the-line should be increased to a figure of forty-five, a proposal that was then decreed unanimously. Such a show a unanimity would become increasingly rare in the Assembly. One can only assume that the proposals were thought sufficient to meet the concerns of the both the Left and Right. Not only was the Spanish alliance now deemed to be in conformity with French 'national' interests, as the Right had claimed, but an expansion of the active French fleet did not present, in the minds of the Patriots, the kind of threat to the Constitution that a similar 'mobilisation' of the royal army may have posed. Above all, it was only through this means that it was hoped that a war between Britain and Spain, and which might thereby include France, could be averted, and that French global interests could consequently be safeguarded.[38]

The only problem with this proposition was whether it would work, whether by this means France could both retain the Spanish alliance and preserve the peace. There were a number of factors across the second half of 1790 that would make the two aims increasingly difficult, and even impossible, to reconcile. One was the attitude of the Spanish government. Faced with the effective French 'neutrality' on the issue of Nootka Sound, and having hence been already forced to agree to British demands for satisfaction, the Spanish had all but lost any faith in the reliability of France as an ally, ceasing even to inform the French Ministry of the details of their negotiations with the British. Nor did it help that the Spanish king evidently abhorred France's seeming decline into revolutionary anarchy and popular government, and that he had

---

[38] In the short but heated discussion on this issue on 26 August, Fréteau, another (and leftist) member of the Diplomatic Committee, took the floor to inform the Assembly of several conferences held between the Committee and the Foreign Minister from 10 August onwards, in which Montmorin warned them of the continuing mobilisation of the British navy. *Ibid.*, 26 August 1790, p. 293.

moved to close the Franco-Spanish border in the hope of containing the revolutionary 'contagion'.[39]

The second major factor in the failure of the dual objective of preserving both peace and the Spanish alliance was the attitude of the British government, which was to maintain an implacable determination to press further demands on the Spanish government regarding commercial and maritime access to the Americas. In early October the British issued an ultimatum demanding that Spain henceforth agree to confine its claims to the sovereignty of the west coast of North America within certain specified limits, and recognise British rights to fish in the Pacific Ocean. With this ultimatum, the Anglo-Spanish crisis entered its most critical phase. Though the terms of the ultimatum were secret, they were generally assumed to be so humiliating that Spain was expected to go to war rather than submit to them.[40]

The final major factor was the situation in France, and the attitude of the French government, the National Assembly and its Diplomatic Committee. In the two months following the decree of 26 August, there was, reportedly, a pronounced strengthening of feeling in and around the the French Assembly against the idea of France going to war in defense of Spanish global pretentions. In his despatches from Paris, the British Ambassador was even suggesting, by late October, that the French 'Popular Party' might prefer an alliance with Britain than one with Spain.[41] Historians such as Oscar Browning and John Holland Rose have given credence to this suggestion that there was, during this time, an apparent shift in public feeling away from support of Spain and toward Britain. They alleged, firstly, that this was a shift not merely in public opinion, but also in the policy stance of the Diplomatic Committee, and, secondly, that it was the intercession finally of British gold (and Mirabeau's cupidity) that was crucial here in bringing about such a reconsideration of French committment. More recent historians such as Howard Evans, finding no evidence for this thesis, have pointed more to the progressively leftward shift within revolutionary politics throughout 1790, as well as the lobbying, respectively, of the Jacobin

---

[39] Blanning, *Origins of the French Revolutionary Wars*, p. 62; Sorel, *L'Europe et la Révolution Française: les moeurs politiques et les traditions*, p. 379.

[40] See, for example, La Luzerne to Montmorin, 19 October 1790, AAE-CP-Angleterre-575, f. 82.

[41] Oscar Browning (Ed.), *Despatches of Earl Gower* (Cambridge, 1885), p. 39.

club and the Diplomatic Committee by British agents such as William Miles and Hugh Elliot.[42]

However much one may credit the evidence for a growing public disinclination to go to war in support of Spain, a similar reluctance on behalf of the Assembly should not be understood as constituting a shift in either the orientation or in the substance of French foreign policy. Rather, it should be seen as perhaps more of a realisation and response, among the separate bodies who now directly controlled this policy, to the incompatibility of their shared primary objectives, which had in fact remained constant throughout the crisis: the preservation of the Spanish alliance, and peace with Britain. Though a 'war party', led most popularly by Lafayette, may well have desired combat with Britain, it is clear that elsewhere in the Assembly and the royal government war was not merely regarded as abhorrent, but as an impossibility. For Montmorin, the need for peace, particularly with Britain, had, from the beginnings of the Revolution, become the *sine qua non* of French foreign policy. The Foreign Minister, like many others, knew full well the paralysis into which the financial crisis had thrown French power from 1787—88, and that the continuation of financial problems and the rising dissension and anarchy in French public life and the armed forces across 1790 delayed any serious hopes for the restoration of that power and influence. As we have already seen, it was such an understanding of French impotence that at least partly determined Montmorin to delay consideration of the Spanish request in June, so as not to encourage Spanish obstinacy in the crisis. While not wanting to lose the Spanish alliance, Montmorin and his master were nonetheless most anxious that a reasonable Anglo-Spanish accommodation could be reached.[43]

This was the hope that had also underpinned Mirabeau's speech of 25 August, with its recommendation that France expand its active naval footing to thirty ships-of-the-line. Thereafter, both Montmorin and the Diplomatic Committee endeavoured to walk the very fine line between trying to reassure Spain of French support, while neither provoking Britain or jeopardising the prospects for peace. For the Committee, though many among the Left had earlier decried the practice in international diplomacy of secrecy and dissimulation, this

---

[42] Evans, 'The Nootka Sound Controversy in Anglo-French Diplomacy', pp. 609-611, 633-634.

[43] In a despatch of 12 October, Montmorin instructed La Luzerne to impress upon the British Ministry that 'nous n'avons dans ce moment aucun projet de réunion, ni de co-opération avec l'Espagne puisque nous conservons l'espérance que les choses s'arrangeront'. Montmorin to the marquis de La Luzerne, 12 October 1790, AAE-CP-Angleterre-575, f. 39.

effectively meant talking in two tongues: for their desire for peace led during October to a number of unofficial and clandestine meetings between Elliot, Pitt's secret agent, and members of the Committee. These secret meetings were intended to allay apprehensions between Britain and France, and to convey a mutual desire for peace.[44] On the official level, Montmorin worked similarly to quell British fears, responding to British ambassadorial protests regarding the projected arming of forty-five ships-of-the-line with confidential verbal assurances that this armament would only proceed with "la plus grande lenteur", and that they were intended only to protect France's Caribbean colonies. Necker even went so far as to admit to the British Ambassador that in fact "the fear of disobliging Spain was the real cause of so extravagant a decree", in other words, that it was intended specifically for Spanish consumption.[45]

In the end, the dual objective held by Montmorin and the Diplomatic Committee—of preserving both peace and the Spanish alliance—would prove unsustainable. When news of the final Spanish capitulation reached the Assembly in November, it was greeted with great relief and elation by the deputies.[46] Despite this elation, it is evident in hindsight that the only real victor in this affair was Britain. Although France had once again, as in the Dutch Crisis, avoided being drawn in to a ruinous war for which it was poorly positioned, and unwilling, to fight, it had only escaped war at the cost of abandoning another major ally. The belated support in the Assembly for measures in support of Spain ultimately had little effect on either the Spanish or British governments, and had in any case been undermined by the French themselves. Thus, while Montmorin would continue to hope that the longstanding Spanish alliance could somehow be salvaged intact from this affair,[47] the Spanish capitulation had in fact only signalled its final deathknell. Peace had been preserved, but only at the cost of deepening France's diplomatic isolation.

---

[44] Pitt's motives in sending Elliot, who was an old friend of Mirabeau, were not actually to promote the idea of an Anglo-French alliance. Rather, Pitt's aim was merely to induce the French not to fulfil the Family Compact and support Spain. See Evans, 'The Nootka Sound Controversy', p. 638.

[45] Gower to Leeds, 27-29 August, in Browning (Ed.), *Despatches of Earl Gower*, p. 28.

[46] AP, Vol. 20, 25 November 1790, p. 739.

[47] See, for example, Montmorin to the marquis de La Luzerne, 23 January 1791, AAE-CP-Angleterre-563, f. 252.

Prussian Feelers and the Mirabeau-Montmorin Coalition

On the very same day, 27 July, as alarms were being raised in the National Assembly over a projected passage of Austrian troops over French soil, the Convention of Reichenbach was signed in Germany between Austria, Prussia, Britain and Holland. Sponsored by Britain, this treaty more or less arrested the drift toward a general European war, by requiring Austria to end its involvement with Russia in the Turkish war, and by also forestalling an imminent Prussian invasion of Austrian-ruled Bohemia (in support, supposedly, of Prussia's recent ally, the Turks).[48]

As Peyssonnel and various deputies had earlier noted, the prospect of an Austro-Prussian peace contained certain dangers for France, in that it opened up the possibility of collusion between the two major German powers in an attack both on France and its Revolution. Now that such a peace had actually been concluded, what would be the response of the revolutionaries and of French foreign policy-makers to the question of diplomatic counter-measures, that is, the formation of a Franco-Prussian alliance? There were, at least in theory, as Peyssonnel had outlined in his speech of 10 May, a number of compelling reasons for another dramatic 'revolution' in France's alliance system: the switch from an Austrian to a Prussian alliance, and the protection of an independent and pro-French Belgium. Aside from checking and diminishing Austrian power on the continent by exploiting Prussia's own desire to achieve this, it was also presumed to carry important secondary benefits to France's strategic and economic position in a more global sense. Not only would a switch to a Prussian alliance be far more consonant with the remainder of France's alliance-system, especially in regard to Turkey, but it would indirectly assist in

---

[48] This was a real coup for the British, who had not wished to see any marked shift in the balance between the two strongest German powers in the old Holy Roman Empire. They also wanted to prevent any potential conflict with Spain becoming part of a larger war in Europe. For the Austrians it meant, above all, a timely reprieve. Though they had experienced some successes in their war against the Turks, the rumblings of potential ethnic rebellion elsewhere in their dominions (in Italy and Hungary) had loomed as a grave threat to the very existence of the Austrian Empire. Disengaging from the Turkish war would now allow Leopold II, Joseph's recent successor, to forestall these further rebellions and thus preserve the security and integrity of the Austrian Empire in central Europe. The terms of the Reichenbach Convention also made provision for the reconquest of the so-called Austrian Netherlands, to be effected as soon as convenience allowed. Blanning, *The Origins of the French Revolutionary Wars*, p. 54-55.

improving France's prospects in its maritime rivalry with Britain. As Jean Favier had argued thirty years before, and the recent Balkans war had amply demonstrated, commitments to mutual defence with Austria were contradictory to France's long-standing and important relationship with the Ottoman Empire. It weakened this relationship with the Ottomans while in itself holding few compensating benefits.[49] Removing that contradiction might now help thwart recent British attempts to supplant France as a primary ally and major trading partner with the Ottoman Porte, thus protecting France's valuable Levant trade. Furthermore, detaching Prussia from Britain might also allow France to regain its recent alliance with Holland, which, together with Spain, would greatly bolster France's position in the maritime and colonial balance of power.

During 1790, conditions in Europe indeed seemed more ripe than ever for another 'Diplomatic Revolution', the reverting of France to a Prussian alliance. The Prussians, who were increasingly frustrated with their supposed ally Britain, were now keen to pursue their expansionist aims, primarily in Poland, with the help of either a French or an Austrian alliance. Hence, from late 1790 and into 1791 the Prussian government, far from being immediately hostile to the French Revolution, endeavoured to interest the French authorities in the possibility of an alliance. In the summer of 1790 an unofficial Prussian envoy, the banker Ephraïm, was sent to Paris to open up negotiations with the French government, and to encourage anti-Austrian sentiment among the revolutionaries.[50] Meanwhile, from Berlin, the French Ambassador the comte de Moustier reported to Montmorin the Prussian frustration with their British ally, and their desire for a French alliance (in opposition to Austria and Russia), writing that the Prussian king "font sentir plus vivement combien l'appui de la France et un concert entre les deux Cours seraient plus utiles que des combinaisons avec l'Angleterre, dont la Prusse n'est qu'un instrument secondaire".[51]

---

[49] Jean Favier, *Observations de Favier*, p. 27.

[50] Blanning, *The Origins of the French Revolutionary Wars*, p. 81. Between December 1790 and April 1791 the British agent William Miles reported from Paris that Prussian agents were not only in negotiation with the French government, but also actively working to encourage the revolutionaries to renounce the Franco-Austrian alliance. See Miles, *Correspondance of W. A. Miles*, Vol. 1, pp. 179, 255, 275.

[51] Moustier to Montmorin, 4 February 1791, cited in AP, Vol. 49, 31 August 1792, pp. 153-154. Elsewhere in this dispatch de Moustier wrote that "le roi de Prusse et son ministère, loin d'avoir des vues hostiles contre nous, désireraient, au contraire, que nous fussions tellement unis avec le Prusse, que cette alliance

Such a dramatic reversal of alliances was, however, staunchly opposed by both Montmorin and Mirabeau, then the two most influential figures in the formation of French foreign policy. To Moustier Montmorin replied flatly that "il ne peut, Monsieur, nullement être question dans ce moment-ci, d'une alliance avec la Prusse".[52] The king, he explained, was indeed concerned to build good relations with the Prussian ruler Frederick William, but not to the extent of breaking the French alliance with Austria. Part of the reason for this disinclination was that Prussia, a restless power, appeared to be angling for a role as an arbiter of Europe, a role Montmorin implied was the natural preserve of France. France, after all, did not wish to become the unwitting plaything of Prussia, and a dupe to the Prussian king's scheming ambitions. "Il faut attendre", instructed Montmorin, "que le chaos où se trouve la politique soit débrouillé pour juger sainement des principes et des vues de la Cour de Berlin".[53]

Despite the growing unpopularity of the Austrian alliance in French public opinion, Mirabeau and the Diplomatic Committee were also concerned not to effect any 'innovation' in the French alliance system. This Mirabeau had more or less implied in his report of 25 August 1790 on the Spanish Affair, where he stated, on behalf of the Committee, that France should continue to observe all of its existing treaties, tactfully avoiding any specific mention of the hated Austrian alliance, France's other major strategic pact. Although Mirabeau went no further here in rationalising this general position, one may deduce that it was the imperative need for peace that was the chief reason for the Committee to want to maintain the diplomatic status quo. Whether or not a switch to a Prussian alliance would result in immediate war with Austria (which was arguable—Austria was still recovering from its war with the Turks), there was a strong possibility that in the context of the Nootka Sound dispute, such a move would provoke, before too long, a British attack on the French colonial Empire in anticipation of a French move into the Low Countries. As we saw in the previous chapter, the deputies were acutely conscious that the French position, particularly in the West Indies, was increasingly fragile by mid-to-late 1790. The Constituents were indeed greatly concerned to maintain the

---

offrit a Sa Majesté prussienne une garantie contre les attaques de l'empereur, dont la puissance est aujourd'hui la principale cause de l'appréhension de la cour de Berlin".

[52] Montmorin to de Moustier, 4 February 1791, cited in AP, Vol. 49, 31 August 1792, p. 155.

[53] *Ibid.*, 23 January 1791, cited in AP, Vol. 49, 31 August 1792, p. 151.

integrity of the French colonial Empire as a whole, and thus keen to avoid making—for as long as France remained weak and riven by internal chaos—any military or diplomatic moves that might precipitate a British attack or retaliation. Unsurprisingly, then, the matter of the Austrian alliance would not be raised either in this report, or in any other submitted by the Diplomatic Committee during the period of the Constituent Assembly. For the reasons of peace, and French global security, the deputies thought it necessary to defer that question for as long a time as possible.

There was also the question of Mirabeau's relationship with Montmorin. By the winter of 1790—91 public pressure on the royal ministers had become so great that all but Montmorin were compelled to resign.[54] Of the original ministers from the start of the Revolution, only Montmorin, it seemed, had retained the confidence of the Assembly. In the new ministry, he was also to be the only minister whom Louis XVI now trusted, being the last remaining minister he had freely chosen. It was around this time that the Foreign Minister entered into a deeper alliance with Mirabeau, a secret coalition whose object was to save the constitutional monarchy in France. At the base of this alliance was a plan concocted by Mirabeau entitled *Aperçu de la situation en France et des moyens de concilier la liberté publique avec l'autorité royale*, by which Mirabeau and the Foreign Minister would together work to reconcile the Monarchy with the Revolution. Their hope, ultimately, was to control the Revolution and thereby forestall a further radicalisation and polarisation of revolutionary politics. Once order, stability and confidence in the monarchy had returned, it was assumed that a new constitution endowing the monarchy with real as opposed to nominal power could be negotiated. Only then, with a strong executive, would France be able to reap the benefits of its 'regeneration', emerging immeasurably stronger from the crucible of Revolution.[55]

The diplomatic component to this plan was simple enough: the maintenance both of peace and the diplomatic status quo, in hopeful

---

[54] Following a closely defeated motion in the Assembly on 19 October 1790 to demand the dismissal of the Ministry, and in the face of continued public agitation in support of this motion, Louis XVI's ministers finally opted to resign, La Tour de Pin on 21 October, La Luzerne on 23 October, Champion de Cicé on 21 November, Lambert on 30 November and Saint-Priest on 24 December 1790. See Luttrell, *Mirabeau*, pp. 234-35.

[55] See Luttrell, *Mirabeau*, pp. 237-47, See also, E. Dumont, *Souvenirs sur Mirabeau et sur les deux premières assemblées législatives* (Paris 1832), Ch. 13, p. 257.

anticipation of a return of stability and the restoration of French power and influence in Europe. In short, in spite of the profound ideological shift in the constitution of the French state, and the implicit threat that this seemed to pose to aristocratic-absolutist regimes elsewhere in Europe, the Montmorin-Mirabeau coalition would endeavour, in general terms, to provide some continuity in the relations between France and its neighbours. In specific terms, this meant avoiding direct confrontation over such issues as the seigneurial rights of the German princes, and the discouragement of any spread of counter-revolutionary support in Europe.

To this end, Mirabeau attempted to reassure the Assembly on the 28 January 1791, on behalf of the Diplomatic Committee, that in spite of the dispute with the German Princes France had little to fear from its continental neighbours. It was, he said, in the interest of France's neighbours to settle the above dispute through negotiation, and otherwise to maintain the peace. As for the *émigrés*, they were merely vicious yet deluded agitators, having neither means nor allies. After all, "Quelle grande nation épousera leur vengeance, leur fournira des armes et des subsides, leur prodiguera le fruit de ses impôt et le sang de ses citoyens?".[56] If France had anything to fear, it was, he proposed, not open war, but, firstly, the clandestine activities of the British government, which might hope to profit from the continuation and encouragement of discord and agitation in France, and, secondly, internal counter-revolutionary intriguers, whose greatest damage was in exciting an unnecessary degree of anxiety and agitation among the populace. "Où donc", he posed, "est la source de cette anxiété, qui, se propageant dans tout le royaume, y a provoqué non seulement l'énergie et la fierté du patriotisme, mais encore son impatience? Le zèle n'a-t-il point exagéré nos périls?". Though counter-revolutionary activity existed, he thus asserted that its capabilities had been blown out of all proportion.[57]

Mirabeau then announced, to the applause of the Assembly, measures designed to address these anxieties, and to combat the source of the revolutionaries' fears. Seconding Alexandre de Lameth's report on the need to strengthen France's internal defences, Mirabeau then affirmed the importance of ensuring that all France's representatives abroad were faithful servants of the new regime in France, and not the old. From November 1790 all diplomatic officials high or low had already been

---

[56] AP, Vol. 22, 28 January, p. 536.
[57] *Ibid.*, pp. 536-37.

required to swear an oath of allegiance to the new regime,[58] but now, he said, a more careful review of personnel was necessary:

> Tout le monde reconnait depuis longtemps, et le ministre des affaires étrangères a rappelé plus d'une fois au comité diplomatique, la nécessité d'employer désormais, pour nos relations extérieures, des hommes qui ne compromettent pas la puissance française par des doutes sur nos succès, qui ne soient pas en quelque sorte étrangers au nouveau langage dont ils doivent être les organes...[59]

By this means both Mirabeau and Montmorin hoped that they could discourage the popular belief in France that the king's officials, particularly his representatives in foreign courts, were, as aristocrats and courtiers, naturally antagonistic to the Revolution and the new constitution, and hence sympathetic to the spread of domestic and foreign counter-revolution.[60] This in turn would hopefully discourage the growth of radicalism, bolster the popularity of the Monarchy and strengthen its position vis-à-vis the constitution.

Foreign Affairs and the Crisis of 1791

It hardly needs stating that these efforts failed to restore the popularity of the monarchy, or to stem the tide of radicalism that had increasingly characterised revolutionary politics. What little hope Mirabeau's plan had of success was dashed with his untimely death in April 1791. Thereafter, in the remaining months of the Constituent Assembly, a series of events and circumstances would propel France into a progressive polarisation of domestic political opinion into those more zealously for and those more steadfastly against the Revolution. This was precisely the outcome that Mirabeau had sought to avert. Rather than reconciliation and a return to stability, France experienced further agitation and a deepening of public discord.

---

[58] As Thompson notes, those few who had refused to swear this oath were promptly recalled by the French Government. E. Thompson, *Popular Sovereignty and the French Constituent Assembly 1789-91* (Manchester, 1952), p. 149.

[59] *Ibid.*, p. 537.

[60] In accordance with Mirabeau's proposal, on 27 March 1791 the King ratified seven new nominations, proffered by Montmorin, for diplomatic posts, respectively, at Rome, Stockholm, Venice, St. Petersburg, The Hague, Dresden and Liége. See Masson, *Le département des affaires étrangères*, p. 88.

The role that France's foreign relations may have played in this process of polarisation has long been the subject of debate among historians. As Blanning recounts in his work *The Origins of the French Revolutionary Wars*, a number of historians have, over the years, concluded that the eventual outbreak of war in 1792 between France and the German powers was more or less inevitable, in so far as it amounted to a violent and unavoidable clash of principles between the defenders of the old regime in Europe, and the proponents of a new, 'revolutionary' transformation of European state and society.[61] Other historians, however, have argued that the war of 1792 was far from inevitable, and that the supposed 'collision' of revolutionary and Old Regime principles has been much overstated, at least as a source of armed conflict. Blanning, for example, has argued that despite the Old Regime monarchs' fears about the spread of some 'revolutionary' ideas, there was nothing in the outstanding points at issue in French foreign relations in 1791—the French occupation of the Papal territories of Avignon and the Comtat Venaisson, and the abolition of the seigneurial rights of the Rhine princes—that in fact constituted a challenge to the state-building practices of the old order, and that could not have been resolved through negotiation.[62]

One could argue, furthermore, that there was, at least during the time of the Constituent Assembly, real potential for the on-going and peaceful co-existence of revolutionary France and the German powers. Not only has it been established that the Austrian rulers Joseph II and Leopold II were strongly sympathetic to various aspects of the Revolution, but that they had been most reluctant—in spite of the Padua Circular and the Pillnitz Declaration in June and August 1791—to actually intervene on behalf of either the Rhine princes or the French Royal Family. They had, furthermore, scorned and discouraged the activity of *émigré* counter-revolutionaries.[63]

There is also evidence to suggest that the relationship between the French revolutionaries and the Prussian monarchy was far from instrinsically antagonistic. Even as late as October 1791, at the start of the Legislative Assembly, it was reported to William Miles that Prussian agents were still trying to detach France from Austria, and procure a Franco-Prussian alliance.[64] It is also evident that many revolutionaries

---

[61] Blanning, *Origins of the French Revolutionary Wars*, pp. 69-73.
[62] *Ibid.*, pp. 77-79. See also, Hampson, *Prelude*, p. 138.
[63] Blanning, *Origins of the French Revolutionary Wars*, p. 78.
[64] On 4 October 1791, an unnamed member of the National Assembly wrote to the English agent William Miles, informing him that "tout ce que je vous ai dit ...

(including Brissot) favoured such a union. So strong was the dismay and disappointment about the eventual failure of France to procure a Prussian alliance, that the fact that Montmorin had worked to prevent it was the substance of a formal accusation later made against him in the Legislative Assembly.[65]

It should be noted, finally, that following the death of Mirabeau in April 1791, the Diplomatic Committee, in conjunction with Montmorin, more or less continued to adhere to a 'pacifist' foreign policy, and continued to negotiate with foreign states over such thorny issues as the papal territories and the claims of the Rhine princes.[66] The broad tenor of French foreign policy hence remained largely unchanged in the final months of the Constituent Assembly. This has led Norman Hampson to conclude that by the end of September 1791, in the area of foreign policy, "nothing irrevocable had been done and nothing suggested that France was on the threshold of twenty years of virtually uninterrupted aggressive war".[67]

* * * *

If relations between the National Assembly and the foreign powers subsequently deteriorated, this was not directly due to the supposed impact of revolutionary principles, but to a combination of different factors. Chief among these factors was, firstly, the failure of the National Assembly to 'close' the Revolution in September 1791 and thus provide a return to political stability in France, and, secondly, the formation of a strategic environment in Europe which facilitated a *rapprochement* between Prussia and Austria during 1791, and the apparent creation of a counter-revolutionary coalition.

---

relativement aux menées du Roi de Prusse était bien vrai; il a un agent ici actuellement. ... Une personne de confiance a été envoyée au Roi de Prusse de la part de l'Assemblée Nationale, et on est très bien disposé à rompre toute liaison avec la Cour de Vienne, dont on n'est pas trop content; mais la Reine, qui se mêle de tout, s'y oppose, ainsi que Montmorin et Lessart, et il y a lieu de croire qu'il y a sur le tapis quelque chose qui doit changer la face politique de toute l'Europe". Miles, *Correspondence of W. A. Miles*, Vol. 1, p. 315.

[65] See the 'Affaire de Montmorin', AP, Vol. 49, 31 August 1792. The unfortunate Montmorin was subsequently murdered by a mob during the September massacres.

[66] Following the death of Mirabeau, the moderate and no less wily Talleyrand was elected to replace him on the Diplomatic Committee, while Fréteau became its *rapporteur*.

[67] Hampson, *Prelude to Terror*, p. 138.

The first of these factors—the deterioration of the internal situation and the failure of the Constitutional Monarchy—has been a central subject of much of French Revolutionary historiography. According to most recent historical accounts, there are numerous reasons why the closure of the Constituent Assembly failed to produce a return to stability. Most of these reasons have to do with the events in France leading up to the finalisation of the constitution in August-September 1791, and may be said to include: the inability of Louis XVI to accept a constitution and a regime which had failed, in his view, to address adequately the financial problems of the French state, and which had merely turned France into a 'crowned republic', and an ungovernable one at that; the resultant Flight to Varennes in June 1791, which only discredited the Monarchy in the eyes of the populace and led to an explosion of republican sentiment; the increasing national influence and radicalisation of the Jacobin club; the refusal of the Right in the National Assembly to co-operate with Feuillant constitutionalists in order to revise the constitution in favour of a stronger and more independent executive; the Civil Constitution of the Clergy which alienated most of the upper and lower clergy, and popularised the cause of counter-revolution; the extremist fulminations of both Right and Left-wing journalists, which stoked an ongoing atmosphere of fear and suspicion and contributed to public unrest; and the partial disintegration of the armed forces and the inability of the Government to restore public order, particularly in the provinces.[68]

All of these factors together contributed to the progressive polarisation of revolutionary politics throughout 1791, and to the ultimate fragility of the constitutional monarchy leading into the Legislative Assembly. To this, according to Blanning, may be added another factor which quickly emerged following the opening of this new Assembly in October 1791: namely, the efforts of the minority Fayettist and Brissotin factions to exploit popular fears of an alleged foreign counter-revolutionary conspiracy, in order to excite support within France for an armed confrontation with Austria. Both these groups—the Fayettists and Brissotins—hoped to benefit politically from a limited war in which they expected France would be quickly victorious.

---

[68] See Doyle, *Oxford History of the French Revolution* (Oxford, 1990), Ch. 6; Hardman, *Louis XVI*, Ch. 14; Blanning, *Origins of the French Revolutionary Wars*, Ch. 3-4; W. Murray, *The Right-Wing Press in the French Revolution* (Woodbridge, 1986).

There were two further major factors which, Blanning asserts, then propelled France and the German Powers into a war that was to prove neither short nor limited in scope. Firstly, was the grave miscalculation of the Austrian ruler Leopold, who assumed—as it turned out, incorrectly—that talk of tough action in support of the Rhine Princes might intimidate the more radical elements of the Patriot party, and hence have a moderating effect on the Revolution.[69] Instead, it merely inflamed the situation in France, inadvertently providing Brissot and his confederates with a platform upon which they could stir up war fever in the National Assembly, and persuade the many non-aligned deputies to overturn the 'pacifist' policy of the Feuillants.

The second further factor was the death of Leopold, and the accession of Francis II at the beginning of March 1792. Unlike his two recent predecessors, Francis was genuinely hostile to the Revolution in France, and far less flexible in his attitude toward it. Hence, when the French issued Francis with an ultimatum later that month—namely, to renounce such threatening treaties as the Pillnitz Declaration—he refused point blank to submit to the French demands.[70] Not long thereafter, on 20 April 1792, Louis XVI, at the behest of the Legislative Assembly, declared war on "Francis II, King of Hungary and Bohemia".[71]

Because this declaration, and the statement on foreign policy which preceded it,[72] were couched in ideological terms, some historians have assumed that the war of 1792 arose out of an inevitable clash of principles. Yet, one may also argue, in conclusion, that there was the potential—at least before the end of 1791—for peaceful co-existence between the Revolution and the powers of continental Europe. The fact that some of the principles promoted by the Revolutionaries were arguably in opposition to those of the old regime, and caused anxiety to some European rulers, did not necessarily mean that armed conflict would inevitably ensue. As we have seen, the larger German powers,

---

[69] He had come to this assumption by attributing to Austro-Prussian sabre-rattling across the summer of 1791 the slight swing to the right instituted by the Feuillants in the last months of the Constituent Assembly. See Blanning, *Origins of the French Revolutionary Wars*, pp. 102-103.

[70] Leopold, through his chancellor Kaunitz, had responded to an earlier 'ultimatum' in February 1792, protesting the his desire for peace and his acceptance of the French constitution, while yet condemning "the provocations and dangerous conspiracies of the Jacobin party". Stewart (Ed.), *A Documentary Survey of the French Revolution*, p. 282.

[71] *Ibid.*, p. 287.

[72] See Stewart (Ed.), *A Documentary Survey of the French Revolution*, pp. 283-286.

Austria and Prussia, gave evidence in the period 1789—91 that the founding of a new regime in France would not even necessarily inhibit or negatively affect their relations with that country. For their part, the foreign policy-makers of the Constituent Assembly explicitly promoted the pursuit of peaceful co-existence between France and its larger neighbours, employing a language of foreign policy leavened with equal elements of idealism and pragmatism, and which placed emphasis on the preservation of the French diplomatic status quo. However, for this position to remain tenable required both the stabilisation and moderation of the political situation in France, a prospect which in fact became increasingly unlikely across 1791 due to a range of contingent factors. These factors allowed a more radical, less compromising political language to come to the fore in the making of foreign policy, a rhetorical language that would soon place Revolutionary France and the supposed forces of liberty in a state of war with the old regime and all the supposed forces of monarchical despotism.

8 Conclusion: Continuities and Discontinuities in French Global Policy, 1787—1791

A certain image of the deputies of the National Constituent Assembly has seemed to prevail in classic historical accounts of the French Revolution, such as Alexis de Tocqueville's *Old Regime and the French Revolution*. The majority of these deputies, the Patriots or *nationaux*, have been traditionally portrayed as enthusiastic and uncompromising 'enlightenment' rationalists who were inexperienced in practical politics, beguiled by the notion of the general will, and who were 'naively'—and, as it turned out, tragically—optimistic about the prospects for a successful and mostly peaceful revolutionary transformation of French state and society. The deputies' apparent determination to formulate a constitution and regenerate French society on the basis of the natural and fundamental 'Rights of Man' gave force to this image. As the historiography has depicted, the deputies of the Constituent Assembly believed themselves to be breaking with a morally degenerate past, the Old Regime, in creating—root and branch—a new society based on 'enlightened' and rational principles.

The decree of the National Assembly of 22 May 1790 declaring illegal the making of offensive war, or the forming of offensive alliances, may be considered evidence—among other major pieces of legislation—of an apparent desire among the deputies to create a new moral order, to set an example of enlightened policy that they hoped the rest of Europe would eventually follow. Many deputies, particularly those on the Left, hoped that the decree of 22 May had indeed inaugurated a new era of international relations in Europe, in which peace, stability and justice would come to rule in place of the incessant conflicts associated with dynasticism and absolutist government.

The recent work of Timothy Tackett has, however, shown that this characterisation of the deputies must be viewed with a strong degree of circumspection. His examination of previously neglected evidence suggests that, while certainly optimistic, the deputies were generally less influenced by enlightenment rationalism than has up to now been assumed. Furthermore, while they were perhaps novices as politicians, the deputies were often better informed on issues of public affairs and technical matters relating to government than they had previously been given credit for, and had had varying and sometimes considerable experience of public administration. The efficiency and thoroughness with which the Assembly's various committees undertook their assigned tasks, combined with the fact that much of their contribution to the restructuring of French administration persists to this day, demonstrated the skill of the deputies in this regard. In addition, Tackett notes that the deputies were not only conscious of moral imperatives as laid down in the 'Declaration of the Rights of Man', but were also often acutely aware of their own material interests and those of their particular constituencies.[1]

As this study has shown, the deputies were also often highly conscious of the material interests of the nation as a whole, as they perceived them. In marked contrast to their image as naive ideologues obsessed with enlightenment values, the Patriot deputies also appeared to demonstrate a degree of cautiousness, common sense and pragmatism in several important areas of policy-making. Their materialism and pragmatism may be seen, in particular, in the Assembly's response to legislative issues pertaining to global policy: foreign affairs and trade, and colonial trade and administration. In this respect, many of them could be described as practical and hard-headed realists. First, despite the deputies' repudiation of Old Regime dynasticism, and their demand that henceforth alliances be rigorously measured against a publicly-defined concept of the national interest, they were nonetheless careful not to dissolve existing treaties and alliances, however unpopular or apparently prejudicial to French interests they appeared to be, lest this lead to a war that neither France nor the Revolution could afford. The deputies of the Constituent were also careful to avoid provoking foreign powers in relation to issues pertaining to the nationalisation of French sovereignty, such as the issue of the German Princes and the Papal territories.

Secondly, despite the popularity of physiocratic and free trade ideas among many of its most prominent members, the Assembly as a whole displayed a cautious pragmatism when it came to commercial policy, and a wariness in regard to abstract and innovative economic theory. For the deputies, the key fact of the French economy—in contrast to

---

[1] See Tackett, *Becoming a Revolutionary*, Ch. 2, *passim*.

that of Britain—was that the corporate strictures of the Old Regime had previously kept it in a chronically underdeveloped state. Now, with the creation of a unified national market and customs union, they believed the French economy could finally develop to its fullest potential. The deputies' subsequent introduction of a staggered but generally moderate tariff policy showed that they no longer fully accepted as valid previous 'mercantilist' assumptions about the nature of national wealth. Yet it also showed their persistent faith in the necessity of protective external tariffs. These tariffs—when combined with a regime of internal free trade—would, they believed, stimulate internal growth and foster a competitive and robust manufacturing and agricultural economy. The Assembly's introduction and maintenance of a range of bounties and subsidies for local industries reflected the desire of the deputies to maximise the potential growth of the French economy, and their belief that the state had an important role in overseeing and nurturing national economic development. Overall, this commercial policy stemmed from the deputies' skepticism about the benefits of a completely free external trade, and their desire above all to protect nascent French industries from the harmful effects of 'unequal' foreign competition.

Colonial policy was another area where the Assembly demonstrated a strong degree of pragmatism. Despite their description of individual liberty, security and legal equality as the "natural and imprescriptable rights" of all men, the deputies were determined not to challenge a regime of black slavery in the French colonies—and one that was particularly brutal and oppressive—lest this alienate the planter-colonists and jeopardise France's highly lucrative colonial trade. In a similar concession to colonial interests, the majority of deputies were also prepared ultimately to allow free blacks and men of colour to be denied—simply on grounds of race—the political rights to which as propertied men they might otherwise have been entitled. From another angle, despite the principle of self-determination implied in the Declaration of the Rights of Man, the National Assembly was determined not just to retain ultimate legislative sovereignty over their colonies. The deputies also insisted on maintaining a national monopoly of colonial trade, in spite of the pleas and objections of the colonists themselves. In material terms, the deputies thus intended little or no innovation in the relationship between France and its colonies, or in the position of non-whites in the slave-holding colonies, in spite of the problems this seemed to present in terms of moral consistency.

Looking at the responses of the Constituent deputies to these various issues, one might surmise that much of this evident pragmatism, and many of the apparent compromises effected in these policies, were only temporary, and driven by political expediency—an effort, in other words, to prevent any avoidable haemorrhaging of support for the Revolution that might result from a threat to the material bases of French prosperity. From the evidence adduced in this study, one may surely consider this to be a significant factor. Yet, one may also draw two further and no less significant conclusions. First, the evidence would suggest that this collection of policies constituting the Constituents' global policy was not just the product of short-term political expediency, but also reflected a general concern among the Assembly's policy-makers as to the long-term interests of the French nation.

Secondly, one may conclude that, in spite of the contrasts between the Old and the New Regime in relation to political culture and ideology, the respective responses of the monarchy and National Constituent Assembly to the question of global policy were similar in terms of material substance. That is, if the Assembly's public declaration renouncing offensive war was certainly unprecedented, and may be regarded as a distinct departure from the foreign policy practices of the Old Regime, it may be asserted that the global policies of the Assembly and of the previous royal government were basically similar in their overall structure and material goals. Both regimes, firstly, seemed to follow policies in regard to metropolitan and colonial trade that seemed to draw their inspiration from similarly contrasting principles: on the one hand they each extended a measure of liberalism into the trade between France and other countries, while they sought, on the other hand, to maintain a seemingly 'mercantilist' monopoly of trade between France and its plantation colonies in the West Indies.

This collection of seemingly inconsistent policies was not simply a response by the National Assembly to a range of separate and temporary exigencies, such as the need to placate various French port towns. It was, rather, a reasonable and pragmatic response by these successive national policy-makers to the evolving conditions of the eighteenth century, and the diverging economic realities pertaining specifically to metropolitan core and colonial periphery. By the late-eighteenth century European powers still tended to view their overseas colonies in traditional, 'mercantilist' terms: as the source of cheap and highly sought after commodities which the mother-country was itself unable to produce, and as a captive market for its manufactured goods. Overall, the chief purpose of colonies was to enhance the economic power of the mother-country by providing it with a more favourable balance of trade, and indirectly, to enhance its strategic power, the taxable wealth generated from colonial ventures being translated into military power on the continent of Europe and on the high seas. In this respect, colonial competition still seemed to be viewed—and measured—in zero-sum terms, with economic and geostrategic imperatives closely entwined.

At home in Europe, however, the situation was changing. The nature of international competition in the European theatre was evolving throughout much of the eighteenth century. Old mercantilist assumptions about the nature and source of national wealth were rapidly losing their force, autarchic notions of national development giving way to an emphasis on production and international exchange. Growing levels of economic interdependence between European states increasingly encouraged many larger states to moderate their previously prohibitive tariff regimes, and introduce more liberal commercial treaties and trading arrangements. This added a new level of complexity to international relations in Europe: for while the military balance of power could continue to be measured in largely zero-sum terms, economic and commercial relations were beginning to appear less directly combative. In the making of foreign policy, strategic imperatives had thus increasingly to be balanced against conflicting economic or commercial imperatives, since these different forms of national competition were no longer always subject to the same dynamics, at least within Europe. This generally required a greater subtlety in approach on behalf of the diplomats and policy-makers of the European states, and a more careful assessment and balancing of the various elements that comprised national interest.

The respective global policies of the last years of the absolute monarchy and the National Constituent Assembly may hence be said to together constitute a coherent and tailored response to this emerging 'bifurcation' in the nature of international relations, between the specific and complex dynamics of European international relations, and those of colonial competition outside Europe. Whereas in Europe the relationship between strategic and economic imperatives was becoming less direct, though still important, in the colonial and extra-European sphere those relationships remained as strong and as direct as before. As such, this multi-faceted structure of French global policy may also be considered to comprise a significant element of continuity in the period 1787—91.

This continuity might also be said to extend to the ultimate goals of these successive global policies. Again, despite the great ideological gulf that separated the absolutist government of Louis XVI and the National Constituent Assembly—for instance, in their contrary definitions of sovereignty—their respective global policies were both similarly ambitious and yet at the same time restrained, even conservative. They were similarly ambitious in so far as they together envisioned a France that would be able to reclaim its former role as the principal arbiter of the European balance of power. They were similarly restrained in so far as that this resurgence of French influence would derive not from a policy of aggression and conquest—a course which both eschewed as morally unacceptable either in Europe or beyond—but from the power that would naturally accrue from France's long-term economic development and increasingly dominant position in European and global trade. Louis thus hardly conformed to the image of an aggressive old regime military despot that had been decried by various Patriot deputies in the May debate of 1790, but was himself in fact a most reluctant warrior and the author of a moderate, albeit ambitious, foreign policy. Finally, these policies were similarly conservative in so far as their mutual emphasis was on the preservation of the existing diplomatic status quo in Europe, as well as on the need to curb and restrain the growth of both Britain and the eastern powers Austria and Russia. In these respects, there would indeed seem again to be a strong element of material continuity in French global policy between 1787 and 1791.

In that these global policies of the pre-revolutionary royal government and the National Constituent Assembly were structurally similar, they may also be said to have suffered from many of the same difficulties and weaknesses. Firstly, in their separate deliberations on commercial and foreign policy, both the royal government and the deputies of the National Assembly may be considered to have overestimated the prospects for future stability within the European balance of power, and of French capacity—even as arbiter—to curb or delimit the expansionist ambitions of such powers as Prussia, Austria or Russia. For instance, the deputies appeared on many occasions to acknowledge that a state's prosperity and economic strength could, though not always, translate into a proportionate measure of strategic power and political influence abroad. They also recognised, particularly in the debates on commercial policy, that states often used such measures as tariffs and subsidies in a targeted fashion in order to maximise both their advantages in international trade and the development of their own economies.

Despite this, the deputies seemed, surprisingly, not to have given much consideration to the potential of foreign powers to react negatively to a regeneration of the French economy, and the strengthening of its commercial power. Would Prussia, Austria and Russia simply have allowed France to assert its supposed 'natural' economic dominance, without taking measures to protect themselves, and thus maximise, however artificially, their own possible gains? It seems hardly likely. These powers would have been all too keenly aware that such a regeneration and economic expansion of France would measurably decrease their own economic and political leverage in Europe, by tilting the balance of power against them. Thus, although they may have been prepared to reconcile themselves to a basic change in political culture in France, their own ambitions would not have let them countenance such a degree of French dominance, when they could potentially prevent it by exerting control over their own economies, and by using trade themselves in a politically targeted way. From this it is hard to imagine how in the long-term France could have prevented or contained the ongoing expansion of the eastern powers, and the major conflicts that such expansionism would surely have provoked within Europe and the Levant.

Whether or not a *Pax Francia* in Europe could reasonably have been expected to last, the economic transformation wrought by the Revolution would certainly have left France stronger than before, and hence better equipped to enter into any armed struggle on the continent. Yet what of French power in the colonial and maritime sphere? Here the key factor was the relative strength of Britain and the nature of Anglo-French relations. Given that Britain had been able to translate its commercial and imperial successes into a preponderant influence in continental Europe, French policy under Louis XVI had stressed the importance of containing and reducing British global power. This containment of their principal global rival, Vergennes had hoped, would allow France to regain from Britain—and, hopefully, also from Russia—its former position as the arbiter of Europe. In this regard, however, the same contradictions that had beset Vergennes' global strategy also continued to plague the global policy instituted by the Constituents. The prime difficulty faced here by both sets of policy-makers was that of sustaining a simultaneous 'containment and rapprochement' strategy with Britain. Contrary to Vergennes' expectations, this had eventually paralysed French diplomatic influence and overseas power rather than strengthening it. In Europe, despite closer economic ties between Britain and France, the persistence nonetheless of an intense diplomatic rivalry had compromised French efforts to contain the expansion of the eastern powers, and prevented them from playing a mediating role in the war that erupted between Austria, Russia and the Ottoman Empire, or in the Northern War between Sweden, Denmark and Russia. Outside Europe, particularly in India and the Indian Ocean, French activity had only excited British fears, further propelling the British into strengthening and expanding their already substantial colonial power in the region. The French strategy of containment was thus also a failure in that it had in fact acted as a spur rather than as a brake to British imperial expansion.

In retrospect, one may conclude that France had two alternatives in its 'Atlantic' policy. One was to go beyond the extention of commercial ties and enter into a formal alliance with Britain, as the duc d'Orléans and others had suggested. The other was to go to war once again with Britain, as Castries had wished, in the hope that France could effect a more decisive defeat of British maritime and colonial power, and the removal of British power, in particular, from India. It was only then that Vergennes' overall strategy could take force without perhaps being beset with such crippling contradictions.

In the first case, the forming of a strategic alliance with Britain would arguably have presented, again in retrospect, a most favourable outcome for France. It would have allowed Britain and France to finally present a united front in discouraging the expansionist ambitions of the eastern powers, and to preserve the territorial status quo in Eastern Europe and the Balkans. Furthermore, for as long as the alliance lasted, it would not only have removed the prospect of an dual threat to French metropolitan and colonial security, but it could also have allowed a 'regenerated' France to expand its trade and influence in Europe more or less unhindered, to the point where it could even have eventually eclipsed Britain as the superior partner in that alliance. In the immediate term such an alliance would most likely have protected a weakened France from the predatory ambitions of Prussia and Austria, not only enhancing French security but also diminishing to some degree the sense of threat held by the revolutionaries in France, and strengthening their negotiating position with regard to issues such as the claims of the Papacy and the Rhine Princes. By this means the ultimate rupture between France and the German powers may perhaps have been avoided. Through an Anglo-French alliance France could ultimately have achieved by stealth many of the goals of Vergennes' system, at least in regard to the French position in Europe, at a time when France was otherwise crippled by financial paralysis and internal dissension.

As Murphy has noted, however, the fact that such an alliance never materialised was not merely due to the incapacity of the French to overcome their longheld mistrust of the British, but to a persistent climate of *mutual* suspicion between the two powers.[2] Hence, even if

---

[2] "Perhaps the most tragic diplomatic failure of the last years of the Old Regime", Murphy comments, "was the inability of France and Britain to break through

the French Ministry had sought in 1790 to negotiate an Anglo-French alliance, there is evidence to doubt that Pitt's government would have been seriously interested in any case. With France in such a state of paralysis at home and abroad, and with Britain now the apparent arbiter in Europe and supreme on the high seas, the British government would have doubtless concluded that such an alliance was far more advantageous to French interests than to its own. However sincere the French desire for peace in 1790, British statesmen and diplomats would have been fully aware of how quickly foreign policy intentions could change, particularly if subject to the shifting will of a popular assembly. The British could have hence placed little faith in an apparent French desire for peace. For them the imperative was to put a cap on French *capabilities*, making impregnable British power in the maritime and colonial sphere.

If an Anglo-French alliance in the late 1780s and during the Constituent Assembly was hence unlikely, the second option for the French government—war with Britain—was impossible, or at least highly imprudent. First, with the deep financial and political problems gripping French government and society during this period, France could barely have been able go to war against Britain, let alone expect to emerge decisively victorious over a country that actually presented a stark contrast to French weakness. Compared to France, Britain was stable, effectively governed, and increasingly strong in its finances, its naval power and its colonial defences. This being the case, the consequences for France of a failure in this war would have been plainly catastrophic: it would have probably led to the irreversible demise and dismembering of the French colonial empire. Moreover, in the heated atmosphere of revolutionary politics, there was evidently some danger that the French ministry, the monarchy, and even the National Assembly might not have survived the popular wrath if it had declared war on Britain in 1790. This option was hence considered by the French government to be neither reasonable nor practicable.

Given that neither of these above alternatives were really feasible, one may hence conclude that the French policy-makers in the last years of the old regime and under the Constituent Assembly had little choice but to persist with the diplomatic and strategic 'system' implemented by Vergennes in the early to mid-1780s. The significant difference was that the policy-makers of the Constituent Assembly assumed that a 'regenerated' France—with a stronger national economy and much

---

their inherited suspicions and build an understanding based on mutual confidence and interests". See Murphy, *The Diplomatic Retreat*, p. 168.

sounder finances—would be better able to take advantage of this system than the previous regime. Although the deputies thus made some adjustments to their general commercial policy, in line with their creation of France's first genuinely national economy, in other respects they endeavoured to maintain the status quo with regard to the other major components of this global policy, and, where possible, in the current global balance of power. They were thus concerned at all times to retain and protect their precious sugar islands in the Caribbean, to maintain and assert French superiority in the Mediterranean, and even to at least partially restore a French military presence on the Indian sub-continent.

Aside from the question of material continuity, one may make the further point that there existed in the Constituent Assembly different 'languages' of foreign policy, even within the dominant group of Patriot deputies. Although an appreciation of Rousseauean values may well have permeated most groups in the Assembly, particularly among the Patriots, there were major differences as to how such 'enlightened' values were to be applied in French foreign policy. Some more radical Jacobin deputies wished France to have no truck whatsoever with the supposedly corrupt practices of the past, such as secret dealings and alliance diplomacy, or with notions such as the international balance of power. They also tended to see revolutionary France as naturally and unavoidably contraposed to all those regimes supposedly still under the sway of monarchical absolutism and the Old Regime. The majority of Patriot deputies, however, in particular those who would emerge as the 'Feuillants', had a more flexible and pragmatic view. Although they also wished to see the emergence of a new, 'enlightened' era in international relations in Europe and abroad, they nonetheless accepted that French security and national interest required a policy which was attuned to the prevailing dynamics of international affairs, and which presupposed a period of peaceful co-existence with Old Regime powers. This was a view that with the increasing polarisation of political groupings and attitudes in France, and the emergence of the Jacobins and the popular movement as potent political forces, was increasingly difficult to sustain. A process of continuing radicalisation within France eventually led to a deterioration of relations with France's Old Regime neighbours, to the overturning of the Feuillants' 'pacifist' policy, and ultimately, to war.

In conclusion, it is clear from the evidence produced in this study that international exigencies were indeed of central importance in the general framing of French policy throughout the period 1787–91. It has been established that in the pre-Revolution, the French government did

Conclusion 255

by no means 'abandon' foreign affairs, but was in fact stricken by an involuntary and crippling paralysis that was both financial and diplomatic in nature. This led to what many in government assumed and hoped would only be a temporary 'implosion' of French global power. From 1789, perceptions of French global interests and aspirations also played a significant role in shaping policy, it being assumed that the 'regeneration' of France would also finally allow the country to not only mount a global resurgence but also to fulfill its supposed destiny as the primary 'arbiter' of Europe and the leading global superpower. Despite the profoundly different understanding and political culture represented by the Old and New Regimes in France, their respective global policies reveal a significant continuity from the last years of the Old Regime to the end of the Constituent Assembly. Both sets of policy-makers appeared to share similar conceptions and operative understandings of international political economy. Finally, their global policies seemed to not only share many of the same goals, but also many of the same flaws and limitations. France could not, after all, easily escape from the dilemmas of its own 'amphibious' geography, of being both a major continental and Atlantic power.

Appendix

Decree of 22 May 1790 on the Right of War and Peace

Art. 1: The National Assembly decrees as constitutional articles the following:
 The right of war and peace belongs to the Nation.
 Declarations of war can only be decided by a decree of the Legislative body, after it has received the formal and necessary proposition from the king, and sanctioned by His Majesty.

Art. 2: The responsibility for watching over the external security of the kingdom, of maintaining its rights and possessions, is delegated to the king by the Constitution of the State; as such, he alone can undertake external political relations, conduct negotiations and choose his agents, make preparations of war proportionate to those of neighbouring states; allocate land and sea forces as he deems appropriate, and to direct them in case of war.

Art. 3. Where hostilities are imminent or already begun, where an ally is to be supported, where a right needs to be upheld through force of arms, the executive power will be required to give, without any delay, notification to the Legislative body, and to inform it of the causes and reasons; if the Legislative body is on vacation it will reassemble immediately.

Art. 4. Upon this notification, if the Legislative body deems that the existing hostilities amount to an unjustified aggression on behalf of ministers, or some other agent of the Executive power, the author of this aggression will be subject to the charge of lèse-nation; the National Assembly should declare, to this effect, that the French nation renounces the undertaking of any war with the aim of making conquests, and that it will never employ its forces against the liberty of any people.

Art. 5. Upon the same notification, if the Legislative body decides that war ought not to be made, the Executive power will be required to take immediate measures to halt or prevent all hostilities, the ministers remaining responsible for delays.

Art. 6. All declarations of war will be made in these terms: "On behalf of the king, in the name of the nation".

Art. 7. During the course of war, the Legislative body will be able to require the Executive power to negotiate peace, and the Executive power will be required to comply with this order.

Art. 8. At the instant war ceases, the Legislative body will fix a time by which the number of troops levied beyond peacetime needs ought to be demobilised and the army reduced to its permanent state.

The troops' pay will only be continued until that point, after which, if the number of troops exceeding peacetime-needs remain assembled, the responsible minister may be charged with lèse-nation.

To this effect, the committee of the Constitution will be required to report regularly on its work regarding the method of ministerial responsibility.

Art. 9. It is up to the king to conclude and to sign with foreign powers all the conventions necessary for the well-being of the State; and treaties of peace, alliance or commerce will be enacted only once they have been ratified by the Legislative body.

(Source: AP, Vol. 15, 22 May 1790, pp. 661-662.)

Bibliography

Archival Sources

Archives de la Marine, Vincennes:
Série 37-H-21

Archives du Ministère des Affaires Etrangères, Quai d'Orsay, Paris:
Mémoires et Documents-Angleterre-18, 65
Mémoires et Documents-Asie-17, 18, 19
Mémoires et Documents-France-587
Mémoires et Documents-Turquie-15
Correspondance Politique-Angleterre-559 à 575
Correspondance Politique-Hollande-571, 574

Archives Nationales, Paris:
Archives Privées-306-21, 19
Série AD-XV-38
Fonds Colonies-C1, C2, C4

Bibliothèque Nationale, Paris:
Nouvelles Acquisitions Françaises-9434

Printed Primary Sources

Anon., *L'Esclavage des nègres aboli, ou Moyens d'améliorer leur sort*, (Paris, 1789).
Arnould, A., *La balance du commerce et des relations commerciales extérieures de la France, dans toutes les parties du globe, particulièrement à la fin du règne de Louis XIV, et au moment de la Révolution* (Paris, 1791).
Arrêtés des bureaux de l'Assemblée des Notables; présidés par Monsieur et par le Prince de Conty, n.p., 1787.
Aulard, F. (Ed.), *Histoire des Jacobins; Receuil des documents pour l'histoire du Club des jacobins de Paris*, 6 Vols., (Paris, 1889-97).
Bergasse, N., *Considérations sur la liberté du commerce; ouvrage où l'on examine s'il est avantageux ou nuisible au commerce, que le transport des denrées et des marchandises soit réduit en privilege exclusif* (London, 1788).
Boyetet, [n.i.], *Recueil des divers mémoires, relatifs au traité de commerce avec l'Angleterre* (Versailles, 1789).

Brissot, J.-P., *Mémoire sur les noirs* (Paris, 1790).
Brissot, J.-P., (Ed.), *Le Patriote français: journal libre, impartial et national*, 8 Vols. (6 May 1789-2 June 1793), (Reprint: Paris, 1989).
Browning, O. (Ed.), *Despatches from Paris 1784-1790*, 2 Vols., (London, 1909).
Browning, O. (Ed.), *The Despatches of Earl Gower* (Cambridge, 1885).
Cassan, M., *Considérations sur les rapports qui doivent existes entre les colonies et les métropoles, et particulièrement: Sur l'état actuel du commerce français dans les Antilles, relativement à celui qu'y font les étrangers* (Paris, 1790).
Clercq, A. (Ed.), *Recueil des traités de la France*, 22 Vols., (Paris, 1880-1904).
Cordier, H. (Ed.), 'La Correspondance générale de la Cochinchine', *T'oung Pao*, 7 (1906).
Cormeré, G. *Situation exacte des finances à l'époque de 1er janvier 1792, ou Lettre de Mahé de Cormeré à M. le président & à MM. les députés composant le comité des contributions publiques, de l'Assemblée nationale* (Nantes, 1792).
Davenport, B. (Ed.), *A Diary of the French Revolution by Gouverneur Morris 1752-1816* (London, 1939).
Dupont de Nemours, P.-S., *Lettre à la Chambre du Commerce de Normandie sur la mémoire qu'elle a publiée relativement au Traité de Commerce avec l'Angleterre* (Rouen & Paris, 1788).
Dupont de Nemours, P.-S., *Le Pacte de Famille et les conventions subséquents, entre la France & l'Espagne; avec des observations sur chaque article* (Paris, 1790).
Farçot, J.-J.-C. *Questions constitutionelles sur le commerce et l'industrie, et projet d'un impôt direct, sur les commerçans & gens à l'industrie, en remplacement des impôts quelconques sur le commerce & l'industrie, proposés à l'Assemblée Nationale par des Négocians Français* (Paris, 1790).
Favier, J. *Observations de Favier, sur la maison d'Autriche, et particulièrement sur le Traité de Versailles, du premier Mai 1756; Entre le Roi et l'Imperatrice Reine de Hongrie* (New Edition: Paris, 1792; originally published: London, 1778).
Forge, [n.i.], *Mémoire tendant à l'extension du Commerce extérieur, à la sûreté du Commerce intérieur, et à l'accroissement de la marine militaire, présenté par M. de Forge, Chevalier, ancien Ecuyer de main du Roi*, n.d.
Frossard, B. *Les cause des esclaves nègres et des habitans de la Guinée, portée au tribunal de la justice, de la religion, de la politique; ou Histoire de la traite & l'esclavage des nègres, preuves de leur illégitimé, moyens de les abolir sans nuire ni aux colonies ni aux colons* (Lyon, 1789).
Gerbaux, F. & Schmidt, C. (Eds) *Procès-verbaux des comités d'agriculture et de commerce de la constituante, de la législative et de la convention*, 5 Vols. (Paris, 1906-37).
Gilchrist, J. & Murray, W. (Eds), *The Press in the French Revolution*, (Melbourne, 1971).
Girault de Coursac, P. (Ed.), *Louis XVI à la parole* (Paris, 1989).

Goudard, P. *Rapport présenté à l'Assemblée Nationale, au nom du Comité d'Agriculture et du Commerce, sur la situation du commerce extérieur de la France pendant la Révolution, en 1789* (Paris, 1791).

Lansel, J. *Necessité d'un régime pour conserver et faire fleurir le commerce et les manufactures* (Paris, 1791).

Lecointre-Marsillac, J. *Le More-Lack, ou Essai sur les moyens les plus doux & les plus équitables d'abolir la traite & l'esclavage des nègres d'Afrique, en conservant aux colonies tous les* avantages *d'une population agricole* (Paris, 1789).

Madival, J. & Laurent, E. (Eds) *Archives Parlementaires de 1787 à 1860: recueil complet des debates legislatifs et politiques des chambres françaises* (Paris, 1862).

Mallet de Maisonpré, C. *Mémoire sur les demandes de la colonie de Pondichéry* (Paris, 1791).

Malouet, P.-V. *Mémoires*, 2 Vols. (Paris, 1874).

Miles, C.P. (Ed.) *Correspondance of W. A. Miles on the French Revolution 1789-1817*, 2 Vols. (London, 1890).

Plon, Henri (Ed) *Réimpression de l'ancien moniteur, seule histoire authentique et inalterée de la Révolution Française depuis la réunion des états-generaux jusqu'au Consulat (Mai, 1789-Novembre, 1799), avec des notes explicatives* (Paris, 1858-63).

Pouliques, M. (Ed.) *Doléances des Peuples Coloniaux à l'Assemblée Nationale Constituante 1789-1790* (Paris, 1790).

Procès-verbal de l'Assemblée des Notables, tenue à Versailles, en l'année 1787 (Paris, 1787).

Stewart, J.H. (Ed.) *A Documentary Survey of the French Revolution*, (New York, 1951).

Thébaudières, A. *Vues générales sur les moyens de concilier l'intérêt de commerce national avec la prosperité des colonies* (Paris, 1789).

Secondary Sources

Acomb, F., *Anglophobia in France 1763-1789: an essay in the history of constitutionalism and nationalism* (Durham, N.C., 1950).

Anderson, M., 'Eighteenth-century Theories of the Balance of Power', in R. Hatton & M. Anderson (Eds), *Studies in Diplomatic History* (London, 1970).

Baker, K., (Ed.) *The French Revolution and the Creation of Modern Political Culture*, Vol. 1 (London, 1989).

Baker, K., *Inventing the French Revolution* (Cambridge, 1990).

Beik, P., *A Judgment of the Old Régime: Being a survey by the Parlement of Provence of French Economic and Fiscal Policies at the Close of the Seven Years' War* (New York, 1944).

Best, G., *War and Society in Revolutionary Europe, 1770-1870* (London, 1982).

Black, J., *Natural and Necessary Enemies: Anglo-French Relations in the Eighteenth Century* (London, 1986).
Black, J., *The Rise of the European Powers 1679-1793* (London, 1990).
Black, J., *British Foreign Policy in an Age of Revolutions, 1783-1793* (Cambridge, 1994).
Blanning, T., *Origins of the French Revolutionary Wars* (London, 1986).
Bosher, J., *The Single Duty Project: a study of the movement for a French customs union in the eighteenth century* (London, 1964).
Bosher, J., *French Finances 1774-1795: from business to bureaucracy* (Cambridge, 1970).
Bowden, W., Karpovich, M., Usher, A., *An Economic History of Europe since 1750* (New York, 1937).
Brinton, C., *A Decade of Revolution* (New York, 1934).
Castries, Duc de., *Le Maréchal de Castries* (Paris, 1956).
Chartier, R., *The Cultural Origins of the French Revolution* (Durham, N.C., 1986).
Cobban, A., *Ambassadors and Secret Agents* (London, 1954).
Confer, V., 'French Colonial Ideas before 1789', *French Historical Studies*, 7:4 (1972), pp. 338-359.
Cormack, W., *Revolution and Political Conflict in the French Navy 1789-1794* (Cambridge, 1995).
Crout, R., 'In Search of a "Just and Lasting Peace": The Treaty of 1783, Louis XVI, Vergennes and the Regeneration of the Realm', *International Historical Review*, 5:3 (1983), pp. 363-398.
Crouzet, F., 'England and France in the Eighteenth Century: A Comparative Analysis of Two Economic Growths', in R. Hartwell (Ed.), *The Causes of the Industrial Revolution in England* (London, 1967).
Darnton, R., *The Literary Underground of the Old Regime* (Cambridge, Mass., 1982).
Davis, R., *The Rise of the Atlantic Economies* (London, 1973).
Doerflinger, T., 'The Antilles Trade of the Old Regime: A Statistical Overview', *Journal of Interdisciplinary History*, 6:3 (1976), pp. 397-415.
Donaghay, M., 'The Maréchal de Castries and the Anglo-French Commercial Negotiations of 1786-87', *The Historical Journal*, 22:2 (1979), pp. 285-312.
Donaghay, M., 'The Ghosts of Ruined Ships: The Commercial Treaty of 1786 and the Lessons of the Past', *The Consortium on Revolutionary Europe 1750-1850* (1981), pp. 111-118.
Donaghay, M., 'The Vicious Circle: The Anglo-French Commercial Treaty of 1786 and the Dutch Crisis of 1787', *The Consortium on Revolutionary Europe 1750-1850* (1989), pp. 447-456.
Doyle, W., *The Old European Order, 1660-1800* (Oxford, 1978).
Doyle, W., *Origins of the French Revolution* (Oxford, 1980).
Doyle, W., *The Oxford History of the French Revolution* (Oxford, 1989).
Duffy, M., *Soldiers, Sugar and Seapower* (Oxford, 1987).

Dull, J., *The French Navy and the War of American Independence: A Study of Arms and Diplomacy 1774-1787* (Princeton, 1975).
Dull, J., 'France and the American Revolution seen as Tragedy', in R. Hoffman and R. Albert (Eds), *Diplomacy and Revolution: The Franco-American Alliance of 1778* (Charlottesville, 1981).
Dull, J., 'Vergennes, Rayneval and the Diplomacy of Trust', in R. Hoffman and R. Albert (Eds), *Peace and the Peacemakers*, (Charlottesville, 1986).
Egret, J. *The French Prerevolution 1787-1788* (Eng. Trans., Chicago, 1977).
Evans, H., 'The Nootka Sound Controversy in Anglo-French Diplomacy—1790', *Journal of Modern History*, 46 (1974), pp. 609-640.
Fehér, F. (Ed.), *The French Revolution and the Birth of Modernity*, Berkeley, 1990.
Fieldhouse, D., *The Colonial Empires* (London, 1966).
Ford, F., *Europe 1780-1830* (London, 1970).
Frost, A., *Convicts and Empire* (Melbourne, 1980).
Fugier, A., *Histoire des relations internationales*, Vol. 4 (Paris, 1954).
Gaziello, C., *L'Expédition de Lapérouse 1785-1788* (Paris, 1984).
Gershoy, L., *From Despotism to Revolution* (New York, 1944).
Gilbert, F., 'The "New Diplomacy" of the Eighteenth Century', *World Politics*, 3 (1952), pp. 1-38.
Glachant, R. *Suffren et le temps de Vergennes* (Paris, 1976).
Goldstone, J., *Revolution and Rebellion in the Early Modern World*, (Berkeley, 1991).
Gottschalk, L. & Maddox, M., *Lafayette in the French Revolution: From the October Days through the Federation* (Chicago, 1973).
Gruder, V., 'A Mutation in Elite Political Culture: The French Notables and the Defence of Property and Participation, 1787', *Journal of Modern History*, Vol. 56, 1984, pp. 598-634.
Guiffrey, J., 'Les Comités des assemblées révolutionnaires, 1789-1795: le comité d'agriculture et de commerce', *Revue Historique*, 1 (1876), pp. 438-484.
Hampson, N., *A Social History of the French Revolution* (London, 1963).
Hampson, N., *Prelude to Terror* (Oxford, 1988).
Hardman, J., *Louis XVI* (New Haven, 1993).
Harlow, V., *The Founding of the Second British Empire*, Vol. 1 (London, 1952).
Haswell, J., *The Battle for Empire,* (London, 1976).
Henderson, W., 'The Anglo-French Commercial Treaty of 1786', *Economic History Review*, 10:1 (1957), pp. 104-112.
Holland Rose, J., 'The Franco-British Commercial Treaty of 1786', *English Historical Review*, 23 (1908), pp. 709-724.
Horner, F., *Looking for La Pérouse: D'Entrecasteaux in Australia and the South Pacific 1792-1793* (Melbourne, 1995).
Hyslop, B., *French Nationalism in 1789 according to the Cahiers* (New York, 1968).
Jones, P., *Reform and the Revolution in France: The Politics of Transition, 1774-1791* (Cambridge, 1995).

Kennedy, B., 'Anglo-French Rivalry in India and the Eastern Seas, 1763-93: A study of Anglo-French Tensions and of their impact on the consolidation of British power in the region', Unpublished Ph.D, Australian National University, 1969.

Kennedy, P., *The Rise and Fall of the Great Powers: Economic Change and Military Conflict from 1500 to 2000* (London, 1988).

Kwass, M., 'The Kingdom of Taxpayers: State Formation, Privilege, and Political Culture in Eighteenth-Century France', *Journal of Modern History*, Vol. 70, 1998, pp. 295-339.

Labourdette, J.-F., *Vergennes: Ministre Principal de Louis XVI* (Paris, 1990).

Lê, N.-D., *Les Missions-Etrangères et la pénétration française au Viêt-nam* (Paris, 1975).

Lemay, E., 'Une minorité au sein d'une minorité: un banquier et quelques négociants à l'Assemblée constituante 1789-91', *Studies on Voltaire and the Eighteenth Century*, 217 (Oxford, 1983), pp. 49-64.

Lemay, E., (Ed.) *Dictionnaire des Constituents, 1789-91* (Paris, 1991).

Letaconnoux, J., 'Le comité des députés extraordinaires des manufactures et du commerce de France et l'oeuvre économique de l'Assemblée constituante (1789-1791)', *Annales Révolutionnaires*, 6, 1913), pp. 149-208.

Lokke, C., *France and the Colonial Question: A Study of Contemporary French Opinion, 1763-1801* (New York, 1932).

Luard, E., *The Balance of Power: the System of International Relations 1648-1815* (London, 1992).

Luttrell, B., *Mirabeau* (Hemel Hempstead, 1990).

Marion, M., *Histoire financière de la France depuis 1715* (Paris, 1914).

Martray, J., *La destruction de la marine française par la Révolution* (Paris, 1988).

Masson, F., *Le département des affaires étrangères* (Paris, 1877; Reprint: Geneva, 1977).

Murphy, O., 'Charles Gravier de Vergennes: Profile of an Old Regime Diplomat', *Political Science Quarterly*, 83:3, (1968), pp. 400-418.

Murphy, O., 'The Conservatism of Charles Gravier, Comte de Vergennes'', *Consortium on Revolutionary Europe 1750-1850*, (1981), pp. 119-130.

Murphy, O., 'The View from Versailles: Charles Gravier Comte de Vergennes's Perceptions of the American Revolution', in *Diplomacy and Revolution: the Franco-American Alliance of 1778*. Hoffman, R. & Albert, R. (Eds), (Charlottesville, 1981).

Murphy, O., 'Louis XVI and the Pattern and Costs of a Policy Dilemma: Russia and the Eastern Question, 1787-1788', *Consortium on Revolutionary Europe 1750-1850* (1986), pp. 264-274.

Murphy, O., *The Diplomatic Retreat of France and Public Opinion on the Eve of the French Revolution, 1783-1789* (Washington D.C., 1998).

Murray, W., *The Right Wing Press in the French Revolution 1789-92* (Woodbridge, Suffolk, 1986).

Norris, J., 'Policy of the British Cabinet in the Nootka Sound Crisis', *English Historical Review*, 70 (1955), pp. 562-580.
Nussbaum, F., 'The French Colonial Arrêt of 1784', *South Atlantic Quarterly*, 27 (January, 1928), pp. 62-78.
Nussbaum, F., 'The Formation of the New East India Company of Calonne', *American Historical Review*, 38:4 (1933), pp. 475-497.
Ozouf, M., 'War and Terror in French Revolutionary Discourse (1792-94)', *Journal of Modern History*, 56 (1984), pp. 579-597.
Padover, S., *The Revolutionary Emperor: Joseph II* (New York, 1934).
Parry, J., *Trade and Dominion: European Overseas Empires in the Eighteenth Century*, London, 1971.
Perkins, M., 'Montesquieu on National Power and International Rivalry', *Studies on Voltaire and the Eighteenth Century*, 238 (Oxford, 1985).
Perkins, M., 'Voltaire's Concept of International Order', *Studies on Voltaire*, 36 (Geneva, 1965).
Pluchon, F., *Histoire de la colonisation française* (Paris, 1991).
Price, M., *Preserving the Monarchy: The Comte de Vergennes, 1774-1787* (Cambridge, 1995).
Priestley, H., *France Overseas through the Old Régime: A Study of European Expansion* (New York, 1939).
Pugh, W., 'Calonne's "New Deal"', *Journal of Modern History*, 11:3 (1939), pp. 289-312.
Quinney, V., 'The Committee on Colonies of the French Constituent Assembly, 1789-91', Unpublished PhD dissertation, University of Wisconsin, 1967.
Riley, J., *The Seven Years' War and the Old Regime in France. The Economic and Financial Toll*, (Princeton, 1986).
Rosow, S., 'Commerce, Power and Justice: Montesquieu on International Politics', *Review of Politics*, 46:3 (1984), pp. 346-366.
Rothaus, B., 'The War and Peace Prerogative as a Constitutional Issue during the First Two Years of the Revolution, 1789-1791', in *Proceedings of the First Annual Meeting of the Western Society for French History* (New Mexico, 1974), pp. 120-138.
Saintoyant, J., *La Colonisation française sous l'ancien régime*, 2 Vols., (Paris, 1929).
Saintoyant, J., *La Colonisation française pendant la Révolution*, 2 Vols., (Paris, 1930).
Savage, G., 'Favier's Heirs: The French Revolution and the Sécret du Roi', *Historical Journal*, 41:1 (1998), pp. 225-258.
Schama, S., *Patriots and Liberators* (New York, 1977).
Schroeder, P., *The Transformation of European Politics 1763-1848*, (Oxford, 1996).
Scott, W., 'Commerce, Capitalism and the Political Culture of the French Revolution', *History of European Ideas*, 11 (1989), pp. 89-105.
Sée, H., 'The Normandy Chamber of Commerce and the Commercial Treaty of 1786', *Economic History Review*, 2 (1929-30), pp. 308-313.

Sée, H., *Economic and Social Conditions in France during the Eighteenth Century* (New York, 1935).
Sen, S., *The French in India 1763-1816* (New Delhi, 1971).
Sewell, W., 'Ideologies and Social Revolutions: Reflections on the French Case', *Journal of Modern History*, 57 (1985), pp. 57-85.
Showalter, D., 'Ni tumulte, ni grandeur: Revolution in Pondicherry', *Journal of Indian History* (Golden Jubilee Volume, 1973), pp. 577-593.
Skocpol, T., *States and Social Revolutions* (Cambridge, 1979).
Sorel, A., *L'Europe et la Révolution française: les moeurs politiques et les traditions; les nouveaux principes*, 7 Vols., (Paris, 1902).
Sorel, A., *Europe and the French Revolution* (Eng. Trans., London, 1969).
Stein, R., *The French Slave Trade in the Eighteenth Century: An Old Regime Business* (Madison, Wis., 1979).
Tackett, T., *Becoming a Revolutionary: The Deputies of the French National Assembly and the Emergence of a Revolutionary Culture (1789-1790)* (Princeton, 1996).
Thompson, E., *Popular Sovereignty and the French Consittuent Assembly 1789-91* (Manchester, 1952).
Vines, P., 'The Slaving Interest in the Atlantic Ports, 1763-1792', *French Historical Studies*, 7:4 (1972), pp. 527-543.
Welch, O., *Mirabeau: A Study of a Democratic Monarchist* (London, 1951).
Whiteman, J., 'Tocqueville and the Two Faces of Modernity: Current Liberal Historiography and the French Revolution', Unpublished M.A. thesis, University of Melbourne, 1993.
Williams, E., *The Ancien Régime in Europe* (Harmondsworth, 1970), 1972.

Index

Adhémar, 53, 80, 81
Aiguillion, 121, 223
André, 222, 225
Austria, 6, 18, 20, 26, 64-69, 73, 102-103, 107-112, 115, 123, 135,136, 165, 221-224, 233-236, 239-243, 250-252

Barnave, 98, 119, 133, 180-188, 190-191
Barthélemy, 52, 54, 57, 61, 72, 78, 80, 81
Begouen, 156, 158
Belgium, 107-115, 222, 233
Bengy de Puyvallée, 126
Bérardier, 200, 201
Biron, 119
Blin, 176-178
Boisgelin, 129
Boislandry, 151-154, 159, 160, 167
Boyetet, 79, 80, 143
Brienne, 49, 56, 57, 60, 63, 77, 81-84
Brissot, 173, 207, 218, 240, 242
Britain, 3, 6, 15-30, 32-36, 40-41, 44, 46, 48, 52-55, 57-65, 67, 69, 71, 73, 75-80, 86, 89-90, 92, 94-96, 101-109, 111-112, 114, 117, 123, 128, 129, 132, 136, 138, 140, 142, 143, 146-148, 150, 155, 157, 158, 161-163, 165, 166, 170, 174, 182, 183, 195, 199, 200, 202, 205, 207-209, 215-217, 220, 223-226, 229-234, 247, 250-253
Bruny d'Entrecasteaux, 33
Bussy, marquis de, 30, 38

Calonne, 15, 23, 24, 26, 27, 31, 32, 34, 43-49, 60, 79, 82, 142
Carmarthen, 52, 53, 55, 62, 72
Cassan, 174
Castries, maréchal de, 15, 16, 18, 21, 22, 28-30, 33-34, 36, 39, 41, 52, 54, 56, 57, 59, 60, 63, 77, 81, 84, 85, 89, 91, 92, 95
Catherine II, 15, 26, 32, 64, 67
Cazalès, 129
Châtelet, du, 128, 130, 225
Chilleau, 172, 173
Choiseul, 18, 21, 23
Clermont-Tonnerre, 124-126
Cochinchina, 91-96, 174, 201, 204 211, 212
Colbert, 146, 148, 171
Condorcet, 173
Conti, prince de, 49
Convention of Reichenbach, 233
Conway, comte de, 75, 76, 89, 90, 92, 94, 95
Cossigny, 39, 212
Custine, 125

Delattre, 158, 160-164, 189, 192, 209, 210
Dorset, Duke of, 107
Dubois-Crancé, 221
Dupleix, 200, 207
Dupont de Nemours, 20, 24-26, 79, 80, 119, 127, 145, 154, 155, 156, 157, 217, 218, 221
Duport, Adrien, 98, 173
Dupré, 195
Duquesnoy, 134
Duval d'Eprémesnil, 192, 200

Eden Treaty (1786), 20, 27, 34, 40, 51, 52, 78-81, 123, 135, 138, 143, 147, 148, 150, 154, 157
Eden, William, 73
Elliot, Hugh, 231, 232
Ephraïm, 234

Farçot, 149-154, 174, 175
Fernan-Nunez, 216
Fontenay, 147, 195, 196
Francis II (Austria), 242
Franco-Austrian alliance, 64, 109, 110, 112, 123, 136-138, 221, 234-236
Franco-Cochinchinese treaty (1787), 93, 94
Franco-Dutch alliance, 29, 35, 36, 39-40, 54, 55, 58, 64, 68, 75, 76, 79, 92, 234
Franco-Spanish alliance, 116, 123, 129, 216-220, 231, 232
Frederick William II (Prussia), 60, 61, 235
Fréteau, 131, 135, 136, 222, 224, 225

Gallisonnière, 126
Gibraltar, 16
Gillet de la Jacqueminière, 196
Goudard, 142, 147-154, 155-158, 168
Goupil de Préfeln, 132
Grenville, 62
Guinebaud, 194

Hailes, 62, 73-75, 77
Hernoux, 193, 195

India, 16, 28-33, 35-41, 51, 54, 74-77, 88-91, 93-96, 170, 177, 179, 191-194, 196-210, 212, 252, 254

Jallet, abbé, 121
Joseph II (Austria), 60, 64, 66, 239

La Luzerne, comte de, 77, 85-90, 107, 147, 172, 201-202, 210, 202, 210, 236
La Luzerne, marquis de, 67, 72, 73, 75, 76, 102, 104-105, 116, 215, 216, 219, 220, 231
La Pérouse, 32
Lafayette, 108, 110, 114, 120, 173, 219, 231
Lambert, Contrôler-général, 147
Lameth, Alexandre de, 98, 119, 173, 181, 217, 222, 223, 237
Lameth, Charles de, 122, 131, 173
Landsdowne, 51
Le Chapelier, 118, 128, 139, 181, 198
Le Couteulx, 157, 193, 194, 200
Le Pelletier de Saint-Fargeau, 132
Lévis, du, 119, 121
Louis XVI, 9, 15-17, 21-25, 29, 32, 33, 36, 39, 43, 44, 48-50, 55, 56, 60, 61, 63-67, 71, 72, 76, 83, 85-87, 90-93, 95, 96, 99-100, 106, 113, 114, 116-120, 122-123, 129-131, 133, 184, 187, 188, 209, 219, 220, 225, 228, 235, 236, 238, 241, 242, 249-251

Malesherbes, 56
Mallet de Maisonpré, 209
Malouet, 125, 126, 128, 130, 152, 156, 198, 205
Maury, abbé, 126-130, 193, 194, 200
Menou, 119, 123, 131, 132, 222, 225
Miles, William, 217, 218, 231, 234, 239
Mirabeau, Gabriel-Honoré, 98, 118, 120, 132-136, 147, 173, 196-198, 210, 211, 218-219, 225-228, 231-233, 235, 236-238, 240
Miromesnil, 48
Monneron, 39, 204-209
Montesquieu, abbé, 125, 128
Montlosier, 126, 127, 129

Montmorin, 50, 53, 54, 56-62, 64, 66-68, 72-74, 77, 78, 80, 93, 102, 103, 105-107, 109, 110, 113, 116, 117, 147, 157, 215, 216, 219-221, 223-225, 229, 231-240
Moustier, comte de, 234, 235

Nairac, 195-200
Necker, 17, 45, 48, 232
Nguyen-Anh, prince, 92-94, 212

Ogé, Vincent, 187, 188
Ottoman Empire, 64-69, 73, 74, 103, 112, 140, 164, 165, 234, 233-235

Padua Circular, 239
Pétion, 120-123, 126
Peyssonel, 110-114, 137, 233
Pigneau de Behaine, Bishop of Adran, 92, 93, 95, 204, 212
Pillnitz Declaration, 165, 239, 242
Pitt, 53, 54, 69, 77, 102, 105, 116, 217, 232, 253
Praslin, duc de, 126, 128, 131
Prussia, 6, 18, 20, 26, 58-61, 64, 69, 73, 107-109, 112-114, 135, 136, 148, 153, 223, 224, 233-235, 239, 240, 242, 243, 250, 252

Quadruple alliance, 65, 69, 73, 74, 75, 102

Rabaut Saint-Etienne, 218
Rayneval, 50-52, 65, 67, 69, 78
Rewbell, 119, 121, 131
Ricard, 229
Robespierre, 119, 221, 223
Roederer, 198
Roussillou, 147, 155, 158-160, 162, 168
Royou, abbé, 224
Russia, 6, 20, 24, 26, 34, 48, 64-69, 73, 74, 102, 103, 147, 148, 159 164, 166, 233, 234, 250, 251

Saint-Pierre, abbé de, 126
Saint-Priest, 55
Sartine, 18
Ségur, 54, 65, 97
Sérent, 128, 130
Shelburne, 16
Sillery, 120, 122
Sinéti, 126
Smith, Adam, 126, 139, 150, 153, 162, 167
Souillac, 38, 39
Spain, 15, 16, 40, 50, 65, 74, 92, 102, 112, 116, 117, 119, 122, 127, 128, 135, 148, 157, 164, 165, 182, 207, 215, 218-220, 224, 226-234

Tippoo Sultan, 38, 39, 75, 77, 78, 205, 206, 210
Treaty of Paris (1783), 16, 21, 22, 209

United Provinces (Holland), 15, 29, 35, 36, 38, 39, 48, 53-64, 66, 68, 69, 73, 76, 79, 84, 92, 107-109, 127, 135, 142, 147, 160, 163, 182, 195, 235
United States, 18, 157, 172, 178

Vergennes, 15-26, 28, 29, 31, 32, 34-37, 40-42, 43, 50-52, 58, 59, 64-68, 71, 78, 91, 101, 102, 251, 252, 254
Virieu, 128
Voidel, 222, 223
Vonck, 114, 115

West Indies, 16, 28, 55, 60, 62, 87, 88, 169, 170, 172, 179, 181, 183, 185, 187, 191, 206, 207, 212, 232, 235, 248, 254

Young, Arthur, 143